THE CROSS,
OUR ONLY HOPE

"In *The Cross, Our Only Hope*, there is a profound simplicity that refuses to shirk difficult questions; a consistent stress on the beauty and dignity of the human person in sorrow and joy alike; and, above all, a consoling and inspiring invitation to see conformity to Christ crucified and risen as the source of our only, and transfiguring, hope."

Sr. Ann Swailes, O.P.
Lecturer at Blackfriars, University of Oxford

"A splendid treasury of stories and reflections in the Holy Cross tradition to inspire and challenge all disciples of Christ."

Rev. Wilfred Raymond, C.S.C.
President of Holy Cross Family Ministries

"This second edition expands and updates the original publication in both scope and breadth. I am especially taken by the personal experiences that ground each reflection, clear evidence of the multicultural reality of Holy Cross and the universal faith community of the Church."

Br. John Paige, C.S.C.
President of Holy Cross College

"*The Cross, Our Only Hope* is a gift for any spiritual seeker looking to grow in faith while incorporating prayer as a priority amidst life's busyness. This indispensable daily devotional builds upon the spiritual gifts of such saints as St. Andre Bessette and Blessed Basil Moreau by offering us wisdom from scores of gifted modern-day shepherds from the Holy Cross community. A beautiful way to start and end every day as we turn our hearts toward the saving grace of the Cross. I look forward to praying with this treasure in our home for years to come!"

Lisa M. Hendey
Founder of *CatholicMom.com* and
author of *The Grace of Yes*

"*The Cross, Our Only Hope* provides readers access to the primary texts influencing the Congregation of Holy Cross, while linking them with modern reflections from Holy Cross religious throughout the world. I'm grateful for this work and believe it will serve as a meaningful witness to the Catholic faith."

Rev. Pete McCormick, C.S.C.
Director of Campus Ministry at the University of Notre Dame

"This collection of reflections offers an intimate view of the Congregation of Holy Cross, and their charisms of familial spirit, hospitality and fellowship, education of the whole person, abandonment to Divine Providence, apostolic zeal, and hope in the Cross of Christ. Particularly helpful are the integration of quotes from founder Blessed Basil Moreau, the Holy Cross *Constitutions*, and Fr. Edward Sorin, C.S.C., with each daily reflection. This enables deep insights into the way the charisms of the founder are being actively lived out in the Congregation today."

Peter Kilpatrick
McCloskey Dean of Engineering at the University of Notre Dame

"The reflections shared by members of the Holy Cross family in the first edition of *The Cross, Our Only Hope* rekindled my appreciation of our *Constitutions* and of two towering figures in the history of the Congregation, Blessed Basil Moreau and Fr. Edward Sorin. The many new reflections offered in the second edition will generate even more insights. Thanks to both contributors and editors for giving us all a superb spiritual resource!"

Br. Patrick Sopher, C.S.C.
Executive Director of Planning of the Congregation of Holy Cross

"*The Cross, Our Only Hope* leads the reader into a fresh encounter with Jesus through rich stories and insights from the collective ministry of the Congregation of Holy Cross. What a gift to have this wellspring of teaching, experiences, and fresh applications, the fruit of religious community and zealous service to draw disciples of Jesus deeper into his life."

Jason J. Simon
Executive Director of the *Evangelical Catholic*

"My hope for this new edition is that it helps us all to answer the call of Pope Francis, the call of Blessed Moreau, and ultimately the call of Jesus himself."

Rev. Richard V. Warner, C.S.C.
Superior General of the Congregation of Holy Cross

"What is the deep true nature of the men of Holy Cross, their idiosyncratic characteristic thing and flavor and charism? What differentiates them from other Catholic orders? This is the only book I know that pokes after shy answers: their blunt honesty, their refreshing lack of ego, their absolute conviction that the divine is the ocean in which we swim every minute of the day."

Brian Doyle
Author of *A Book of Uncommon Prayer*

Revised Edition

THE CROSS, OUR ONLY HOPE

Daily Reflections
in the Holy Cross
Tradition

Edited by
ANDREW GAWRYCH, C.S.C.,
and KEVIN GROVE, C.S.C.

With a Foreword by Richard V. Warner, C.S.C.

AVE MARIA PRESS AVE Notre Dame, Indiana

Founded in 1865, Ave Maria Press is a ministry of the United States Province of Holy Cross.

www.avemariapress.com

Paperback: ISBN-13 978-1-59471-653-9

E-book: ISBN-13 978-1-59471-654-6

Cover image © Corbis.

Cover and text design by John Carson.

Printed and bound in the United States of America.

FOREWORD

IN MY MANY years as a Holy Cross religious, October 17, 2010, stands out as one of the greatest and most beautiful days. That day, I was privileged to be in St. Peter's Square in Rome—representing not just the Congregation of Holy Cross, but the wider Holy Cross family, including our colleagues, students, parishioners, and many friends—as Pope Benedict XVI canonized Br. André Bessette, C.S.C. This humble, prayerful, loving religious brother became the first canonized saint of the Congregation.

St. André Bessette's canonization was not just an affirmation of his own saintliness, but it was also an affirmation by the Roman Catholic Church that the charism, spirituality, and tradition of Holy Cross is a way of following Jesus and living the Gospel that can lead to our own sanctification if we are faithful to the God who loved us first and who is full of mercy and forgiveness. It was the way of discipleship that was first given through the inspiration of the Holy Spirit to our saintly founder, Blessed Basil Moreau, whose own eventual canonization we await in joyful hope. Since then, it has been the way of discipleship that thousands of Holy Cross priests and brothers have followed: in imitation of Christ, to make God known, loved, and served as educators in the faith and as religious called to serve in the mission of teaching and engaging in direct service to the poor.

I am delighted at the publication of this new volume of *The Cross, Our Only Hope*. The original volume in 2008 by the Congregation of Holy Cross was a significant step which enabled us to share our spirituality and tradition not only with those we minister with and to, but also with Christian believers within the Catholic Church as well as many others. This new volume both dives deeper into our charism through new sources and reveals more of the growing international face of our Congregation through new contributors. I hope you will find these reflections by Holy Cross priests and brothers a real treasure for your daily prayer life and walk with the Lord.

With great energy and joy, as well as an inspiring personal witness, Pope Francis has challenged the Church to go to the peripheries of our world and to take on the smell of the sheep in order to share the hope and joy of the Gospel. This call of the Holy Father fully resonates with our Holy Cross history and tradition, since from the earliest days of Holy Cross, more than one hundred fifty years ago, Blessed Moreau was sending the members of his religious family to the peripheries of the world—from the poor, rural towns in France to the dangerous East Bengal Mission that no other religious community was willing to take. He also called on Holy Cross religious truly to plant the Congregation and their lives where they served, to be not just servants but also neighbors to those they served, to be with them and of them.

My hope for this new edition of *The Cross, Our Only Hope* is that it helps us all—members of Holy Cross and others alike—to answer the call of Pope Francis, the call of Blessed Moreau, and ultimately the call of Jesus himself, that in knowing ever more the love of God for us, we might live and minister among people of many cultures and ways of life in order to proclaim that the Cross of Christ is, indeed, our hope.

Richard V. Warner, C.S.C.
Superior General of the Congregation of Holy Cross

ACKNOWLEDGMENTS

WE ARE GRATEFUL for the support of the United States Province of the Congregation of Holy Cross, in particular our Provincial Superior, Fr. Thomas O'Hara, C.S.C., for the permission to undertake this project.

We also thank Tom Grady and his team at Ave Maria Press not only for their work on the first volume but also for their enthusiasm and care for this second edition.

Above all, we are deeply grateful to the over two hundred men, our brothers in Holy Cross, who contributed reflections for this book. Although we were their editors for this project, they are mentors and friends, and their lives dedicated in service of the Lord are inspiring models to us. More than we could have imagined, this book has profoundly shaped and influenced our own lives in Holy Cross.

A. G. and K. G.

INTRODUCTION

It is bold to claim that the Cross of Christ is our hope. It is even bolder to believe and live the Cross as our only hope. Yet we in the Congregation of Holy Cross, a Roman Catholic religious order of priests and brothers, profess this truth as the center of our spiritual tradition. Our motto is: Ave Crux, Spes Unica—*Hail the Cross, Our Only Hope. And for more than one hundred fifty years, our priests and brothers have worked to bring the hope of the Cross to schools, universities, parishes, and other ministries on five continents of the globe.*

—Introduction to the first edition of
The Cross, Our Only Hope

IN 2008, WE first compiled a book of reflections in order to share the spirituality of Holy Cross so that others might grow closer to God through reflection and prayer with us. The success of that book far outstripped all expectations. But since that time, much has happened in the Congregation and the world that makes a new and updated edition timely both for seasoned readers of the 2008 edition as well as for those who might be encountering the Holy Cross tradition for the very first time.

Since the 2008 edition, the Congregation of Holy Cross has been blessed with its first saint by the Catholic Church: Br. André Bessette, C.S.C., canonized by Pope Benedict XVI on October 17, 2010. The collected writings of the founder,

Blessed Basil Moreau, have been published in English for the first time in *Basil Moreau: Essential Writings* (Notre Dame: Ave Maria Press, 2014). Holy Cross history and spirituality are now being taught in university courses and seminars. Pilgrimages have begun from around the world to the new International Shrine of Blessed Basil Moreau, located at the church Fr. Moreau himself built: Notre Dame de Sainte-Croix in Le Mans, France. This second edition, in one sense, continues this movement of hope. In another sense, however, it is merely a response to ever-increasing demand.

The basic narrative structure of this second edition remains the same. Reflections for each day of the year follow the rough outline of the Church's liturgical year, highlighting in a special way the feast days of Holy Cross—St. Joseph, the Solemnity of the Sacred Heart of Jesus, and Our Lady of Sorrows. Each reflection begins with a text from Holy Cross's spiritual writings, followed by a reflection written by a brother or priest of the Congregation.

This volume presents an expansion both in the source texts and in the international diversity of the contributors. The first edition included writings of Fr. Moreau; Fr. Edward Sorin, C.S.C. (one of the original members of the Congregation, an essential figure in its early development, and its third Superior General); and Fr. Jacques Dujarie (the founder of the Brothers of St. Joseph who became the Brothers of Holy Cross when joined with Fr. Moreau's Auxiliary Priests) as well as excerpts from the present-day *Constitutions of the Congregation of Holy Cross*. This second edition adds newly translated writings of Blessed Moreau as well as some of the very few preserved writings of St. André Bessette. This volume also includes new reflections from both seasoned authors as well as those who have recently professed final vows in Holy Cross. Though the community has mourned the death of some of the luminaries whose reflections continue to grace these pages, it also enjoys its highest levels of vocations in decades. This edition celebrates both the lives of those we have lost and the new life that has burst forth.

In the introduction to the first edition, we provided a brief summary of the genesis and early history of Holy Cross in order to draw out the spirituality of our religious community that grew up in post-Revolutionary France and quickly spread—even before it had sufficient personnel and resources—to be educators in the faith throughout the world. This time we wish to deepen our understanding of the Congregation: What holds the spirituality of Holy Cross together? What grounds our mission? How is it of use to all who are trying to follow Jesus in our daily lives?

Conformity to Christ

These reflections are a living proof that for Holy Cross and for those with whom and for whom we serve a life "conformed to Christ" is lively, exciting, and all-encompassing. This conviction threads its way through all of the spiritual sources, from the opening and closing lines of our *Constitutions*, which speak of God's call to follow Christ, to the exhortations of Blessed Moreau, St. André, Fr. Sorin, and Fr. Dujarie. The sentiment itself is as old as the conviction of the earliest Christians and is borne out by the writers of the New Testament. Fr. Moreau, like the thinkers of his time, seized on it and planted it at the heart of all that his religious were to do and become. One of his favorite exhortations to the community was that of St. Paul, "It is not I who live, but Christ who lives in me" (Gal 2:20). Fr. Moreau always reminded his religious to place themselves in the scenes of salvation—to stand with the Magi adoring the infant Jesus at Epiphany or to hold Jesus along with Mary after he is taken down from the Cross.

As this book attests, the spirituality of Holy Cross operates on the same sort of principle. Our daily lives are a participation in Christ's. We do that incompletely now, but always concretely—in flesh and blood. The reflections in the book are a testament to the ways in which conforming one's life to Christ might be fulfilling and salvific. Found in these pages are the meditations of priests and brothers who, just like our readers, are works in progress. Coming not just as servants but as neighbors, we journey right along with those around us, such that conformity to Christ is not an unachievable ideal but as ordinary as the work we undertake in the course of a day, the prayers we pray with others and alone, the bumps in the road as well as the spiritual heights, the grave situations and also the good humor. Christ transfigures every one of us, writers and readers alike. He draws us along as the members of his own body, and blesses us and those around us in a faith that is honest, practical, and practiced.

Christian Education

For all disciples of Jesus, our living a life conformed to Christ is living a life committed to each other. Fr. Moreau and all Holy Cross religious since have understood this mutual commitment in the Body of Christ in familial terms and with a familial spirit, looking to the Holy Family as a particular inspiration. Jesus' dying desire was that we be united not just with him but also with each other, that we all may be one as he and the Father were one. We experience this dynamic most powerfully in the Eucharist, in which we are drawn into communion with Christ and together become his body. Because a life in Christ is in essence one lived with others, Holy Cross's apostolic mission has always looked outward to its neighbors, both near and far. Drawing from the Spirit's inspiration of our founder and our founding charism, Holy Cross understands that outward mission as serving as "educators in the faith."

The sheer number of different ministries in this book shows that such a charism takes unique forms, from university professor to parish priest, campus minister to missionary, servant of the poor and the migrant to one who cares for the young seminarians or the elderly of the Congregation. Even more, it extends to parents and grandparents, to sisters and brothers, to catechists and coaches, to nurses and executives, in a word, to all Christians sent by Jesus to announce the kingdom of God in this world.

Education in the faith is an important way to consider these reflections. For since the founding of Holy Cross, generations of priests, brothers, sisters, and many lay collaborators have continued to labor under a profound assumption: a Christian education is not only the way to prepare a society for better times than our own but it is also a part of the road to heaven together as family. In this way, the ministry of the Congregation is not simply making sure that people receive the finest possible education that can be provided—though this is true from the magnificent opportunities given to young people from the University of Notre Dame to the newest college that Holy Cross has started in Mymensingh, Bangladesh. Rather, Holy Cross religious take for granted that we should not want, as Blessed Moreau stated, our students to be ignorant of anything that they should know.

What renders that regular learning unique, however, is the learning of the ways of Jesus Christ, guided by the Spirit, in order to know the Father. And so, a Christian education is not merely learning facts about Christ—though, of course, it requires sitting down and studying the faith—but it is the very act of participating fully and actively in Christ's body. When we "learn" about Christ in this way, we are learning our very own death and Resurrection. So, when Blessed Moreau tells us that education is a work of the Resurrection, he is suggesting that our normal understanding of education aims far too low. A proper education is much more exciting, much more dynamic, and involves all of who we are, from now to eternity. The reflections in this book are from priests and brothers who are committed to be both ever students and ever teachers. It is also an invitation to all who wish to be fellow students and teachers of such a dynamic faith, one in which we learn together the first fruits of the Resurrection.

Hope

The lasting mark of the Congregation of Holy Cross is sharing hope. The congregational seal is composed of a cross and two anchors, with the latter, from the dawn of Christianity, signifying unwavering hope. The *Constitutions* of Holy Cross refer to the members as "men with hope to bring." Like the Congregation's understanding of education, this is not the hope of a small order, such as might be the slogan of a campaign or social movement. This is a hope that cuts to the heart of human longing, a longing for sacrifice, love, fullness, joy, and grace. It is a hope that emerges from the worst of suffering and shame, not only that it might not be broken or inaccessible to any who suffer or are shamed but also that it might truly make all things new. It is hope in the Cross of Christ Jesus. It is hope that we might have life, have it abundantly, and in him rise again—forever.

Of course, hope would be cheap if it did not know the full range of human experience—from devastation to transfiguration. That is why the Cross and hope go so intimately together. It is also why the religious of Holy Cross do not shy away in these texts from describing the difficulties of human life along with the joys. We know we are not alone in experiencing these highs and lows. We are blessed very often to pray with and for people at the hours of their death; we have stood alongside peoples as they suffer; we have learned from the plight of the poor and felt the frustrations of moments when, despite our best efforts, all does not go according to plan; we even have known our own personal weaknesses and failures. But in those moments—which appear in stark honesty in some of these reflections—just as much as in good times, we trust that Divine Providence wastes absolutely nothing.

The men who have written these reflections are all Holy Cross religious, committed to vows of poverty, chastity, and obedience. A number of the reflections treat these vows and the experience of living them. This subject matter might at first sound odd or inapplicable to an outside reader, but we hope to show that is not the case. In fact, each of the vows names something very deep about humanity and how we relate to the world around us and ultimately to God. Poverty treats the desire we have to own and control that which is around us. Chastity treats all of the desires of our physical bodies and our hearts. Obedience concerns our will and the power that each of us has in relation to others.

In Holy Cross, as a religious congregation of educators, these vows represent a "school" or means of learning the ways of conformity to Christ. They are not, of course, the only way in which one can be educated. But inasmuch as the vows that mark the lives of Holy Cross religious treat human realities, hopefully they will provide solid spiritual fodder for all who reflect on the goods they own, their physical and affective longings, and their own wills. Holy Cross priests and brothers understand their vows as nothing less than expressions of love for the God who first loved them. As these pages tell of moments luminary as well as ordinary, it is important to know that all of them are considered the expressions of love from ongoing students of such a school of conformity to Christ. The vows are inherent in the very expression of hope that Holy Cross religious live and teach.

For many in the world, the claim of the Congregation of Holy Cross and of this book—that the Cross of Christ is our one and magnificent source of hope—might seem rather strange or even outlandish. But for priests and brothers of Holy Cross, that claim reshapes all else. It inspires compassion in the face of sin, insurrection amid injustice, sacraments for a world searching for God in its experiences, and communion when tempted by the needs of the self. For all of us, this hope has to be learned, practiced, relearned, and perfected in us by our God from now until the day we rise again.

In that way—namely, the way of continual practice—the work of the first edition of this text was necessarily incomplete. Yet we could not be more excited to walk and pray with you the journey that marks the pages that follow. For although the steps we take are as small as the reflections that mark each day, they are steps we take together as one, whole Christ—the young and the old, the weak and the strong, the confident and the unbelieving, the poor and the rich. We are delighted to share—with all humility—the hope we have found, to be bold with it, to imagine it for all eternity, and to let it draw forth from us here and now more than we knew we could have or give. Please come and see with us how all of us might learn together to listen and to discover, as our *Constitutions* say, "It is the Lord Jesus calling us. Come, follow me."

Andrew Gawrych, C.S.C., and Kevin Grove, C.S.C.

January 1

May we start on this new year with a firm conviction that, having enrolled ourselves and pledged our lives under the glorious standard of the holy Cross, we must, to the last breath, further or check its progress according to how we fight vigorously or cowardly the battle in which we are engaged.

—Fr. Edward Sorin, C.S.C.

THE START OF a new year is often a time to focus on self-improvement. The idea of a New Year's resolution may be a bit of a cliché, but it's still a time of year when people buy a lot of gym memberships and nicotine patches. Often that's a good thing; it's certainly good to take inventory of our lives periodically and address areas that need some work. The problem with New Year's resolutions, of course, is that they often get broken—quickly. This is especially true if we view resolutions as an all-or-nothing proposition. If February rolls around and we've slipped, we often give up or wait until next year to try again.

Hopefully, some of our New Year's resolutions involve being a stronger Christian. We promise to pray every day or to go to confession every month. Perhaps we resolve to get involved with a charity or to overcome finally that nagging sin with which we struggle. Like all worthwhile goals, these are difficult. We always struggle; we often fail. But that doesn't mean that we simply discard these resolutions and wait for next year. Instead, we keep trying because we aspire to more than mere self-improvement. We aspire to conversion. Conversion is not a one-time self-improvement project. It's the everyday work of being a Christian, the work we will do every day for the rest of our lives.

So as this new year begins, we cannot be afraid to set the bar high and to reach for it every day. Some days we will come close; some days we will fall short. But when we give thanks for our daily successes and learn from our daily failures, we will find that Jesus Christ—our crucified yet risen Savior—can work through both of them to draw us closer to himself.

Steve Lacroix, C.S.C.

January 2

The sacraments are the most tangible proof of the love of Jesus Christ for us.

—Blessed Basil Moreau

SOMETIMES WORDS ARE insufficient. A gesture is needed to complement them. In the musical *My Fair Lady*, a suitor, Freddy, keeps speaking sweet words to Eliza. One day she goes into a tirade, saying that she is sick of his many words. If he truly loves her, she begs him to show her.

Jesus needed a means to be with his Church in every generation. His enduring presence would be supported by more than his powerful and beautiful words. Thus, he gave the Church the gift of seven sacraments. They are words combined with gestures that make tangible his saving presence. In Baptism, we are called by name and immersed through water in the life of the Triune God. In Confirmation, we are sealed with the Holy Spirit as sacred oil is placed upon our foreheads. In the Eucharist, bread and wine are blessed by the priest and thus changed into the Lord's body and blood.

I recall perhaps most of all the literally thousands of the sick and dying with whom I have celebrated the Anointing of the Sick. I have observed the power of this sacrament, as peace overcame fear, trust overtook anxiety, and a deep awareness grew of Jesus' abiding presence. The mood of the patient, spouse, and family changed as the sacrament put Jesus' love for them not only into words but into action.

Seven sacraments in their words and gestures have graced millions over the centuries. Jesus remains present to us—welcoming, strengthening, feeding, forgiving, healing, marrying, and ordaining. We can't help ourselves. We keep coming back to his sacraments time and again, just as Eliza sang, "Don't speak of love. Show me!" In the sacraments, Jesus visibly shows us his love while touching and healing our minds, hearts, and spirits.

Michael D. Couhig, C.S.C.

January 3

Bear in mind and do not forget that just as Divine Providence has willed its greatest works to begin in humility and abjection, it has also decreed that they should expand only at the price of difficulties and contradictions, trials, crosses, contempt, calumny, and detraction. Its purpose in so decreeing is that the first materials of these spiritual edifices may be tried as gold in the fire.

—Blessed Basil Moreau

FROM THE PERSPECTIVE of the Christian faith, encountering the Cross is more than a probability; it is an inevitability. Trials—of whatever kind and in whatever dimension of life—will not rank among our favorite moments, but neither can they be avoided. In fact, consciously trying to avoid these difficulties might be the worst thing that we could do. For, as Blessed Moreau points out, God's greatest works usually begin in small, humble circumstances. Scripture testifies to this truth; we need only recall the stable in Bethlehem to remember the power hidden in unassuming beginnings. And, as Blessed Moreau goes on to say, these works progress and expand through trials. Scripture testifies to that also; we need only envision the hill outside Jerusalem to bring to mind the saving victory wrested from seeming defeat.

These are not merely the truths of scripture; they are embodied in the very history of Holy Cross, and they are experienced daily by all who follow Christ. Yet we live in settings that often deny pain and pretend it away. We ourselves may even try to discard or erase the memories of our encounters with the Cross. The great risk in this is that we also discard the grace that accompanies painful, difficult, or confusing times. We might, instead, reflect on the graces that God is offering us through these trials and thus find the strength to embrace them. For each encounter with the Cross is the Lord's invitation to us to grow ever more fully into the persons God made us to be.

Joel Giallanza, C.S.C.

January 4

*Let the humble, candid and guileless souls of our Con-
gregation gather around the poor, dear little Babe in
his crib, and present him with the gold of their charity,
the incense of their prayers, and the myrrh of their
penitential life!*

—Fr. Edward Sorin, C.S.C.

WHEN I WAS studying in Japan, a group of sisters invited me to
preside at Mass in their convent. After Mass, the nuns presented
me, their visiting American priest, with a holy card featuring
the Blessed Mother. The image of Mary was one with distinctly
Japanese features and dress; she was wearing a kimono. At that
point, I had just come from the main university church in
downtown Tokyo, where the statue of Mary had distinctly Ger-
manic features. It struck me that the historical Mary, a young
Jewish girl in Palestine, probably had little physical resemblance
to either image.

The little Babe in his crib, born of the young Jewish mother,
is at once the Savior of all the world, the Deliverer of every people, and also a particular human being, fully present in time and
space, with physical features and a cultural context determined
by the circumstances of his birth. He belongs to every people
and also to the Chosen People. Every nation wishes to claim him
as its own, to depict him in familiar fashion, and yet he appears
as a helpless baby at a specific place in a particular moment
in history through the mystery of the Incarnation. We are all
challenged to respond to this act of extraordinary generosity, to

embrace both the universal mission and the very real humanity of our Savior through lives of charity and prayer—not only for our people but for all the peoples of the world.

Art Wheeler, C.S.C.

January 5

Our calling is to serve the Lord Jesus in mission not as independent individuals but in a brotherhood. Our community life refreshes the faith that makes our work a ministry and not just an employment; it fortifies us by the example and encouragement of our confreres; and it protects us from being overwhelmed or discouraged by our work.

—Holy Cross *Constitutions*

AS A SEMINARIAN, I learned how to be a good brother in community by watching how the finally professed religious at Moreau Seminary acted. I remember one day early in formation when after ministry I returned to the seminary disappointed and upset. I was frustrated with the people to whom I was ministering and beginning to question whether this was the life for me. My frustration must have been quite evident as Br. John Platte, C.S.C., one of the wisdom figures in the seminary community, took one look at me, gave me a hug, and invited me to the refectory for a bowl of ice cream. As we ate, Br. John listened to me complain, smiled knowingly, and told me that I was going to be just fine. It was exactly what I needed to hear.

I am sure that every Holy Cross religious could tell a similar story of a time in which a community member came to his aid. For me, these stories get at what it means to share in the brotherhood of Holy Cross. As brothers in community, we are called to be present to each other through the ups and downs of religious life. In sharing these moments, we make Christ's deep and abiding love for us real, and our faith is renewed.

This call to accompany others is not unique to Holy Cross but is instead the call of every Christian. Whether we live in a religious house, as part of a family, or as a single person, all of us are called to bring the love of Jesus Christ to those we encounter. That is what it means to be a good community member and part of the Body of Christ.

Christopher Rehagen, C.S.C.

January 6*

After seeing and adoring the Infant Savior, oh, for his sake, for the sake of our holy faith, for the sake of our beloved family, we, too, shall return from the stable by a different road.

—Fr. Edward Sorin, C.S.C.

AFTER THE MAGI reached Bethlehem, they had every reason in the world to be overjoyed. They finally had found the newborn Jesus whom they had been seeking and presented him their wonderful gifts. In fact, we might think they were also deeply satisfied and ready to declare "mission accomplished." But instead, as

Matthew's gospel recounts, they were scarcely halfway through their long journey. Having received instructions in a dream to avoid King Herod, they returned home by a different road.

Fr. Sorin plainly saw a significant lesson in this episode from Christ's Nativity that applies to us as well. The command that we go back differently than the way we came puts us in the position of the Wise Men, who saw and believed, and who now carry the Good News of God's presence among us, in place of gold, incense, and myrrh. But this obligation to take another route also resonates with the great arc of the biblical drama, which begins in an earthly garden and, after taking a surprising path from the tree of knowledge of good and evil to the very wood of the Cross, ends in a heavenly city. The paths we are called to follow are often strange and new, teaching us to trust in the Spirit. They bring us into contact with unfamiliar people who enrich our knowledge of the image of God. These roads often confront us with difficult choices and challenging situations, which become so many opportunities for a new epiphany as we follow the Way, the Truth, and the Life.

Patrick D. Gaffney, C.S.C.

* Although the Church in the United States celebrates the Feast of St. André Bessette today, the day of his death, the Congregation of Holy Cross and most of the Church in the rest of the world, including in his home country of Canada, celebrate St. André on January 7. This difference is due to the fact that most local churches celebrate the Solemnity of the Epiphany on January 6, rather than moving it to the nearest Sunday after the New Year, as is the custom in the Church in the United States.

January 7—Feast of St. André Bessette

*God does not ask the impossible. God asks that we
offer our good intentions, accept the inconveniences
that come with each day, and offer our daily work.*
—St. André Bessette

THIS IS THE formula that Br. André used throughout his life,
and it led him to sainthood. Simple and straightforward, his
words reflect a profound trust that God is and remains faithful,
that God will use our usual daily activities to bring us to holiness. St. André needed that trust throughout his life, from his
entrance into Holy Cross to the development of the Oratory
of St. Joseph. He trusted even when confronted with misun-
derstanding and lack of support. St. André nurtured that trust
with the truly essential works of his life: faith, prayer, service.

St. André believed that he would enter Holy Cross; he
believed that he could make a contribution; he believed the
Oratory was possible. And all of that came to be. He would say
to others, "If you do not believe in God, you will get nothing."
He believed, and today we see the fruits of his faith and the ways
that he continues to touch so many people. So it must be for us.
How does our faith enable us to touch the lives of others and so
make a difference in our world?

St. André prayed. Eyewitnesses testified that when he prayed
he looked as if he was speaking to someone from whom he
expected an answer. His prayer to God—often through St.
Joseph and Mary—was, above all, a personal relationship from
which he drew strength and encouragement for the work before

him. He believed that God was very close to anyone who prayed. As he would say, "When we pray, God's ear is pressed to our lips." So it is for us. How is our own prayer a relationship?

St. André served others to the best of his ability, not allowing his limitations to shrink his openness to whatever God and St. Joseph wanted to accomplish through him. We could consider his work for the development of the Oratory and his ministry of healing as the primary activities in his life. His own perspective, however, was much more Gospel-based: "We cannot love God without loving our neighbor." He understood his main vocation in life was to love even as Jesus loved. So, too, for us. Beyond the arenas of family and profession, in which ways do we serve others?

Believe, pray, serve, and, by all that, trust God. It is a simple enough regimen for a full spiritual life. It is a simple enough formula for sainthood. A regular recommendation from St. André was: "Be saints." In his mind, this was not an impossible task for he knew God would not ask that of us. Rather, this is what we were created to be: saints.

Just before he died, St. André's last words were, "This is the seed." He was a seed, a small seed—he would say an insignificant seed—but one that was watered by God's grace and grew in the fertile soil of faith and prayer and service. He was a seed that became a saint. And so it is for us because, after all, God does not ask the impossible.

Joel Giallanza, C.S.C.

January 8

*Once entered into the house, having found the Child
with Mary, his mother, and fallen down to adore him,
let us pause awhile in their holy presence, forgetting
the world with its vain noise and treachery. And, opening our only treasure, our hearts, let us make him our
richest offering, our whole being, that he may dispose
of it as he pleases.*

—Fr. Edward Sorin, C.S.C.

THOUGH I HAVEN'T experienced the joys and challenges of
fatherhood, I am privileged to have eight nieces and nephews.
Now a new generation is arriving—six great-nephews and three
great-nieces grace the family hearth, including one from his
place in heaven. I'm at a stage in life and ministry that I call
"spiritual grandpa-hood"—baptizing the children of the children I baptized those many years ago.

How easy it is to give one's heart to an infant. Our attention
is focused solely on that little child. Outside distractions fade
away. We marvel at the tiny physical features, feel the clasp of
small fingers, and lose ourselves in the depths of the little one's
eyes. We get down on the floor and play with rattles and squeaky
toys. We make silly faces. The "conversation" between ourselves
and the infant is perfectly understandable to both of us. In other
words, it's all right for us to let go of our adultness. An infant
gives us permission to be a child ourselves.

So, too, it is with Jesus. True, we won't relate to him as
though he were a baby, nor does he expect that. But how deeply

Jesus desires the clasp of our hands, our gaze into his eyes. He longs for the language of our heart speaking to his heart. Playfulness is welcomed and cherished. We can let ourselves go with Jesus, just as we do with an infant. Yet one huge difference remains between Jesus and an infant. Sooner or later the infant's attention shifts to something different. Jesus never tires of us.

Herbert C. Yost, C.S.C.

January 9

Even in this life God blesses human efforts surprisingly, when the cause of his Holy Mother is interested in them. Whoever neglects her deprives himself of something essential to success.

—Fr. Edward Sorin, C.S.C.

IN MY FIRST few days as a new provincial, I received from a predecessor a storied rosary that was well-used, old, and fragile. According to him, the rosary first belonged to Fr. Edward Sorin, C.S.C. Fr. Sorin had given it to Notre Dame faculty member Fr. Cornelius Hagerty, C.S.C. Fr. Hagerty had mentored the young Patrick Peyton, C.S.C., at Notre Dame and had given this precious rosary to him. More than fifty years later, as he lay dying, Fr. Peyton, the American Apostle of the Family Rosary, passed the rosary on to his provincial superior at the time. And, in turn, it was given to me.

Two years before ordination to the priesthood, Patrick Peyton had been diagnosed with terminal tuberculosis and advised by doctors that he should try prayer since they had exhausted all of their remedies. He returned to Notre Dame from Washington, DC, to die at the community infirmary. Fr. Hagerty, his favorite professor, visited him at the infirmary and told him, "Mary is alive. She will be as good to you as you think she can be. It all depends on you and your faith." He told Patrick to pray to the Mother of God that he might be healed through her intercession—if it be God's will. He and his friends in Holy Cross prayed the Rosary for that intention.

Later, perplexed doctors examined him carefully and confessed their bafflement. He was going to live. He was ordained Fr. Patrick Peyton, C.S.C., two years later and spent fifty-one years as a priest enriching and strengthening the lives of families all around the world. God, indeed, will bless our efforts if we seek the help of his Holy Mother.

Willy Raymond, C.S.C.

January 10

The more Divine Providence is pleased to bless the works which it has confided to us and for which we are jointly responsible, the more keenly do I feel the weight of my responsibility and the more deeply I am convinced of the need of personal holiness if I am not to be an obstacle to God's design for each one of you.
—Blessed Basil Moreau

DIVINE PROVIDENCE IS neither magic nor attainable by mere human achievement. Instead, it is the marriage between divine initiative and human response. It is the reality we experience when we stop seeing God's design as something foreign to us and begin to see ourselves within that design. Divine Providence is not a suit we must go out to buy, be fitted for, and then live in. It is a reality already at work in us into which we awaken through prayer and attentive listening.

In awaking to the design that God has already inscribed on our hearts, we discover that our only responsibility is to respond. Ultimately, this response does not consist of a list of things to do but is a call to wake up and be—for personal holiness is a way of being in the world. As I discerned my own call to the priesthood, it did not come down to whether I believed I could do everything God might ask of me. The real question that haunted me, the real weight of the responsibility I felt, was whether I could be who he was asking me to be. And that question could only be answered through listening and then responding to what God had already planted within my own heart.

Thus, if we truly seek to do God's will, we cannot rely on our will alone nor can we count on our lives magically unfolding. The only way to fulfill God's designs for us is to listen and to respond continually to the workings of grace in our lives, thereby creating that union between our human response and God's initiative that is Divine Providence.

Jeffrey Cooper, C.S.C.

January 11

Once in their life the shepherds and the Magi beheld him in the manger; but I, every day, poor sinner, receive him, not in my arms, but in my own bosom, in my very heart, so that I may say with St. Paul: "I live: no, not I, but Christ lives in me!"

—Fr. Edward Sorin, C.S.C.

I HAVE OFTEN taken the daily reception of the Eucharist for granted. It becomes quite easily just another routine component of the Mass. More often than not, I get the most meaning from the well-read epistle or gospel, the nicely crafted and well-delivered homily, or the beautifully moving music. And then, on cue, I rise and follow the crowd to take nourishment. Regrettably, there are times when all this happens and I am completely unaware of the monumental value of the moment.

But when I am focused, it is then that I am overwhelmed with awe by the gift that Christ is giving to me and that I am receiving. The body and blood of the Lord, once shed for me on Calvary's height, now dwell mysteriously within my very heart, transforming myself and all who receive him into his Body—the Church. The concept is so awesome, so divinely generous, that it completely escapes not only my reason but my power truly to believe it. And yet it is real—it was, and it will always be.

Perhaps it would have been eminently better for me to have been present with the shepherds and Magi—physically to have witnessed the Savior incarnate in the world. Perhaps in that one spectacular event, I would have believed totally. But even now,

Christ lives and breathes and transforms me. It happens each time I receive his body and blood in bread and wine. Ever so slowly, it is not I who live, but Christ who lives in me.

Philip Smith, C.S.C.

January 12

In our attempts to love others, Jesus Christ is our model. Notice what great charity he practiced in his public life. This charity was evident everywhere, especially in his bearing, his reserve, and his constant patience with others. There was no distinction; he cared for everyone.

—Blessed Basil Moreau

NOTICING TWENTY OR so bodies of children—infants, really—piled limp and doll-like, three and four deep on metal racks in a sweltering hospital morgue in Haiti, my students stood in stunned silence. When they asked about the horror before us, I did not have a particularly good response. I muttered something and suggested a quick prayer to remember these kids whose lives had obviously ended prematurely and who were probably now saints. Most died for no good reason—hunger and its illnesses, a minor accident left untreated for lack of a physician, the absence of life-saving vaccines due to a corrupt official looking for a bribe, or a simple infection grown fatal because of filth. As a priest and biologist working in Haiti, I have witnessed all these stories. Destitute poverty and early death evoke a reaction in us of shock—then empathy. Yet the reaction of these children's parents is even more surprising. They often speak of the hope they find in Jesus Christ and his sacraments.

The degree to which the sacraments nourish the soul is vividly apparent in a place like Haiti. Our Lord was correct. Blessed are the poor. They can find comfort and grace where we see tragedy. Everywhere we followers of Christ serve the poor, we can help to make the charity of Jesus more evident through word and sacrament. We manifest his charity when we work to heal. We do this not because we will solve poverty or because any particular person deserves our charity. Our actions come from our following Christ because, yes, we try to model his love for others.

Tom Streit, C.S.C.

January 13

We shall always place education side by side with instruction; the mind will not be cultivated at the expense of the heart. While we prepare useful citizens for society, we shall likewise do our utmost to prepare citizens for heaven.

—Blessed Basil Moreau

THESE WORDS OF Blessed Moreau are very familiar to us in Holy Cross and to our many lay colleagues who minister alongside us. I walk by them every day, for they are framed outside of my office at Stonehill College. These words speak to our core educational values of assuring that our students not only grow in wisdom but also develop as men and women of highest character and integrity. They also describe the ultimate outcome of a Holy Cross education: to inspire young people to live lives that embody those virtues that bear fruit not only in this life—in service to neighbor and the common good—but for eternity.

In choosing the word "cultivate," Blessed Moreau reminds us that it is God who plants within the heart and mind of each of our students the grace to come to know of his loving presence. For us as educators in the faith, we seek to help our students integrate both the mind and the heart in their academic studies, as well as within their daily lives. We know that learning happens not only in the laboratory or classroom but also on the athletic field, in their residences, and in both the local and global neighborhoods through their many acts of service. I have witnessed this integration most especially when I have participated with our students in service immersion programs. As students reflect on their experiences, they draw connections between their readings and study and the lived experience of their neighbor.

This integration of mind and heart is hopefully the aim of all of us who work with young people. As cultivators of God's grace in their education and lives, we pray to empower them to become engaged citizens, shaping a more just and compassionate world.

John Denning, C.S.C.

January 14

One of the surest and safest means to prevent the collapse of society is to bind and to hold more and more strongly bound the child's heart to the parents' heart, to the family, to home, to primitive and innocent affections.

—Fr. Edward Sorin, C.S.C.

ONE OF THE strongest values in most African societies is family. I have learned this firsthand through living and working in our Holy Cross community there. Unlike in most Western societies, with their heavy emphasis on thinking, African cultures tend to stress belonging. Rather than, "I think therefore I am," their fundamental understanding of themselves is, "I am because we are."

Every time I am privileged to visit an African family, I strongly experience this oneness. Great reverence is always shown to guests, and they are made to feel part of the family. Upon entering their home, guests are taken to the sitting room and then all the family members come to greet them, grandparents and parents, uncles and aunts, and all of the children. It is very important for each family member to shake hands and greet the guests by bowing and even kneeling before them. Then the family serves them tea and something to eat. At this point, the guests already feel strongly bound to the family.

This strong commitment to family forms the backbone of these African societies. In addition, it has made me value my own natural family even more. It serves not only as an example for us in Holy Cross but for all families as we strive to form the strong and lasting bonds that unite us to each other as communities, societies, and ultimately one human family.

Alan Harrod, C.S.C.

January 15

The love with which the Sacred Heart of Jesus burned for us stripped him of his glory, clothing him in the form of a slave and making him be born in a stable; this love made him live among trials and sufferings; this love made him sad until death in the Garden of Olives and crucified him on Calvary; this love holds him still among us veiled in the Eucharist and unites him so closely to our souls that we must therefore say with him: see how he loved!

—Blessed Basil Moreau

MANY OF US know the challenge of being engaged in work that is not directly connected to our vocation, at least not in an obvious way. As a priest, I once administered a Catholic high school of almost nine hundred boys in New York. I spent a lot of time dealing with budgets, personnel, the maintenance of the building, and politics. But then there was always that moment, that phone call, the interruption, that brought me back to the Heart of Jesus, to the heart of the priesthood, to the center of my real vocation.

One year, I presided at the funeral of the husband of one of my teachers. He was forty-two years old and left behind his wife and their eleven-year-old son. At the homily, no one cared if I could read a balance sheet or understand the complexities of education law. What they cared about was my faith and especially my ability to comfort that little boy. One only does that by speaking from the heart—indeed, about the heart: about the love that made the Lord Jesus live among suffering and trials, about the love of his Sacred Heart that brought him close to us, without glory, to bring compassion upon the world. In joy and in sorrow, in everyday things as well as at extraordinary times, we are united with the Lord through his presence in the Eucharist, where heart speaks to heart. That is the truest vocation of every Christian.

Walter E. Jenkins, C.S.C.

January 16

Our consecration is a public one, for we are called to stand forth in service and witness. It is desirable therefore that we ordinarily be known and seen as members of the congregation. The symbol of the congregation, the cross and anchors, is worn to identify us as members of Holy Cross.

—Holy Cross *Constitutions*

HAVING THE CROSS and anchors as our congregational symbol leads to confusion at times. People see us wearing it and ask, "Are you in the Navy?" I am often glad they at least ask because it gives me the opportunity to explain who I am and what the symbol means. Our cross and anchors are an image of our motto: *Ave Crux, Spes Unica*—Hail the Cross, Our Only Hope. The cross stands upright with two anchors laid over it, the anchors being an ancient Christian symbol of hope.

In reflecting on our congregational symbol, I have always been more intrigued by the anchors than the cross. I have wondered frequently why exactly anchors have been a longstanding symbol of hope for Christians. Anchors keep ships secure amid stormy seas. They are immensely heavy and sturdy and yet seem so small in comparison to the objects they hold in place. They have two arms reaching out to grasp the ocean floor to resist the force of the unstable ship. Oh, how much like hope they are! Hope settles us amid the turbulence of our lives. Hope weighs heavily on our hearts and yet seems so insignificant when our worries and cares are larger than life. Hope is our arms grasping for anything that will root us against the forces moving us away from God. As Christians, our hope in the Cross is all of this and the firm comfort that, through our faith, this Cross leads to the Resurrection.

Gregory Haake, C.S.C.

January 17

It is not merely we who pray, but his Spirit who prays in us. And we who busy ourselves in announcing the

*Lord's kingdom need to come back often enough and
sit at his feet and listen still more closely.*
—Holy Cross Constitutions

VOCATUS ATQUE NON *vocatus, Deus aderit.* When I served as
novice master, I gave this inscription on a laminated card to
every novice who entered the Holy Cross Novitiate. It was also
inscribed on a bronze plaque in my office. It means, "Bidden or
not bidden, God is present." At the same time that I presented
this card to the novices, I asked them to go through a kind of
detox, giving up their cell phones, the Internet, and all of their
electronic toys for the year. It is not an easy task for anyone.
Can we imagine our lives without all of these props? Without
all the noise? Without all the busyness? To discover joy, renewal,
and refreshment in the silent presence of the One who is always
present to each of us is what we learn at the novitiate. Once
we have experienced this gift of sacred time, sacred space, and
intimate relationship with the Lord, then the line from Psalm
46, "Be still and know that I am God," becomes real.

All of us grow anxious and busy with many good things,
especially the mission of Jesus Christ in the world today. We
all need to maintain an awareness of Jesus' presence with us
whether we are active and busy or not. We all need to carve out
some sacred time and sacred space to sit at the feet of Jesus, to
be still, and to listen to the voice of God. Then our relationship
with the Lord will deepen, and we will be conformed all the
more to Christ, who will send us back out into the world of our
busy lives refreshed and renewed.

Tom Lemos, C.S.C.

January 18

For human beings, imitation is a necessity. It is also their life. Children retrace in their own persons the good as well as the bad characteristics of their parents; servants, those of their master; soldiers, those of their captain; friends, those of their closest friend. Understand, then, to what great glory your God wants to raise you up when he calls you to imitate his only Son who became human like you so that you might all the easier imitate him.

—Blessed Basil Moreau

"MIMESIS, MIMESIS, MIMESIS . . . this is how you become good writers!" This was the constant refrain of Ron Karrenbauer, my revered high school English instructor. To an impatient high school student, the advice was unwelcome: Was one not supposed to be finding one's own voice? "Mimesis"—imitation or copying—seemed uncreative, tedious, beneath us. But history and life teach otherwise. We learn by doing; we grow in virtues by exercising them. We are well served to place ourselves in the tutelage of a master before we know what we are doing.

The composer Chopin would spend an hour or even two playing music from J. S. Bach before he would compose his own. The author James Gurney, reflecting on Chopin's exercise of imitation in this way, wrote that when Chopin "played Bach's music he felt he absorbed the master through the pores of his fingertips. Why don't we artists do the same thing? Maybe it's because we're taught that it's bad to copy someone else's artwork.

. . . But there's nothing at all wrong with copying as a way to practice and learn. It's the shortest path to understanding. . . . Great illustrators developed [their] own way of painting by absorbing earlier masters. . . . This was considered almost a mystical process of letting the earlier master's spirit into you."

The Christian who wants to embrace fully the glorious freedom of the children of God is invited to adopt the imitation of Christ as a form of life—indeed, to let the Master's Spirit enter into us. When we repeat the Our Father, we pray the words in the first person together with Christ himself—how great a mystery, how great a privilege! Let us also sit with the woman at the well, grieve with Martha and Mary over Lazarus, weep over Jerusalem, and suffer gracefully when life imposes its crosses on us. Such is our way out of the tomb.

William R. Dailey, C.S.C.

☩

January 19

"Come, follow me." It was the Lord Jesus calling us.
—Holy Cross *Constitutions*

I FIRST DISCOVERED my vocation to the priesthood when I was a mere sophomore in high school, but it was not until my senior year in college that I decided to act on my calling. During those in-between years, I routinely entered into "confidential" meetings with my parents to see about the feasibility of living my life as a priest. Every time I would become convinced that Jesus was calling me to the priesthood, I would back off, believing it to be too hasty, too different, too frightening.

After countless late-night conversations, I finally had enough courage to leave home and visit Moreau Seminary at Notre Dame for the first time. When I was just a few blocks away, I pulled over to the side of the road and called home. Upon my dad's answering, I told him that I was going to return home because the seminary just wasn't for me. Being a wise father of six, he responded, "They're priests for goodness sake. Please go and hear what they have to say." I went. And now I am a priest in the Congregation of Holy Cross.

So often we are tempted never to leave what is comfortable or what is familiar in our lives. Yet we are challenged to trust that God is always guiding us along the right path. Trust is an absolutely essential part of our spiritual lives because it triumphs over fear, anxiety, and popular opinion. By willingly following the Lord's call in our lives, we most clearly demonstrate our trust for the One who is always true. "Come," he beckons, "follow me."

Peter McCormick, C.S.C.

January 20—Feast of Blessed Basil Moreau

Far from me be the thought of attributing to myself the merit of the truly providential works which have arisen under my direction. After God, who alone is the author of all good, it is to the devotedness of my fellow priests and to your own that we owe what can be seen today at Holy Cross which astounds everybody. I have

*been but a simple instrument which the Lord will soon
break that he may substitute for it others more worthy.*
—Blessed Basil Moreau

IN THE EARLY decades of the twentieth century, the Holy See
challenged religious communities to reexamine their common
life and ministries in light of the charism of their founders.
This reoccurring theme in the renewal of religious life presented
something of a problem for Holy Cross. At that time, there was
an ambiguous, if not somewhat troubled understanding of the
role of Blessed Basil Moreau. While Fr. Moreau was indisputably
our founder and the architect of our spirituality and apostolic
program, there had been serious tension in the last years of his
life between himself and significant personalities within the
Congregation.

Early attempts to rehabilitate Fr. Moreau's reputation met
with some resistance, especially at the University of Notre
Dame. As late as the 1930s, when the Superior General, Fr. John
Wesley Donahue, C.S.C., was preaching about Fr. Moreau from
the pulpit of Sacred Heart Church on campus, he faced a noisy
walkout by some of the older religious. With the passage of time
and a more serious examination of Holy Cross's history, however, Fr. Moreau's heroic holiness and creative religious genius
came to be recognized throughout the Congregation and, with
his beatification, in the universal Church.

Blessed Moreau wove together different strains of Catholic tradition into what became the Holy Cross charism. He
embraced the incarnational piety of the French school of spirituality. He adapted elements of monastic life and governance
into Holy Cross's rather distinctive familial style. He imitated
the Jesuits with the intentional priority given to the apostolate.

He persistently challenged Holy Cross religious to be educators in the faith in their schools and missions. Fr. Moreau proclaimed that the foundational hope of his community was the holy Cross of Christ, as seen through the faith-filled eyes of Our Lady. Blessed Moreau's dream of a Holy Cross family of priests, brothers, and sisters has known times of challenge, but his inspiring vision persists today.

Two rather similar personal episodes in Blessed Moreau's life epitomize his lifelong zeal. After Fr. Moreau's first Mass at his home parish, someone came in the middle of the night to ask him to substitute for an ailing priest in a neighboring village. Without hesitation, this newly ordained priest got out of bed, left his family, traveled through the night, and then, for what should have been days of rest and celebration, stood in for the ill priest. Then, in the final years of his life, after much suffering—having witnessed the auction of his beloved Notre Dame College and feeling abandoned by his religious family—Fr. Moreau resumed an energetic ministry as a preacher and retreat master. As an old man, in the harsh cold of winter, Fr. Moreau once again traveled to a small country parish to substitute for an ailing priest. He himself became gravely ill, and a short time later he died in Sainte Croix, surrounded by faithful Marianite sisters.

Blessed Basil Moreau was clearly a man with a most generous heart, a man of intense prayer, and a man who loved God and neighbor. Both when it was easy and when it was difficult, he poured himself out in the service of the Church. Not only the Holy Cross family but the whole Church should be very proud of Blessed Moreau. We best honor this saintly man by striving, like him, no matter what the situation, to be simple instruments that the Lord can use for his glory.

Daniel R. Jenky, C.S.C.

January 21

The rule forms our character; it softens our disposition and smoothes rough edges. It roots out faults of mind and heart and replaces them with virtues.
—Blessed Basil Moreau

HUMAN CIVILIZATIONS THROUGHOUT history have used a rule of law to govern themselves. Such systems, at their best, are liberating because they provide a framework in which citizens may live freely and work productively for the betterment of all. Without such laws, society risks falling into chaos. In a similar way, religious life, since its beginnings in the fourth century, has structured itself within a framework that forms the character of the community and its members.

Blessed Moreau wanted his priests and brothers to flourish. Informed by the history of religious life, he knew this would happen best when rules were set and articulated. A religious rule of life requires a certain discipline and forces its adherents to reflect seriously upon their words and actions so as to conform to the higher order and good that the rule demands.

Beyond the confines of religious life, Christianity also is lived within the context of a rule as articulated by the message and mission of Jesus Christ. To follow the ways of the Gospel is very challenging, especially in a contemporary society that often shows little value for Christian ideals. Those, however, who have the courage to follow the narrow path, the way that is often more difficult and filled with obstacles, will experience a sense of peace and manifest the virtue of love, the most fundamental and important of Christian virtues. For it is love that will free us from the bondage of this world. And it is the rule that allows love to permeate our lives and the society in which we live.

Richard Gribble, C.S.C.

January 22

The Lord Jesus loved us and gave up his life for us. Few of us will be called to die the way he died. Yet all of us must lay down our lives with him and for him. If we would be faithful to the gospel we must take up our cross daily and follow him.

—Holy Cross *Constitutions*

"WITHOUT A DOUBT, this is the hardest thing I've had to do," said the elder brother, allowing himself to be dressed by the aide. He was talking about his life, living it, coping with the gap between his memory of being younger and capable—a respected Holy Cross school administrator—and his current state. Catching a glimpse of himself in the mirror across the room, he arched his eyebrows and, with a rueful smile, pulled his shirt smooth. He stood still a moment, remembering . . .

During each stage of our lives, we are brought to a cross. How will we respond? In our earlier years, whether our challenges are troublesome coworkers or a periodic glitch in the plans, we learn to recognize the Cross and to take the opportunity to turn challenges into a brief retreat with him. This builds "The Relationship"—the only one that will make the difference. But, especially in our final stage of life, we may encounter our own poverty in searing ways: aches, of course; loss of physical capacities; and for those of us who live long enough to be once again washed, diapered, and dressed, a humility that allows no pretense. As a final service, we pray that we may allow ourselves to be served and that our helpers may find it a grace to work with us. We pray to have the courage we will need in our last hours. Without a steadily built perspective, a friendship born of years of choices for him who has ever loved us, our aging could be agony, rather than rebirth.

Reverie over, the elder brother, chuckling, shook his head, grabbed the handles of his walker, and headed out of his bedroom to join the group waiting down the hall. "Time for our social!" he crowed.

Mark Knightly, C.S.C.

January 23

Jesus Christ speaks to us in the holy scriptures where we can find his teachings. He speaks by the voice of his ministers, by books of piety. He speaks by the good thoughts he inspires in us, by remorse of conscience

and the interior consolations he has us experience. His
voice is refreshing, persuasive, and touching.
—Blessed Basil Moreau

WORDS AND THOUGHTS are intimately related. We could not even think to ourselves if we had never learned a language. Language is central to our very identity as human beings and to our personal development. It also points to the communal nature of our existence. Significantly, we are taught a language by others. We learn our first words from our parents and teachers. We listen to others and learn from their words as well. We are fed and nourished with words. Words shape and form us.

The most formative word for us is the Word of God. God spoke his Word in the beginning, and all of creation came into being. The Word became flesh through the Virgin Mary and dwelt among us. As one of us, the Incarnate Word touched and healed us; he taught us about the kingdom and how to love the Father and one another in the Holy Spirit.

As followers of Christ, we are formed principally by listening to the Word speaking to our hearts. So above all, we must be men and women of prayer, attentive to the Word spoken to us in scripture, in the liturgy, in quiet solitude at the foot of the Master, and in our consciences. Then, formed by this Word, we go forth as educators in the faith to help God's people re-Word their lives. We speak Christ's language so that our very lives allow others to hear the Voice that is so refreshing, persuasive, and touching to their souls. And thus we make God known, loved, and served.

Terrence Ehrman, C.S.C.

January 24

We forgo the independent exercise of our wills in order to join with brothers in a common discernment of God's will as manifested in prayer, communal reflection, scripture, the Spirit's guidance in the church, and the cry of the poor.

—Holy Cross *Constitutions*

AS PROVINCIAL SUPERIOR, one of my greatest privileges is to meet with individual brothers and priests and explore with them their lives spiritually, pastorally, and even professionally. I am often humbled by our conversations, realizing how committed these men are to living a life of integrity, honest to the vows that we profess. I also have the special privilege of meeting with our young men who are not yet finally professed and who are taking it "one year at a time" as they question if God is calling them to religious life. I am surprised that, quite frequently, the vow that they most question—whether or not they can truly understand it, let alone live it—is obedience.

Perhaps, I ought not to be so surprised. Most of us have been deeply immersed in a culture of self-reliance, individual initiative, individual achievements, and individual rights. It is not so easy to break from that mindset! To think suddenly of decision making as "common discernment" is difficult.

Yet we in Holy Cross view our community as a family. I grew up in a family where we were all expected to sacrifice for one another and for the good of the whole family. It all boiled down to trust. When our parents made decisions, we would eventually trust they saw a bigger picture than our individual desires. The vow of obedience similarly calls us to trust—most especially God, but even the community and fallible provincials. So, too, for us in our families, we place trust in God, in the other family members, even in fallible parents. While such trust might be hard to come by at times, God stands ready both to reinforce our trust and to reward it when we commit ourselves to each other.

Tom O'Hara, C.S.C.

January 25

"I have chosen," says the Lord, "and have sanctified this place that my name may be there forever, and my eyes, and my heart may remain there perpetually." How fervently each of us should wish these words should apply to our own hearts!

—Fr. Edward Sorin, C.S.C.

WE IN HOLY CROSS are used to it. People always seem to want to make us the Congregation of *the* Holy Cross, but we're not. We are the Congregation of Holy Cross. That little definite article might not seem to make much of a difference, yet it reveals an important truth about our community. We are named for the small French town of Sainte-Croix, where Blessed Moreau founded our Congregation. Since then, the particularity of places has been an essential part of our ministries. Both Blessed Moreau and Fr. Sorin understood clearly what Holy Cross might accomplish as a community by working together to sanctify particular places. With this understanding of place, Holy Cross religious have done God's work for almost two centuries, from the classrooms of rural France and Algeria to North America, India, Poland, South America, and Africa. The desire of these countless religious was to fulfill the Lord's stirring command to sanctify whatever piece of the world they were sent to serve.

I can vividly remember all of the places I have been blessed to minister in my over four decades in Holy Cross. I remember the halls of the high schools in Indianapolis, Akron, and Chicago. I remember the campus of Holy Cross College at Notre Dame, and I recall well the bluff on the Willamette River on which sits the University of Portland. We all have places that are seared forever into our hearts. Our hope must be that our lives and efforts there have helped to sanctify those very grounds for the people who will follow after us.

Donald J. Stabrowski, C.S.C.

January 26

We must first seek the kingdom of God and his justice and then trust in Providence. That is why I beg of you to renew yourselves in the spirit of your vocation, which is the spirit of poverty, chastity, and obedience.
—Blessed Basil Moreau

WHEN I TAUGHT college history courses, my students' first assignment was to write their own obituary. It was not a task most freshmen and sophomores relished, but the exercise demonstrated that everyone contributes to history, even if their names never appear in textbooks. It also made them consider, if briefly, how they might want to be remembered in the end.

Interestingly, none ever bragged about accrued wealth and worldly fame. They did not boast about breaking laws or neglecting responsibilities. The universal theme was that they hoped to be loved.

Religious vows are public commitments, but they represent basic aspirations that dwell deep within every heart: to be courageous and generous, self-disciplined and accountable. Drawn out of this desire, religious vows—indeed, every Christian vocation—seek first the kingdom of God and the love for which we all long. Whatever illusions we hold about controlling our lives in our desire for fulfillment, the details of most daily events and encounters seem quite random and unpredictable. Trusting in Providence, however, we learn to greet the sun, acutely aware that the ultimate goal is salvation, and we are little deterred by trials tumbling into our paths.

We are called to shape our days with prayer, knowing that we are and always will be fully embraced by the Divine Presence, even in our folly, and so we strive to dedicate the hours from morning to night to being selfless, faithful, and dutiful. Our common human longing is to die as we have lived. It is our only hope.

James B. King, C.S.C.

January 27

We find prayer no less a struggle than did the first disciples, who wearied of their watch. Even our ministry can offer itself as a convincing excuse to be neglectful, since our exertions for the kingdom tempt us to imagine that our work may supply for our prayer. But without prayer we drift, and our work is no longer for him. To serve him honestly we must pray always and not give up. He will bless us in his time and lighten our burdens and befriend our loneliness.

—Holy Cross *Constitutions*

IN *THE SCREWTAPE LETTERS*, C. S. Lewis stresses that humans are subject to continual change: "Their nearest approach to constancy is undulation—the repeated return to a level from which they repeatedly fall back, a series of troughs and peaks. Interest in work, affection for friends, physical appetites, all go up and down." This Law of Undulation holds true for prayer as well. We have moments when prayer is rich and rewarding; we have moments in which it is dry and dull. This undulation is not our fault; it is how we are made. Nothing is gained by reproaching ourselves for a phenomenon ingrained in our humanity. Instead, we must strive to pray faithfully during troughs as well as peaks.

We tend to focus on work during periods of spiritual bleakness. Ministry provides conscious rewards when prayer does not; however, work is potentially endless. It is all too easy to immerse ourselves in work or ministry, especially during times of aridity. But these are just the moments when we should redouble our efforts to pray. Our ministry must be inspired and informed by our prayer. Our *Constitutions* insist that the more we come through prayer to relish what is right the better we shall work in our mission for the realization of the kingdom. Or, as my first formation director maintained, "You can't give what you haven't got."

In fact, God makes us into the persons he wants us to be through our undulations, especially the troughs. As Lewis says, "Prayers offered in the state of dryness are those which please him best." This is a mystery but a central truth nevertheless. When our Lord prayed at Gethsemane and on the Cross, the Father appeared to have forsaken him, yet these are the prayers most linked with the consummation of Jesus' mission.

Patrick Sopher, C.S.C.

January 28

We will live so that our faith might be so simple, so strong and lively that it not only enlightens the spirit but also inspires our thoughts, feelings, words, and actions.

—Blessed Basil Moreau

WHEN I READ Blessed Moreau describe the ideal faith as simple, I must admit that a part of me bristles. I associate "simple" with negative words like "simpleton," and so I hesitate to endorse the simplicity of faith. And yet religious philosophers like St. Augustine and St. Aquinas remind us that God is by nature simple. How can this be? In what sense can the source of all the universe's complexity be simple?

God is simple because of his essential and eternal unity. God is so pure that his word and his love share his very being. We admire people whose words and actions are consistent with who they really are. God's being and speaking and doing are so consistent that they are truly one. It is in this sense that God is awesomely simple.

And so Blessed Moreau rightly asserts that our simple faith in this simple God will affect a similar unity in us—a unity of spirit, thought, feeling, word, and action; a unity of mind, heart, soul, and strength. Far too often, unfortunately, we endure the frustrations and struggles described by St. Paul as he laments the predicament of a divided self: "For I do not do the good I want, but I do the evil I do not want" (Rom 7:19). When I am divided against myself, I waste so much energy fighting myself that I have little left to give to God and neighbor. By contrast, Blessed Moreau understands that a simple person, a united person, is lively and strong because that person is an image of the living God.

Charles McCoy, C.S.C.

January 29

Our experience in Holy Cross is demanding. It is joyful as well. And so it should give us a life to which we would happily invite others. The Lord's call will be heard in our steadfast witness to the gospel, the companionship we offer one another, the cheerfulness with which we serve in our mission without counting the cost, and the sincere welcome we openly offer men who join us. If we delight in our vocation, we will share it with others.

—Holy Cross *Constitutions*

"LAND OF HOLY CROSS"—Portuguese navigators originally gave that name to Brazil when they landed there in 1500. Some centuries later, in 1944, the first Holy Cross priests arrived in the huge city of São Paulo, followed by the Holy Cross sisters, and then, in the Amazon region, the Holy Cross brothers. Since then, Holy Cross men and women have been faithfully serving in this land. We have a burning desire to make God more known, loved, and served, even in the country with the largest number of Catholics on the globe.

I had the privilege of knowing some of those pioneering brothers. They knew how to invite others happily to the mission. On my first visit to a Holy Cross community in the Amazon, I felt their sincere welcome. They invited me for evening prayer and a delicious supper with good conversation. The hospitality of the brothers made a profound impact on me, and I started saying to myself, "I want to be a man like these men I have met!"

I now work in vocation promotion, charged with inviting young men, like myself, to our life and mission. I know I am only an instrument in the hands of the Holy Spirit, but I delight in my vocation, and so I joyfully share it with others. Yet the work of raising up religious vocations is not mine alone or ours alone as brothers, sisters, and priests; it is the work of the whole Church. As one of the pioneering brothers used to say, we need to be "*núcleos do Reino*"—that is, we need to build communities that have at their core the kingdom of God. In that way, witnessing to the Gospel and welcoming others, we will build together a "land of Holy Cross" wherever we are.

Ronnie Lenno Silva, C.S.C.

✠

January 30

It is this union, the fruit of sanctifying grace, which will strengthen us against the world and the devil, while being at the same time the source of our success and consolations. It is like the mortar which holds and binds the stones of the building we have undertaken, for without it, everything will crumble and fall into ruin.

—Blessed Basil Moreau

REALITY TV PUZZLES me, mostly because of how unreal it is. One of the first and most famous of these shows is *Survivor*, in which people are dropped off on some deserted island where they form tribes and compete against one another to be the last person left. They operate out of some of the most depraved motivations within our human nature. It's about looking out only for oneself so as to win a million dollars.

Each of us has our own "survivor" story, I suppose. Mine has to do with being the ninth of ten kids. (Having three sisters and six older brothers is survival in itself!) But the real test of survival for my family came after my dad died. I had just turned four, my oldest sister was fourteen, and my mom was three months pregnant. Our family was a bit of a tribe on our own island, yet we learned to survive not by being cutthroat but by looking out for one another. We formed coalitions, but they were coalitions to ensure everybody would be okay. We survived not by throwing one another off the island but by reaching out to each other and beyond.

From the first days of Holy Cross, Blessed Moreau offered unity as one of the most fundamental tenants of our being together and in the world. As sisters and brothers in Christ, we reveal the kingdom Jesus came to proclaim by walking and working together. Blessed Moreau echoes St. Paul's letter to the Ephesians, where Paul urges us "to live in a manner worthy of the call you have received, with all humility and gentleness, with patience, bearing with one another through love, striving to preserve the unity of the spirit through the bond of peace" (4:1–3).

Bill Lies, C.S.C.

January 31

The spirit of faith inspires and enlivens zeal, that is, the sacred fire that the Divine Master came to bring upon the earth. So if one has faith and the zeal inspired by faith, that person can never think without heartbreak about the vast amounts of sin in the world. Such a person will be ready to go wherever obedience calls to save souls which are perishing and extend the rule of Jesus Christ on earth.

—Blessed Basil Moreau

As a FIRST-YEAR teacher and coach at a Catholic high school, as well as a new pastoral associate at a parish, I met periodically with a ministry supervisor. He had spent many years in Latin America and was now the head of a Catholic secondary school. Needless to say, I was almost overwhelmingly busy. Yet during the year, I was continually struck by my supervisor's tireless energy, compassion, joy, sense of humor, and willingness to do—as he liked to say—"whatever it took" to make people experience Christ's love and call. He had that twinkle in his eye that instantaneously called forth from others an almost impulsive desire to follow his example. Once I asked him for the secret to his boundless service to the Gospel. He paused momentarily, smiled, and then said simply that God had given him three things—faith, a love of people, and a promise that there would be plenty of time to rest in the afterlife.

I often have reflected on these simple words. They reflect the deep relationship with Christ that has allowed my former supervisor to serve as a priest and religious in the poorest neighborhoods and schools from South America to inner-city Chicago. He had the energy to do this because he realized that this service was not his but the Lord's. I pray often that I can have this same faith, this same love of others, and this same abiding trust that there will be time to rest in the afterlife.

Sean McGraw, C.S.C.

Since God alone provides the means for the successful accomplishment of any task, it really seems evident that a person needs to be called by God to be a teacher if that person is going to be able to be effective.

—Blessed Basil Moreau

TEACHING IS A path to sainthood, or perhaps martyrdom. Either way, being an educator—especially a Catholic educator—is a vocation that demands devotion and humility if one is truly to educate both the heart and the mind.

During my first months of teaching high school, I had one particularly frustrating evening. As I was correcting papers, I came to the realization that several of my students had blown off an assignment that I had worked hard to create. Disheartened and drained by long and thankless days, I cried out to God, "What am I doing wrong?" I walked down the hall and talked to Fr. Sean McGraw, C.S.C., and at his suggestion, I retreated to our chapel, Bible and gradebook in hand.

There, before the Blessed Sacrament, I prayed the words of the parable of the sower and the seed. Christ told his followers that the seed they spread throughout the world would find many different kinds of soil, some rich and some rocky, but their charge was simply to spread the Good News with reckless abandon. I realized that it would not be through my strength that these seeds would take root but only through the power of the Holy Spirit. His was the mission, his would be the strength, and from him alone would come the grace to persevere in teaching each of the names staring at me in my gradebook. This, for me, is the divine call not only of teaching but of all vocations—cooperating with God's grace, spreading the Good News, and then getting out of the Holy Spirit's way.

Nate Wills, C.S.C.

February 2

We have all, doubtless, endeavored to present our-selves to God, like the blessed child, with as much as possible the same pure intention and the same sincere desire to serve him, and serve him alone.
—Fr. Edward Sorin, C.S.C.

IT WAS SIX o'clock in the morning on February 2, 1944, when twelve other novices and I approached the altar at St. Joseph's Novitiate to kneel before the Blessed Sacrament and pronounce vows of poverty, chastity, and obedience in the presence of the community. It was a profound moment of acceptance into Holy Cross. Yet what we didn't realize was that we weren't fully poor, chaste, and obedient at the moment of profession. That would come later when students, parishioners, and the poor called us forth to live those vows.

Our religious vows are meant to free us to love and serve people, to build the kingdom of Jesus' Father, a kingdom of justice, love, and peace. Having made several visits to our missions in East Africa, I found the real meaning of this love and service. The willingness to share and the simplicity of so many poor people touched me greatly. Often there would be a knock at the door with someone bringing a chicken, a few eggs, and some bananas. It was what I might call a reverse mission.

When this life is over and we meet our Creator, God will ask, "When I was thirsty, did you give me drink? When I was a stranger in your land, did you welcome me? Did you care for me in the widow, the unwed mother, the sick, the leper, and the prisoner?" The extent to which we can say yes to these questions is the extent to which we have said yes to our Christian vocations, whatever our state in life. For those who call forth the love and service we Christians profess are the ones who help us to become ever more like Christ.

Renatus Foldenauer, C.S.C.

February 3

Here begins the sacred task to make of the new-comer a Christian and a scholar, for both of which God's grace must be solicited, and suitable attention secured from teachers.

—Fr. Edward Sorin, C.S.C.

EACH MORNING, ONE student would light the candle and lead us in prayer. "O God, come to my assistance," she would proclaim, and the rest of the sixth grade would respond, "O Lord, make haste to help me." After a hymn came a psalm recited by alternating sides of the classroom like monks in choir. Another student then read the scripture passage of the day before that young assembly voiced their prayer concerns, prayed the Lord's Prayer, and offered the closing prayer.

One can't overstate how seriously these twelve-year-olds took their daily prayer and how the ritual and its rhythm settled and focused them each morning. The power of true worship grasped young hearts as they asked God's blessing on sick grandparents and lost cats, on the victims of the recent earthquake, or on those who lost everything in the fire that devastated a neighboring city.

Yet the impact of those brief encounters with the Divine lasted far longer than the prayer itself. Each day's studies were then viewed through the lens of prayer, so that their efforts were understood, in part, though a deeper appreciation of human longing and God's love for us. In turn, their struggle with the themes of literature, the often harsh realities of history, and the complexities of the truths of faith led them back to prayer and a deepening appreciation of the challenges of living a Christian faith.

The process of Christian maturation never ends. Faith must always be informed by study and our studies by faith. For human striving without grace is doomed to fail, but grace without human effort often remains unrealized possibility. And that is a great, and most sad, loss.

Gary S. Chamberland, C.S.C.

*Let us never forget that by praying for our beloved
departed ones we establish for ourselves rights which
eternal Justice will respect when "the hand of God
shall have touched us also."*

—Fr. Edward Sorin, C.S.C.

FR. JOACHIM BIMAL ROZARIO, C.S.C., a fellow Holy Cross
priest in Bangladesh, died unexpectedly on this day in 2007. We
were classmates in seminary. The loss of such a close friend at the
young age of fifty was a shock for me. Since I was studying in the
United States at the time, I was unable to attend the funeral. Yet,
according to our Bengali custom, I observed three days of prayer
for his soul and for his bereaved family and abstained from
eating meat and fish. If I had been in Bangladesh, I would have
joined in the celebration at the end of the third day in which
the family prays together and then shares in a meal. Forty days
later, just as the Church celebrates the Ascension of Jesus forty
days after his Resurrection, the family and friends gather again
to pray for the deceased. His or her good works and example
are fondly remembered and shared by all. On both of these
occasions, if a priest is available, we also celebrate Mass.

These traditional Bengali customs, as well as our Catholic traditions of praying for the dead, are not the worship of
ancestors. They are gestures signifying the bonds that do not
end at someone's death but continue into our eternal life with
God. In remembering and following the good examples of
those who have died, we keep them alive among us. This holy

remembrance helps to prepare each of us for our own entrance into the Communion of Saints in the heavenly kingdom.

Eugene Anjus, C.S.C.

February 5

Here is the secret of success for each and for all—a good will. Let us think less of ourselves and more of our God and of our neighbor.
—Fr. Edward Sorin, C.S.C.

FR. SORIN BIDS us to be of good will by thinking of others first, but this is difficult to do when we are caught up in our own pain. We simply cannot force ourselves to change our feelings and be bright and cheery when despair barges into our lives. Yet being of good will—and not necessarily of good feeling—can work wonders.

Marietta knows this firsthand. A twenty-six-year-old deranged man abducted her seven-year-old daughter, Susie, from the family's tent during a camping trip. He tortured and killed her. Marietta felt intense rage and the need for revenge but tried hard not to overburden others with her sorrows and struggles. She was a being of good will, thinking of others first. Her doing so helped her to carry her unimaginable grief a little more lightly. It also led her to think of what kind of inner torture the perpetrator must have endured to motivate himself to do such a heinous act. With the help of prayer, such consideration led Marietta to have a phone conversation with the man during which she was able to listen caringly and compassionately. This special conversation led the man to reveal inadvertently information that made it possible for the FBI to identify and arrest him.

Continuing to think of others, she succeeded in getting the man a life sentence rather than capital punishment. She did not want to memorialize her daughter's killing with another death, creating only another victim and another grieving family. Marietta knows that being of good will and thinking of others first heals hearts. She now travels the world, offering workshops on the power of forgiveness made possible by God's mercy and compassion for all of us.

Bill Faiella, C.S.C.

February 6

All the members must cultivate the spirit of mutual love and cooperation and have at heart the welfare and success of the association as a whole. Joys and sorrows will be mutual. If anyone fails in health or is incapacitated before his time, the others will support him and provide for his needs. Then it is that we shall taste the happiness of a life of poverty, chastity, and obedience in the midst of the fathers, brothers, and sisters in Jesus Christ.

—Blessed Basil Moreau

A WISE ELDER brother once excused the discontent of two young religious, saying, "Perhaps they haven't needed the community yet." Experience gained through ministry, prayer, and community deepens our realization that we need each other in order to live our vowed life and accomplish our mission. Similarly, another brother in community often reminds me, "We are in this together." Through my brothers' acceptance of me as I am and their encouragement of my ministry, through their sympathy when loved ones have died and their support when I have failed, I have been well instructed in the bonds and responsibilities of community.

Times in which we truly have to depend upon each other underscore our need for community. I learned this as one of four brothers initiating a collaborative project in rural southern Georgia. As pioneers and as members of a Catholic minority, we faced many obstacles in responding to the needs of the local Church. But together we found our way.

We in Holy Cross are strengthened and energized by our diversity and by the dynamics of sharing resources in service of our common mission. Like Holy Cross, all members of the universal Church share the task of cultivating the spirit of mutual love and cooperation in service to the mission Christ entrusted to his followers. We all need each other. We are in this together.

Richard Critz, C.S.C.

February 7

As disciples of Jesus we stand side by side with all people. Like them we are burdened by the same struggles and beset by the same weaknesses; like them we are

made new by the same Lord's love; like them we hope
for a world where justice and love prevail.
—Holy Cross Constitutions

WE ALWAYS TRY to empathize with those we serve, but in this case, it was different. What I experienced was as if the Lord himself was mysteriously speaking to me: "Come with me; find solidarity with my pain." That day, I received a request from a young woman from our parish; she asked me to accompany her to visit a friend's family in which one of the children was sick with cancer and had entered his terminal phase. I went with her and offered to anoint the sick child. The family accepted, but they also asked about the possibility of offering the child his First Communion as well because, with his struggles against cancer, he had been unable to receive it. So that day we celebrated Patricio's First Communion. He was just ten years old—a life that was ending in this world but beginning its fullness in heaven.

Three weeks later, Patricio died. They asked me to celebrate his funeral. It was another call—even harder than the first—to be in solidarity with a family who had lost a child. Like them, perhaps, I felt the sadness and pain. Like them, I did not understand how a child had to suffer, and questions arose about the promises God made to us. In that moment, my priesthood asked of me something more than being empathetic; it asked me to be in solidarity with a family that was searching for answers in its faith, as I myself was seeking the same answers.

And so it is with all of us, disciples of Jesus. In joining in solidarity with others, we, at times, necessarily share even their struggles and questions, yet all so that we might share the same love and hope.

Carlos Augusto Jacobo de los Santos, C.S.C.

February 8

Allow me to hope that yours will be the heritage of Jesus Christ, the heritage which his saints, our fathers in God, have bequeathed to us. It is a heritage of humiliation, poverty, and suffering; of trials, temptations, labors, and persecutions of all kinds. In vain shall we seek any way leading to heaven other than the road to Calvary.

—Blessed Basil Moreau

THE HERITAGE LEFT to the Church by Blessed Moreau is that of Jesus Christ himself, the heritage of the Cross. It is the same heritage handed down to us by the other saintly men and women in Holy Cross, a heritage that was their daily bread. It is not a heritage of money, fame, or earthly power, but it is a solid inheritance, made to last. It rests on the continual cultivation of a virtuous life and a deep, disinterested love of God and neighbor. Anything keeping us from acquiring this heritage must be put aside. Everything that can increase our possession of it must be favored. It is here that we encounter the Cross.

The Cross does not consist in seeking privations or suffering. Rather, the Cross flows from our love of God and of neighbor and our seeking after a virtuous life. The Cross is the result of such a choice, and it is a measure, if not an indication, of our efforts to acquire this virtuous life. The higher we aim, the more certain we can be that we will find the Cross.

There is the question of the stakes involved. Is it all worth it? What, if anything, awaits us beyond these crosses? Heaven is the answer. It is the final goal. It is the summation of our call to follow Christ and to embrace his Cross—to become truly the image and likeness of God.

Mario Lachapelle, C.S.C.

February 9

This does not mean that our Lord forbids foresight and human initiative. He recommends elsewhere work, order, and economy in the use of temporal things, but he forbids all anxiety, because this is a reflection on his paternal providence.

—Blessed Basil Moreau

TO BE SURE, I have anxious moments as we all do. These are the times in life when a given task may seem too large or impossible. As a result, I might feel alone, perhaps even abandoned. But at such times I have only to pause and to reflect on the reality of love that surrounds me—the care and support I know from family, friends, brothers in community, and others who share my life and work. This love is wonderful. It is a sign of God's love for me. It is the way in which God guides me to his end. This is Divine Providence.

So much has been said about God's loving care for each one of us. St. Paul recalls, "In him we live and we move and we have our being" (Acts 17:28). God is the source and sustainer of our lives. All that we are and hope to become is from God. And so we can begin each new day in that sure and confident hope that God provides for us. We are all parts of the marvelous plan that our good and gracious God has for all of creation. To live in Divine Providence, though, means that we can never be passive, simply waiting for God's will to unfold. We are each uniquely gifted with wits, abilities, virtues, and zeal. The more that we come to know that we are loved, the more we will live to return that love to God and to others. For what we lack, the good Lord will provide.

John Conley, C.S.C.

February 10

Interior peace is a habitual disposition of the soul that makes us completely despise the enjoyments of the world and of the flesh, makes us rise above thoughts of sadness and discouragement which sometimes well up from our self-love, and preserves us from this eager, natural impulse as well as from those preoccupations which trouble and disturb the mind. In short, it establishes calmness in the soul along with that gentle quiet, which is the fruit of victory over our passions and the disordered longings of our heart.

—Blessed Basil Moreau

THE FINAL COMMENDATION, giving a dying soul to God, is one of the hardest prayers I have ever said and also one of the most beautiful moments of God's grace. On one occasion, I was called to the hospital by a grandmother because her grandson was dying. My feelings and emotions on the drive were scattered because I knew this visit would be difficult. A man, no older than thirty-five, was dying, and I was going to anoint him and hand his soul to God.

What a powerful moment of God's grace, and yet one that also seemed daunting because he was so young. My prayer in the hospital elevator was simple, "Holy Spirit, be with me as I enter his room." It was a simple prayer asking for God to rest his Spirit upon me so that I could pray for the dying man and with his family. As I began the prayers and the final commendation, I felt immense peace: "Go forth, Christian soul, from this world, in the name of God the almighty Father . . ."

As I said the words, nothing else mattered in the moment. No worldly desire or pleasure mattered. The only thing that mattered was encouraging the dying man to meet God and to begin his new life in the heavenly kingdom. In this moment of grace and interior peace, I was able to be present to the man's family, and my presence seemed to bring them a certain sense of peace and hope despite their pain and sorrow. All of us who follow the Crucified One are to cultivate deep hope in the Cross so that we might have the interior peace to be present and to bring that hope and peace to others in their darkest hours.

Daniel Ponisciak, C.S.C.

February 11

Zeal is the great desire to make God known, loved and served, and thus to bring knowledge of salvation to others.

—Blessed Basil Moreau

LOVE IS A powerful force. It moves spouses to give of themselves in marriage. It compels parents to sacrifice for their children. It inspires priests, religious, and lay ministers to labor for the sake of the Gospel. And it's what prompted Blessed Moreau to give up all to follow Christ and to encourage others to do the same.

At the heart of zeal is the love that moves, compels, inspires, and prompts. At a parish like St. Joseph in South Bend, Indiana, where I served as pastor, zeal was the dynamic, spirited love that motivated us to celebrate the sacraments, visit the sick, feed the hungry, welcome the stranger, and educate children and youth. In worship, service, and education, our community acted to make God known, loved, and served.

Sometimes, however, we can become lukewarm in living out our faith and lose sight of the love of God that expresses itself in good works. The same zeal that motivated Blessed Moreau and his band of religious invites us to reject spiritual lethargy and to renew our own baptismal commitment to spend our lives in the Lord's service. As disciples of Jesus, we must ask ourselves continually if we are willing to make the sacrifices that the love of the Lord and his mission require. If we find ourselves lacking in this zeal, we must let the powerful force of his love rekindle our own and move us to even greater action. For we are called to be men and women of zeal, for the glory of God and the salvation of souls!

John DeRiso, C.S.C.

February 12

God is faithful; he will not suffer you to be tempted above your strength. He will always give you the means to resist your temptations in such a way that you will be able to overcome them. Hence, laying aside the burden of sin which can retard our advance, let us run with constancy in the way which is opened up before us.

—Blessed Basil Moreau

HUMAN LIFE IS no stranger to temptations and trials. Our brother Elijah was ministered to by an angel so that he might be given strength and consolation before he departed for a journey lasting forty days and forty nights. We recall that even our Lord experienced temptation. Situated in the desert for forty days and forty nights, Jesus felt the mental and physical pain and anguish of temptation, but did not succumb. Afterward, he was ministered to by angels.

It is out of this scriptural history that Blessed Moreau wrote this letter of encouragement. He knew then, and communicates to us even now, that we are not strangers to temptation and trial. But Blessed Moreau, always a man rooted in the hope of the Cross, reminds us of the grace of God that is ours. This is what is meant when Holy Cross religious profess their vows and say, "May the God who allows and invites me to make this commitment strengthen and protect me to be faithful to it." We are not ministered to by angels but by Christ Jesus himself. And this is a great consolation to all Christians who strive daily in discipleship, our own forty days and forty nights.

God does indeed give us the means by which to resist temptation and, more importantly, to live well our Christian lives of discipleship with joy and freedom. The task, then, for we Christians who are beset daily by temptations and trials is to accept the gift of grace as it comes to us with joy and faithfulness.

Michael Wurtz, C.S.C.

February 13

Prayer should be the beginning and end of your studies. It should awake with you and take its place at your bedside. It should accompany you even in your recreations and perfume all your occupations as with a divine balm.

—Blessed Basil Moreau

IF SOMEONE ASKED me to describe my years of graduate studies, I would not hesitate for a second in responding, "I've been very blessed by God." I say this because my studies in spiritual theology at the Gregorian University in Rome have been one of the most enriching experiences of my life. Obviously, going back to college meant taking up books again, learning another language, and preparing assignments, presentations, and exams—in a word, a lot of studying!

Blessed Moreau challenges us to make prayer the beginning and end of our studies. My question is, How are we to do that? How are we to combine the life of a student, which involves many duties and lots of work, with a life of prayer? Many times, perhaps, the experience of students is that our lives of prayer and our studies intersect most when the dreaded exams are looming: "Lord, help me get through this well!" Certainly, I believe God hears those prayers, and there are surely many testimonies of his heavenly aid in these moments.

Nevertheless, Blessed Moreau's proposal goes far beyond desperate invocations in our studies or in any other difficult situation in our lives. What he is proposing, and what we all hope for, is that we develop through our personal prayer a spiritual sensitivity that is able to discover in every activity—be it studies, work, or rest—the real presence of God. In other words, we see and study God in all things. When we awaken to the Spirit of God at work in that way, it truly is like a perfume, a divine balm, as it sweetens all of our lives.

Alfredo Ledezma Olvera, C.S.C.

February 14

By our vow of celibacy we commit ourselves to seek union with God in lifelong chastity, forgoing forever marriage and parenthood for the sake of the kingdom. We also promise loyalty, companionship and affection

to our confreres in Holy Cross. Openness and disci-
pline in prayer, personal asceticism, compassionate
service, and love given and received in community
are important supports toward the generous living of
this commitment.

—Holy Cross *Constitutions*

FOREVER FORGOING MARRIAGE and parenthood for the sake of the kingdom is a commitment involving both a promise and a gift. For our celibacy as religious does not find its meaning in what we do without but in what we open ourselves to receive from God. We promise to be there for those who are lonely or hopeless, those who have suffered the loss of a loved one, and those nearing the end of their earthly journey to God. We promise to be there for those following the Lord in the single life, those seeking to confirm their love in marriage and family, and those searching for God's plan in their lives. And in this promise lies the gift. God's grace provides that we might serve and care for all whom we encounter. In love, he draws us into their lives, and in love, he draws them into ours.

For all of us need to love and to be loved. It is our deepest human longing. We celibates also need the loving support of our brothers and sisters in religious life and of our coworkers in the Lord's vineyard to remain faithful and generous in our promise to God. And yet the only way for any of us to find love is by making and keeping a promise. For it is in making and keeping a promise—whether in religious vows, marriage vows, or single faithfulness—that we open ourselves to receive not only the gift of each other's love but ultimately the unparalleled gift of God's love.

William B. Simmons, C.S.C.

February 15

Jesus himself has prepared the delicious food he offers us, and yet he must await our pleasure to partake of it. His flesh will be our food, his blood our drink, his divinity our gift, all at the same moment. His preparations are finished; his holy table is set. It is for us to come to our Communion.

—Blessed Basil Moreau

IN MY TWENTY-THREE years as a Holy Cross priest, I've been fortunate to be able to serve in parish ministry, leadership within the community, and now in college ministry. It has been wonderful to minister to such a wide variety of people, both young and old, lay and religious. One thing I have learned in my years of ministry is that what keeps us from being in a deep relationship with God is the fact that we really cannot believe just how much God loves us. If only we concentrated on the love of God instead of our fears, guilt, or doubt, we would be able to face everything that life throws at us with peace and, yes, even joy, knowing that Christ is with us every step of the journey. But we rarely experience this kind of unconditional love in our lives, so it is hard for us to trust that it is true of God.

That is the wonderful thing about the Eucharist. At each Mass, we celebrate the love of God that is so deep that he offers his very Son for us; so powerful that it conquers sin and death through Christ's passion, death, and Resurrection; and so real that it provides us the body and blood of the Lord himself as the food for our journey to the kingdom of God. This gift is given to us without cost, so that we will come to know, believe, and live in God's love. It is simply up to us to come and eat and live.

Anthony Szakaly, C.S.C.

February 16

We grow close to one another as brothers by living together in community. If we do not love the brothers whom we see, then we cannot love God whom we have not seen.

—Holy Cross *Constitutions*

IT HAS BEEN remarked that we can choose our friends, but we are born into our families and have to make the best of it. People usually join religious communities because, in part, they are attracted by members whom they have met and look forward to enjoying them as friends and companions. But we change over time and can find ourselves at odds with the very folks whom we once regarded as worthy of our friendship. Moreover, in time, others are admitted to the community whose manners put us off and whose opinions on politics, theology, liturgy, and a host of other counts we do not share. It is then that community life can become a challenge rather than a comfort, and we are tempted to draw apart into a small circle of people who are like us.

Our Lord recognized this tendency when he reminded his disciples that their "Father in heaven makes his sun to rise on the good and the evil, and sends rain on the just and the unjust. If you love those who love you, what reward shall you have? Do not even the publicans do that? And if you salute your brethren only, what are you doing more than others? Do not even the Gentiles do that?" (Mt 5:45–47).

Neither the challenge nor the problem is new, and it never has been. But almost two thousand years ago, Jesus, who connected love of God and love of neighbor, charted the path forward and the way to unity: "Forgive us our trespasses, as we forgive those who trespass against us" (Lk 11:4).

James Connelly, C.S.C.

February 17

What shall we gain from knowing and believing that Jesus Christ died for us upon the Cross, unless we are willing to suffer upon it with him?

—Fr. Edward Sorin, C.S.C.

LIVING IN A comfortable world with warm clothing, plentiful food, central heat, and air conditioning, we might be pampered too much. The other morning, although I was warm under the blankets, it was cold in the room where I awoke.

Then the thought crossed my mind of the hundreds of thousands of people in Mexico and Central America who are unable to support their families, people whose relatives I had served in ministry at our parishes in Texas, Arizona, and Indiana. As I struggled with the cold, they were struggling with the difficult decision of possibly needing to leave home and migrate north to the United States. In doing so, they would have to leave their loved ones and face all the dangers of the journey—robbers, extreme heat during the day, cold nights, and poisonous snakes. They had a hard decision. Then I thought of Christ and his passion—the agony in the garden, the scourging and crowning with thorns, the carrying of the Cross, and finally the Crucifixion and death. My faith reminds me that his suffering and death led to his Resurrection and the new life he offers all of us.

My first reaction was to be humbled. My few moments of discomfort would be nothing in comparison with those real sacrifices. And yet I hesitated, which made me question myself and how much I was willing to sacrifice for the good of others, willing to join Christ in his total gift of self. The only way to find out was to get out of bed and start trying.

John S. Korcsmar, C.S.C.

February 18

Consider the great reward promised to those who have taught the truth to others and have helped form them into justice: "They will shine eternally in the skies like the stars of the heavens." With the hope of this glory, we must generously complete the Lord's work.

—Blessed Basil Moreau

I RECEIVED AN e-mail from a man I had taught forty years ago at Moreau Catholic High School in Hayward, California. He wanted to thank me for what I had done for him. He reminded me that I taught him English for two years and religious studies for two years. While I remembered his name, I didn't remember much of what proved to be very important to him as he looked back. I also learned that I had unknowingly been involved in his career choice, which involved writing. Somehow, I had become a star in this man's sky. Such events bring one face-to-face with the responsibilities inherent in being a Holy Cross educator or any other kind of mentor or minister.

While Blessed Moreau's use of the passage from the book of Daniel is intended to encourage educators in what he considers a great calling, it also tries to focus all of us on the long view. Those who want instant gratification in the responses of those with whom they work are often disappointed. As educators, mentors, and ministers, we seldom know those upon whom we will have the greatest impact. Often those who have been most transformed are those who gave us the greatest difficulties or who we thought were not responding. Wherever we go and whatever we do, we leave something of ourselves—especially our view of the universe, God, and eternal realities—with those we meet. That, in a sense, makes us eternal since what we give to others, if accepted, will be passed on to others with whom they journey, especially their families and friends. It is in this way that we hope to change the world: by transforming, often mysteriously, the lives of those with whom we work, one encounter at a time.

Donald Blauvelt, C.S.C.

When we do serve him faithfully, it is our work that rouses us to prayer. The abundance of his gifts, dismay over our ingratitude, and the crying needs of our neighbors—all this is brought home to us in our ministry and draws us into prayer.

—Holy Cross *Constitutions*

IT SADDENS ME to hear someone say, "My work is my prayer." I fear that the work will soon become less of a prayer and more of a disillusioned drudgery followed by a diagnosis of burnout or low-grade depression. To be sure, work can be prayer, but when it becomes our only form of prayer, the emphasis tends to be on our own talents, resources, and ego.

Those of us engaged in the work of the Lord—in the office, on the street, over the counter, at the altar, or around the dining-room table—sooner or later find situations overwhelming and beyond our puny abilities. In short, it becomes too easy for us to lose confidence, give up hope, and change our mantra to "I did all I could."

There comes a time in every endeavor when we conclude we have done everything possible. For example, Blessed Moreau's darkest hour came when he was tested by Satan: "All is lost." It is then that we must join with the psalmist in humbly saying, "My help comes from the Lord" (121:2). It is then that we must ask for the guidance of the Holy Spirit. And it will be then that the embers of burnout will be reignited with the fire of hope and debilitating low-grade depression will be elevated to confidence in the Lord. It is then that we will be able to say, "Our work is sustained by our prayer." Indeed, our work is transformed by our prayer.

John F. Tryon, C.S.C.

February 20

Human life is like a great Way of the Cross. We do not have to go to the chapel or church to go through the different stations. This Way of the Cross is everywhere and we travel it every day, even in spite of ourselves and without being aware of it.

—Blessed Basil Moreau

SO OFTEN I wish that life itself was not a great Way of the Cross, that discipleship and the Cross were not so intimately related. I prefer, like most, to flee from suffering, difficulty, and hardship. I prefer a God whose love saves me from sin, death, and the suffering that links them.

And yet each day I find the invitation to take up the Cross—in the boredom of life's everyday tasks, in the neighbor whose very presence is an affront to my serenity, in a news item that details the suffering of another, in unrequited love, in tasks beyond talents, in the realization of my own pettiness, and in the battles that persist within. At times, I find myself taking up the Cross in spite of myself; it is hoisted upon my shoulders before I realize it. Love—not simply being human—requires it. At times, I run from it, only to fall exhausted into bed, the

Cross nestled beside me preventing me from falling asleep. Other times, I willingly take it up, my heart moved by a love beyond my own loving.

And so, I do not have to find a church to go through the different stations, for I am aware that I walk with him already; rather, he walks with me. I am accompanied by Love itself, a love that has born my infirmities and guilt, a love that saves me from sin and death. I am aware that the Cross, and its daily way, though not my preference, is my salvation. As the Cross is offered to me each day, I beg for the grace to echo the prayer of Jesus: "Father, if it is possible, let this cup pass from me; yet, not as I will, but as you will."

Thomas P. Looney, C.S.C.

February 21

No one outdoes God in generosity. The more precise we are in carrying out his commands, the more attentive he is to pour out his favors on us. A first grace is gained, attracts another one even greater, and this second grace, when well-received, merits still another. Thus, day-by-day fidelity brings an increase of grace and at the same time makes us grow in courage.

—Blessed Basil Moreau

I WAS AT a local BBQ place when a couple came up to me and said, "We really enjoy your homilies and your stories about real life situations." Then the wife said, "Oh yes, and I never get up and leave to go to the bathroom because I feel that you are always looking right at me."

I told her that the most recent story that I had recounted at Mass occurred to me while I was mowing the yard.

Another time a man came up to me and asked, "Father, when are confessions?"

I first told him, "On Saturdays from 4:00 to 5:00." With God's grace, I then added, "If you like, we can talk now."

"I have been watching you for the last three years and looking at how you respond to others," he responded, "and I feel that now I can let go of what has been keeping me from moving forward in my relationship with God."

One morning a student came to me after first-period class, and he was clearly upset. His aunt had passed away four months ago, and it was at that moment in class that all the feelings he had been suppressing came to him.

Over time, I have learned that we cannot control time. Yet when we give up our time, God reveals his grace to us and thus makes us grow in the courage needed to surrender to him and his beautiful designs. For we never know when inspiration will hit or when someone is going to turn to us and need to share their sacred moment with us. Grace often comes at unexpected times. But by giving up our time and entering into the moment, whatever or whomever it may be, we can truly experience how one grace attracts another, and another, and another.

Joseph Moyer, C.S.C.

February 22

Our thoughts are not easily God's thoughts, nor our wills his will. But as we listen to him and converse with him, our minds will be given to understand him and his designs.

—Holy Cross *Constitutions*

IN THE GOSPELS there are few, if any, more strong-willed than Simon Peter. The evangelist probably has kindly edited Peter's response to Jesus' request that he row back to deep waters for the catch that the apostle was certain was not there. Luke tells us that Peter simply said, "Master, we have worked hard all night long and have caught nothing." I can only imagine Peter's response was really a bit lengthier and perhaps more colorful before it ended with his gasp, "But at your command I will lower the nets" (5:5). This is classic Peter, obstinately sure of himself but finally given to temper his own steely will with Jesus' persuasive insistence that he let go of it.

The Holy Cross *Constitutions* recognize the Peter in all of us. They tell us that our thoughts and wills are not easily God's but do not rule out the possibility that they could come to be so, just as Peter's became ever more like God's. But first we need to be humbly honest and recognize that we cannot know God's designs unless we are given to understand them. Otherwise, the more we try, the more frustrated we become because often our own designs, superimposed upon God's, are what we see. So perhaps we need to take "be given to understand" literally and let Jesus lead us to be given to know God's will.

Letting go of our will is not a loss but a gain. When we allow it to become part of something greater, something greater becomes part of it. And in the process, God's greatness overcomes our pettiness and self-interest, and his breadth and depth fill the shallowness of our understanding.

Don Fetters, C.S.C.

February 23

The fast of Lent is instituted for the wisest purpose—to check vices and raise the soul above the desires of the body; to mortify and afflict, but not to disable and incapacitate anyone from duty.

—Fr. Edward Sorin, C.S.C.

WHILE I WAS greeting my parishioners after the noon Mass on Ash Wednesday, a joyful woman with dust on her forehead gleefully smiled at me and clutched my hand as she was leaving. I quickly questioned her, "Why are you so joyful? There is no smiling in Lent." Pulling me closer, she simply stated, "My birthday was last week, and I don't have to fast anymore. I'm too old." With that, she kissed me and hurried down the steps of the church.

Knowing this woman as I did, I delighted in her spirit. She was a typical "church lady" who always arrived thirty minutes before Mass to recite her prayers and light her votive candle. A widow, she lived alone with her cats in a small house one block away from the parish. I knew for a fact she was in her eighties and had been well beyond the recommended age for fasting for quite some time. Her Lenten fast was a fast that continued throughout the year. She had given herself completely over to God by denying herself the pleasures of family, status, and material possessions. She embraced life with a smile and kiss because she had never abandoned her hope in the promise of the Resurrection. Her Lenten fast was a lifestyle that reflected a sincere devotion to and dependence on God.

Lent for us, too, is something we ought to embrace rather than endure. How powerful this season can be—in its fasting, prayer, and almsgiving—when we don't merely choose to live it, but live to choose it.

Michael C. Mathews, C.S.C.

February 24

Let us go with all our illnesses, let us go and find this loving physician, this spiritual Father, but let us go there like the leper with a lively faith, a strong desire for our healing, a firm trust, a sincere humility that brings us to make known the state of our conscience without hiding anything, and especially a strong and generous resolution never again to fall into the same sins.

—Blessed Basil Moreau

I WAS SO recently ordained that it seemed my hands still felt the sacred chrism when a respected professor-priest of the

Congregation asked me to hear his confession. I was so nervous! This was a Holy Cross father I looked up to. Was it taking me by surprise that he could sin? Was he trying to put me to the test once more? No. He simply desired the sacrament. That was all.

Shocked at this man's lively faith and strong desire for spiritual healing, I realized he was affirming me in a way and letting me in on his deep spiritual life. What great trust and sincere humility! Could I be like that one day? His openness was as refreshing as his acknowledgment that he was, in fact, a sinner. It was clear that he knew better than I that loving physician and spiritual Father whose compassionate forgiveness we were celebrating.

Fr. John English, S.J., in his book *Spiritual Freedom*, writes of the great saints: "When they felt themselves to be great sinners, I think all they meant was that their experience of grace was so immeasurably more than their own meager response to grace. It was not that they felt they were going to hell. Rather they were totally conscious of love, and they felt that they were not cooperating fully with it."

I think of this brother in community when I myself do not want to celebrate Reconciliation. He can inspire us all.

Lord, make us like that humble priest. Help us feel your deep love and grace. Let us know that we are forgiven. And beyond that, Lord, let us know that your forgiveness and compassion can flow through us sinners to other sinners, saintly or not.

John Phalen, C.S.C.

☩

February 25

Today, more than ever before, Catholic education means for our youth a knowledge of divine truths, more comprehensive and developed, more visibly sustained by daily Christian practices, cheerfully accepted and faithfully observed by them as an indispensable evidence of their initiation to a Catholic life, of which they may well feel proud all their life.

—Fr. Edward Sorin, C.S.C.

FR. SORIN HARDLY qualifies as a great educational theorist or intellectual. He was neither a regular teacher nor a serious scholar. He contributed relatively little to discussions regarding curriculum at the University of Notre Dame as it slowly evolved into a genuine institution of higher learning. Fr. Sorin, instead, was an ambitious institution builder and a decisive leader. His courage and iron will ensured that Notre Dame survived and eventually prospered despite fires, a cholera outbreak, and a series of financial crises. Yet Fr. Sorin was much more than this. He was a man of deep faith who believed that God and Our Lady had summoned him across the Atlantic Ocean to undertake a crucial work in Catholic education.

From the outset, Fr. Sorin hoped that Notre Dame would develop as a "most powerful means for good" by preparing young Catholics to go forth and serve well in the world. He understood that Catholic education was not only about training minds but also about forming character and shaping souls.

While no great educational theorist, he assuredly got to the heart of the matter.

Catholic educators today at every level might draw inspiration from his example. Our most important contribution to our students is to nurture them in the ways of faith—to provide them with appropriate catechetical and theological formation, to celebrate our faith with them in prayer and liturgy, and to guide them to express it through service of neighbor in the world.

Wilson D. Miscamble, C.S.C.

February 26

It is necessary to be humble, docile, fervent, to take courage and not look behind you, always to move forward until you are in the possession of the glory of God.

—Fr. Jacques Dujarie

ALL OF US have something to be humble about, no matter who we are. After all, we are finite. None of us can claim great wisdom, yet we try to grow in wisdom as we grow older through our education and our life experiences. And the fact is that we do not and cannot move forward without a certain basic humility. It boils down to this: We must realize that we are simply instruments. The instrument does not do the job. The person who uses the instrument does the job. In this way, we open ourselves to the Spirit; we allow ourselves to be instruments in the hands of God. And we give him the credit for what we do because it comes from his inspiration.

The older we get, the more we tend to simplify things, even the religious life. I have read dozens of religious books, but when it all got boiled down and I was on the firing line, the inspiration of the Holy Spirit is what I found most important. Ultimately it is not just a question of being docile but being docile to the Holy Spirit. We need to know and to trust that the Spirit is working through us by virtue of our Baptism. We today have lost a sense of the active, living influence of the Holy Spirit in the life of the Church. We need to be more attentive to the promptings of the Spirit, following his lead. It is then, when we are obedient to the Holy Spirit, that courage comes. For we receive true courage only when we know we are in the hands of God, when we know that God is acting through us for his glory.

Ted Hesburgh, C.S.C.

February 27

We heard a summons to give over our lives in a more explicit way. It was a call to serve all people, believers and unbelievers alike. We would serve them out of our own faith that the Lord had loved us and died for us and risen for us and that he offers us a share in his life, a life more powerful and enduring than any sin or death.

—Holy Cross *Constitutions*

"SERVE MY PEOPLE." That was my more explicit call. I was raised in the practice of the faith. I was taught to pray, to go to Mass, and to strive to know and love God. For that wonderful foundation, I am very thankful to my parents. They taught my siblings and me what it means to be a Christian. All of the baptized are called by Christ to be disciples, to spread the Good News of Christ, and to love God and neighbor. But for me, there was something more, something beckoning me further.

How was God calling me to serve? I knew there were many ways to lead a life of service. Again, my parents were models of how Christians can live out this call with a job and a family. But the desire continued on in me as something stronger. I knew I had been given so much by our loving God. I desired to show my love, my gratitude, by giving something back. But what could I offer?

"Serve my people." My life—I could give God my whole life. I prayed, "I am yours, O Lord; do with me as you will. I give you all that I am, loving God; use my life as you see fit."

This explicit call was asking me not merely to serve but to spend my whole life in service. And so I gave God my life. I consecrated my life in service to God as a religious in Holy Cross.

We religious priests, brothers, and sisters, however, are not alone in being called by God to something more. Through our Baptism, God summons all of us to a particular mission. What can we offer? We can always offer ourselves in response to his call, whatever it may be.

Matt Fase, C.S.C.

☩

February 28

Let us take a holy and firm resolution to steep our-selves anew in the religious spirit by generously offer-ing to God all the little sacrifices demanded by our rules. This is my most ardent wish for the entire family entrusted to me.

—Blessed Basil Moreau

OUR YOUNG MEN in initial formation in Holy Cross often bring a zeal for ministry and religious life that can help us see more clearly the gift that God has given us in our own vocations. Years of ministry and community life and the habits we form can wear away some of our youthful enthusiasm and dull our spirits. Sacrifices that we were once eager to make can come to feel like, well, sacrifices.

If the *Constitutions* that are meant to guide our lives—our call, mission, prayer, brotherhood, vows—are allowed to gather dust, we can drift and lose our focus as individuals and as a community. Only by regularly recommitting ourselves to all of what our *Constitutions* call us to be can we hope to live our religious life in Holy Cross with zeal and generosity.

Similarly, one of the great blessings of parish life is jour-neying with people seeking initiation into our Catholic faith through our RCIA programs. As they progress and grow in their faith, many of them have an enthusiasm that is apparent and infectious. Their zeal and commitment serve as wonderful reminders of the incredible gift of our faith. The stakes of our lives as Christians are high. Who we are and what we do matters.

We live our faith for God and are called as well to offer a witness for God's people. It is important for us, likewise, to return to scripture and the roots of our faith. In this way, we prepare ourselves to renew our commitment, to renew our own baptismal promises once again at Easter.

John Herman, C.S.C.

February 29

It is consoling, it is encouraging, it is wonderfully rejoicing, to breathe a prayer for a friend, for a child whose welfare is as dear as that of oneself.
—Fr. Edward Sorin, C.S.C.

"HOW ARE DON CLEMENTE and Doña Rita?" This is the type of question the students at Our Lady of the Lake University in San Antonio, Texas, asked me whenever I returned from a trip to Mexico. In my work as a campus minister there, I led students on week-long immersion trips to La Luz, our Holy Cross parish across the border in Monterrey. In a single week, in spite of language barriers, I was always blessed to witness the friendships that formed between our young people and the parishioners of La Luz.

While we were at the parish, we spent time with the children, youth, and elderly. We assisted with after-school programs for students. We ate lunch with the older members of the community. We took Communion to and visited with the sick. But mostly we simply spent time getting to know the people in the neighborhoods of the parish. When we returned to the United States, the students talked about their desire to work with the poor and to live more simply. Even more, however, they talked about their friends in Mexico, whether those friends were newly adopted grandparents or children they met in the very poor area of the parish. They spoke sincerely of keeping them in prayer. Likewise whenever I returned to the parish, the people there always asked about their friends in San Antonio and told me that their young American friends were remembered in prayer.

These prayers, as much as they are petitions for the other, are expressions of joy and thanksgiving for the good that God has brought through our relationships. In turn, these prayers keep ever new the grace of these encounters—with Don Clemente, with Doña Rita, and ultimately with our Lord.

Mike Winslow, C.S.C.

March 1

We are a community of pontifical right: men living and working under the approbation and authority of the successor of Peter. We are a religious Congregation composed of two distinct societies of religious, one of religious priests and one of religious brothers, bound together in one indivisible brotherhood.

—Holy Cross *Constitutions*

FROM THE FIRST words of our *Constitutions*, we members of the Congregation of Holy Cross—both religious brothers and religious priests—are reminded that we are men in relationship. We live in relationship with one another and with the entire Church. We are bound together in one indivisible brotherhood. Even when our *Constitutions* speak of our mission, we proclaim to live and work together in the hope that our mutual respect and shared undertaking will be a hopeful sign of the kingdom.

I am often struck by how unique Holy Cross is in the Church. There are other religious congregations composed of priests and brothers, but thanks to our founder, Blessed Moreau, we view this relationship differently. In Blessed Moreau's vision, we are equals because for him it was all about relationship, about union, about community. Blessed Moreau therefore made his religious family of Holy Cross—to include the sisters as well—into a microcosm of the Church. Rooted in the relationships of the Holy Family and reflective of the love of the Holy Trinity, our relationships with each other are to be a living ecclesiology; they are to incarnate for the Church and the world a model for community.

If there is one thing our Church and world are in need of today, it is a model for community. There is so much that divides and separates us today. Yet even more than a model, our Church and world need hope—hope that such community is possible. This is where we come in—not just we in Holy Cross but we in the Body of Christ. In the way we unite together as equals to build a kingdom of justice, love, and peace, we become seeds of that hope.

Thomas A. Dziekan, C.S.C.

March 2

*Let us show by our deeds, especially during this holy
season of penance and prayer, that we believe in our
crucified Redeemer and hope in him.*

—Fr. Edward Sorin, C.S.C.

WITH ITS FINGER pointing, scantily clad characters, and banishment, the story of Adam and Eve has remarkable currency for an ancient description of sin and punishment. But because a return to Eden doesn't figure as prominently in Christian spirituality as does Resurrection, we're better served in Lent by the story of Adam and Eve's children, Cain and Abel.

I learned how relevant Cain and Abel are to our hope of Resurrection when a drunken man came to the rectory late one night. The priests were all asleep, I told him, so perhaps I could help. I was a deacon at the time, yet nothing in my subsequent years of hearing confessions has compared to what he had to say. That's because when I asked him what his name was, he declared, "I'm Cain; I killed Abel."

As it turns out, his name really was Abel, and in a manner that each of us has experienced, an inner struggle had ended badly. Sin had won out, yet only temporarily, for our Redeemer has risen to die no more. His Resurrection begins to fulfill the yearning of Abel's blood as it cries out to God from the ground (Gen 4:10), not for revenge but for a spirit re-created.

Like my friend Abel, we can be our own worst enemy at times. So our spiritual task is to make holy again that ground from which we hear the pleas for mercy emanate. To do so, we must heed the appeals for new life that come from others, for our deeds in service of them will render the Cain within us powerless.

Kevin J. Sandberg, C.S.C.

March 3

Truly, we cannot sufficiently admire God's plan in our regard. After sending us crosses and trials, he now crowns us with success and consoles us with peace both within and without. It is an indubitable proof that he wishes to guide his work himself according to his own admirable designs.

—Blessed Basil Moreau

THERE ARE NO individual examples of God's care for us, if by this we mean special moments when God provides for our needs. At the core of our Christian faith is the trust that every moment is part of God's design. As Blessed Moreau wrote, trials and successes, crosses and consolations, are all part of Divine Providence in our lives.

This faith does not lead us to disdain the material world or to abandon our efforts to accomplish something. We are called to dedicate ourselves to some useful task, and we all share the same human responsibilities—to worship God, to lead an honorable life, to love our neighbor, and to be of some service. In all of these we often fail. But life's ultimate significance does not depend on our worldly successes and failures. Our salvation is the final value, and this is in the hands of God. Blessed Moreau put his hope in the Cross because he found there the revelation that God had rescued us from sin and called us to himself.

Everyone who has lived many years learns the truth of the saying that life is what happens while we are making other plans. But even though our plans are not accomplished, we can be sure that we are part of a greater design not of our making. God's shaping of our lives remains a mystery, yet each day we can lead lives of thanksgiving because Christ has opened for us the gates of heaven.

Louis Manzo, C.S.C.

March 4

To succeed in the important undertaking entrusted to us, we must be, first of all, so closely united in charity as to form but one mind and one soul.

—Blessed Basil Moreau

IN HIS FUNERAL homily for Fr. Theodore Hesburgh, C.S.C., a former president of the University of Notre Dame, Fr. John Jenkins, C.S.C., the current president, mentioned Fr. Ted's many acts of kindness, including an encouraging phone call to Fr. Jenkin's mother. The university newspaper was also filled with many remembrances of kindness shown by Fr. Ted.

Prior to his death, Fr. Ted lived at Holy Cross House, the community's medical facility, because of his impaired vision and failing health. Fr. Paul Doyle, C.S.C., and Fr. Austin

Collins, C.S.C., gave of themselves freely to assist Fr. Ted with his work and travels. When Fr. Ted first asked for their help, little did either know that this service would last over ten years and become more and more demanding. Yet both showed how charity is lived out. The kindnesses they showed Fr. Ted were the same kindnesses Fr. Ted showed others in his seventy-eight years as a vowed religious of Holy Cross.

In today's society, kindness and charity often are interpreted as signs of weakness. At times in politics and in the Church, division seems to be more appreciated than unity. Yet Pope Francis continually reminds us that through our Baptism we are to be messengers of God's mercy and compassion. We are to show God's love by our countless acts of kindness to each other and especially to the marginalized.

For me, it is a daily struggle. So each day when I awake, I pray, "Thy will be done." It is only when we seek God's will that we find the grace from God to do the daily acts of kindness that transform us into people of compassion and unity.

Carl F. Ebey, C.S.C.

March 5

Our concern for the dignity of every human being as God's cherished child directs our care to victims of every injury: prejudice, famine, warfare, ignorance, infidelity, abuse, natural calamity.

—Holy Cross *Constitutions*

"I'M A WORTHLESS, hurting, good-for-nothing," he mumbled to himself. Wounded in a knife fight, stitched up, and still bleeding, he claimed he was going to die of pain. A compassionate parishioner placed her arm around him and brought him in from the street to Mass. "I will ask Father to anoint you and that will help." Quite overcome by her kindness, the man received the sacrament of the Anointing of the Sick and humbly thanked me as well as the parishioners who prayed for him. The next day his physician called to report that his wounds were healed; the doctor offered to send all his homeless patients to our chapel.

Called to express concern for the frail, needy, and those without voice, we are challenged to face up to the truth that all human life is sacred. Comprehending this truth is one thing; practicing it is quite another. Human misery and powerlessness are not welcome friends. Yet, Christ tells us, "When you welcome the stranger, however humble, you welcome me."

Allowing ourselves to get close to suffering and injustice can trigger pain, resistance, or anger in us. Christ up close is very human and sometimes uncomfortable. Yet our care for all God's cherished children brings important blessings. We learn about our inner life, about our hesitations and exclusiveness, about our personal and institutional limitations, about the need for grace and healing within us, our Church, and our world. Those hurting among us could lead us to pray that God might give us eyes to see, ears to hear, and a heart to understand real dignity—that is, Christ among us all.

Richard Berg, C.S.C.

We can, however, teach only what we know well our-
selves, and our living example must be ever the out-
ward expression of our inner life. In a very real sense,
we become what we think upon, and so it is partic-
ularly necessary that we learn how to meditate well.
—Blessed Basil Moreau

WE HAVE MORE information at our fingertips and are more
frequently the target of communication than any humans in
history. Television and radio, smartphones and tablets, e-mail
and the Internet, Facebook and Twitter, Instagram and Yik Yak
(and many others) continually update, entertain, stimulate,
persuade, cajole, pressure, and scold us.

We imagine ourselves to be in control of the information we
take in. "I am the one who listens, evaluates, and decides," we
tell ourselves. But those skilled in marketing know they can, if
they get our attention often enough, shape what we will want,
buy, think, and do. They have grasped the power of Blessed
Moreau's insight: "We become what we think upon."

It is all the more critical in our age that we find time to listen
to the Lord who invites us, his disciples, to come with him by
ourselves to a quiet place (see Mk 6:31). The Lord needs silence
and needs our attention so that we can hear his Word and contemplate his image so that his Word and image can shape us.
He will not call our phone or send an e-mail blast. He waits in
silence for us to come to him in silence.

In a demanding and busy administrative job, I struggle to find time and silence to meditate on the Lord and what he is trying to tell me. I often do not do as well as I should. Yet I know that unless I find time with the Lord, I am being shaped every hour by other messages and other demands, and I will end up teaching what I do not know and trying to give what I do not have.

It is a matter of spiritual life and death that from time to time we turn off the noise, come away with the Lord in silence, and meditate on his Word.

John Jenkins, C.S.C.

☩

March 7

Where then shall we find intelligent, zealous, and devoted teachers for the poor? Only in the inspiration of religion. For religion not only promises that those who have taught justice to their brothers and sisters shall shine as stars in the firmament, but likewise ranks among the proofs of the divinity of Christ's mission the fact that "the poor have the Gospel preached to them."

—Blessed Basil Moreau

THERE IS A poverty that crosses all cultures, social levels, and areas of society. It is a poverty more subtle than what we're accustomed to handle. It has to do with the loneliness and affective emptiness with which all young people wrestle. After many years working with young people from different levels of society in both parishes and schools, I am struck by how this affective need is common among economically and culturally wealthy youth as well as among those from poorer backgrounds. There is no distinction.

All young people have a need to find someone who might pay attention to them. They are immersed in a society that renders them so needy and fragile that it's not surprising that they would so easily join groups and adopt fads and lifestyles that allow them to forget their loneliness and make them feel that they are somebody or part of something that confirms their identity. It is not just their affective lives that are hurt but also their spiritual lives, to the extent that often the only place where they've heard talk about God is in school.

In this context, the role of all Christians as educators in the faith is vitally important. All of us have a part in helping our young people to discover God as the One who gives meaning to our lives and as the Father who welcomes us, listens to us, and reveals our deepest identity.

Jorge Urtubia, C.S.C.

March 8

Some of the most decisive transformations are God's gracious gifts to us not when we conform to his will but when we have gravely failed him. However the benefits of our formation may disintegrate, however we may fall, we need the supportive confrontation

*and sensitive encouragement of our confreres for us
to be rehabilitated. This is the way some of the wisest
and strongest men in our community have, by God's
grace, been raised up among us.*

—Holy Cross *Constitutions*

EARLY IN MY religious life and priesthood, I found myself drifting away from my brothers in Holy Cross. Something was causing my resolve as a religious and priest to be undermined. I fulfilled the duties of my ministry, but I did so mostly for show. I was decaying inside, and the goodness and graces of my formation were slowly vanishing. I was not the person, priest, and religious that I wanted to be, but I was helpless to do anything about my dilemma. I was an alcoholic.

God, however, would not cease loving or pursuing me and would not let me be destroyed totally by my grave failure to conform to his will. My brothers in Holy Cross sensed my dilemma and realized I was struggling with addiction. They confronted me with sensitive but tough love, getting me into treatment and onto the path of recovery. They showed me what community and commitment to each other really means: we stand by each other no matter how much we may have failed. They were the conduits of God's grace and love for me. To this day, they continue to encourage me to grow and use my gifts and talents for the Church and for the community.

We are all challenged to confront and assist those whom God places in our care when they have fallen and need help in finding their way back to him. From our weaknesses and failures we can gain great strength and experience to share with those with whom we walk the journey to him.

Charlie Kohlerman, C.S.C.

☫

March 9

Let us bear in mind that, as it is written, we are temples of God, that his Spirit dwells in us, and that this temple is sacred. These temples of ours are much more sacred than the material edifice where we gather to pray.
—Blessed Basil Moreau

A TEMPLE IS a place where we worship God, a place where God dwells. Our bodies are places of worship. We stand to pray, holding up our empty hands in the ancient sign of dependence, in the universal sign of surrender, in the street beggar's gesture of request. We sit to read, to follow with our eyes the words of revelation, the prayers of the ancients, the petitions of the universal Church. Even in meditation without words, we hold our bodies in a posture of waiting, of expectation. The rhythm of our breathing and the beating of our hearts speak their own prayer, speak to us as well as to God.

No matter where we are, the actions of our bodies and the attitudes that we manifest are holy beyond the holiness of consecrated stones and beams. Our churches themselves are made holy by the bodies of the believers who kneel, bow, and walk in the rituals of the Church.

And when our prayer moves us into service of others, we sanctify our bodies even more. For the same Spirit who gives us the desire and utterance for prayer also provides us with the energy and impetus to love our neighbors. At those times when we tire, when we relent, when we are no longer able or willing to press our bodies into service, it is then that we recognize most clearly the indwelling of the God whose creative power holds us in existence and draws us to himself. Our bodies are places where God dwells; indeed, they are temples of God.

David Sherrer, C.S.C.

March 10

Our Savior works on our maladies of soul the very same miracles of healing he worked on the sick and broken bodies of Judea in the long ago. He is our consolation, and by his bruises we are healed.

—Blessed Basil Moreau

"**MALADIES OF SOUL** . . . by his bruises we are healed." It is important to consider those two phrases together in Christ. One might think that maladies of soul equal personal sin, and that may very well be. Personal sin does have an effect on our physical and emotional well-being. But Jesus was without sin, so how could he be bruised by sin?

We can start by looking at some of Jesus' "bruises." Jesus needed alone time, but everyone wanted a piece of his time and talent. He was impatient when people didn't get it or when they wanted something for nothing. He reacted angrily when deeply held values were violated. He was unjustly accused and also criticized for not obeying the Law or not doing things the approved way. Jesus often had to resist others' expectations as well as negative people who tried to deter him or those whose priorities were different. Friends were not there when he needed them, and he was criticized for spending time with the wrong kinds of people. He often asked others to keep things confidential, but soon everyone was talking about what he said and did. He was mocked because of his ethnicity, birth circumstances, and parentage. And, last but not least, he felt abandoned by God.

Do these sound familiar? Jesus shares our humanity in all things, including those difficulties that affect and bruise our ego, our sense of self, or our confidence. These bruises can often stir up a storm of negative emotions. These emotions in turn corrode our souls, our peace of mind, and eventually affect our bodies.

Gentle and compassionate Jesus, please heal us. Help us to rewrite the negative narrative that comes with these bruises so that our responses may be more like yours. Better yet, help us to sit back and watch you handle it for us.

Herbert C. Yost, C.S.C.

March 11

Let us forget past wrongs. Let us bear in mind the reply of our Divine Lord to St. Peter who, after asking how many times he ought to pardon, received from his sacred lips the equivalent of these words: always and without ever tiring.

—Blessed Basil Moreau

WITHOUT FORGIVENESS THERE can be no community. Without forgiveness human societies and nations fall apart. Holy Cross exists because our founder, Blessed Moreau, understood why Jesus made forgiveness such an important part of his life, both in story and in action. Jesus himself forgives not only his friends the apostles for their cowardice and betrayal but also his Roman enemies who ultimately put him to death. He extends this forgiveness to them when they do not ask for it or even know how.

In this world all too full of conflict, exploitation, and ethnic cleansing, forgiveness can be unfortunately dismissed as a sign of weakness and even as an injustice. How could we ever forgive a betraying neighbor, a torturer, or a killer? Jesus, however, teaches otherwise, calling on us to forgive always and without ever tiring. For him forgiveness is a sign of strength, the only kind of strength from which true justice can come.

And yet the power of forgiveness is so subtle that only a child can do it with grace and love. Maybe that is why Jesus continually invites us to be like little children. We adults must work hard at forgiving and asking for it. Even then, it does not always come easy or end very well. But when it does, it is a pure gift—a divine gift making our very life together in human communities possible.

Claude Pomerleau, C.S.C.

March 12

Little as we may have received, we shall all have some- day to account for it. Whoever has received an obedi- ence, however insignificant it may appear—a common employment—were it only to wash the dishes, or to sweep the floor, has to fulfill it in a religious manner, not indifferently or loosely or carelessly, for in it angels see the will of God.

—Fr. Edward Sorin, C.S.C.

"YOU CAN ALWAYS tell a Holy Cross school," the Sister of Mercy said. "It's clean inside and out." After years in other schools, she had been teaching alongside me for many academic terms in one of our co-institutional secondary schools. It was late Sunday night, and we had just finished cleaning and resetting the high school cafeteria after weekly bingo, finally locking up and shutting off the lights. Consulting her wristwatch, she half-grumbled, "In other places, they'd leave this to 'the staff.'" Then, with an Irish chuckle, she shook her head. "Here, the brothers roll up their sleeves, and somehow we all find ourselves working with you. Well, see you in school tomorrow."

Brothers in a classroom, moms and dads at home, sisters in a medical setting, or priests in a rectory—it's all the same in that everywhere our daily lives are made up of hundreds of discreet tasks. From complex professional or administrative activities to washing dishes and sweeping floors, we perform routine actions so often that we put our minds elsewhere. Before we know it, our commute is ended, our teeth are brushed. But is there a way to labor in a religious manner so that everyday jobs become offerings to God? Fr. Sorin reminds us that the bridge to the Divine is to see the task as worthy, to fulfill it and not just perform it. To do this, we have to approach our daily tasks with full attention, seeking to see and cultivate holiness in them.

Mark Knightly, C.S.C.

But we do not grieve as men without hope, for Christ the Lord has risen to die no more. He has taken us into the mystery and the grace of this life that springs up from death. If we, like him, encounter and accept suffering in our discipleship, we will move without awkwardness among others who suffer. We must be men with hope to bring.

—Holy Cross *Constitutions*

POPE FRANCIS IS lifting up a vision for our Church that is resonating in the minds and hearts of many people, and not only of Catholics. His vision invites disciples of Christ, and all people of good will, to something that seems simple in its conception, yet digs deep into the mystery of grace and of what it means to be human. He asks of us this: to be God's mercy.

His use of imagery, down-to-earth and understandable, situates mercy in every corner and crevice of human experience and, most importantly, in the sufferings and sorrows afflicting souls. He speaks of the Church as being a field hospital, healing wounds and lives. He invites disciples of Christ—aware of our own grief, suffering, failure, and brokenness—to walk through the dark night with others and to help them find God's light and peace. Mercy offers the promise of hope, that all shall be well.

In my work with young adults, I see more and more students suffering with mental illness. It is painful to hear of their struggles. I encourage them to seek help, to find a network of support. I pray with them. Familiar with my own suffering and crosses, I find that sometimes the only thing to do is walk with them in their darkness, to be for them God's mercy. Yet there is hope to bring. The hope is in the search with them to find the light of God's healing and peace.

The Paschal Mystery, Christ's death and Resurrection, is the mystery that rests deep in our human experience. To show mercy to another is to live that mystery. And with that mercy truly shared comes hope—hope that we may all believe in the Lord's promise: "Your faith has saved you" (Lk 7:50).

Bob Loughery, C.S.C.

March 14

Here is what I want you all to be—the guardian angels of the dear young souls Divine Providence entrusts you with.

—Fr. Edward Sorin, C.S.C.

GOING TO SCHOOL in first grade was initially not a happy time for me. I missed my familiar surroundings, my toys, my family, and my friends. Yet one of the earliest catechism lessons that our teacher, Sr. Agnes Angela, C.S.C., taught us was about guardian angels. She explained that God gave each one of us our own special angel. Her kind words reassured me. I even tried to make a little extra room on the seat of my desk so my angel could sit beside me.

At our Holy Cross parishes in the United States with schools, the priests have the custom of helping the younger children out of their cars in the morning when they come to school. One day, early in the school year, when I was at Christ the King School in South Bend, Indiana, a little kindergartner had tears in her eyes as she got out of the back seat. I sensed she was scared, like I was so long ago, about coming to school. I told her what Sr. Agnes Angela had told us: "Don't be afraid. God has given you a special friend called your guardian angel. You can't see him, but it's like having your mom with you when you are away from home."

As she walked off to class, I suddenly realized the deeper truth of what I said to the little girl. We, too, are those special friends sent by God to be there for someone in need. Often, it is just a small gesture—a word of encouragement, a helping hand, or a smile. Sometimes we feel overwhelmed: "Why doesn't God take care of this problem?" But indeed God has. He made you and me.

Tom Jones, C.S.C.

March 15

It ought to be clearly understood among us that in everything we should be governed, not by private views or self-interest, but by principles.
—Fr. Edward Sorin, C.S.C.

ONE OF MY wiser brothers in Holy Cross often reminds me, "Religious life is for the weak." For the weak religious, there is strength in community. It is not simply the strength from trusted brothers who will pick us up when we fall—or when we arrive at the airport late at night—but more importantly it is the collective wisdom that the community offers. The worst of our individual weaknesses can be redeemed by opening ourselves to the best of this collective wisdom. The principles of obedience, prayerfulness, and poverty that organize our lives demand that we tether our personal futures to the community's. They also enable us to do so. To be healthy as religious, we must beg the Lord for the humility, transparency, and simplicity that permit us to embrace our common way of life.

Of course, even if religious are the weakest of Christians, we know that all of us, being human, are weak. Fortunately, the principled life of Christian community offers strength. Principles calling us past selfishness begin at home—obedience to our parents, fidelity to marriage vows, hospitality to guests. These are the beginnings of living for others. Extending outward from the home, we bind ourselves to a parish and the rules of the larger Church—committing ourselves to a discipline not of our individual choosing. Within these strictures, we find ourselves able more deeply to comprehend and embrace our Lord's twofold commandment to love God and others. Indeed, the precepts of scripture and tradition are the true principles giving shape, meaning, and vitality to the principles of our common life. To neglect that reality is to risk that our devotion to common disciplines will become a stifling legalism and an obstacle to the very new life it is meant to foster.

William R. Dailey, C.S.C.

March 16

The mission is not simple, for the impoverishments we would relieve are not simple. There are networks of privilege, prejudice and power so commonplace that often neither oppressors nor victims are aware of them. We must be aware and also understanding by reason of fellowship with the impoverished and by reason of patient learning.

—Holy Cross *Constitutions*

INTERRUPTIONS TO OUR routines can be deliberately sought or surprising, welcome or unwelcome, from within or without, with physical manifestations or nonempirical encounters. Working mostly with economically and socially privileged university-age students at Notre Dame's Center for Social Concerns, we are glad to invite them intentionally to seek such interruptions through encounters with the less privileged, hoping thereby to expand their compassion, deepen their critical insight into social problems, and advance the integration of their faith convictions with their way of being in the world. Such experiences can become transformative when, guided by grace and the Holy Spirit, the face of the Crucified One merges with the face of someone latter-born who is dying, hungry, imprisoned, or lonely. And transformation becomes ongoing when solidarity ensues and our students find their own well-being inextricably linked to those with whom they journey.

Interruptions that prompt such transformation are inevitable when we risk our hearts in caring for another. By embracing the mission of Jesus Christ as his disciples, we seek to lower our quite natural resistance to such interruptions, and to do so not out of love for suffering but out of love of God and God's holy people. We are also motivated by concern to counteract the warping effects of the inevitable sinful conditioning that our lives, like all lives, have undergone. In becoming weak with the weak and standing with others amid their suffering, we seek to allow the mercy of God to moisten the naturally hardened clay of our hearts, unbend our often stubborn wills, and render supple our too-easily stiff necks. Simultaneously, the outlines of sinfully constraining networks that implicate powerful and powerless become clearer. And we know that we can, with divine assistance, overcome . . . and maybe even glimpse how.

Paul Kollman, C.S.C.

March 17

Every action of the Word of God is an action for us to imitate. His life is such a clear model of what our own should be that there is not a single one of his acts of which Jesus Christ cannot say: "I have given you an example so that you can do what I have done." We must look at the Divine Model and know that he wants us to follow him.

—Blessed Basil Moreau

A PENANCE THAT I often give is to spend a few minutes reflecting on an image of the crucifix. I like this penance because it accomplishes two things. First, it reminds us of the depth of God's love for us. Our reflection on the greatness of his love, mercy, and compassion aids us in opening our hearts so that we might be receptive of God's forgiveness and allow it to transform us. Second, in reflecting on the Crucifixion, we are reminded of the model of the Christian life. What we have strayed from is the life to which Christ calls us—the life he models perfectly for us by his sacrifice on the Cross.

There are certainly times when living the life of virtue will appear daunting and difficult. It is certainly the case that living the Christian vocation requires discipline and sacrifice. At times the path of vice, which seems easier, is much more appealing. There are moments when our struggle with a particular sin seems insurmountable, and there is a temptation simply to give in. In these moments, our hope in the Cross becomes particularly profound because there we see the person who sacrificed so much for us. There we see the God who loves us so much that he allowed himself to be nailed to a cross so that he might grant us eternal salvation.

The Divine Model reminds us that even the Cross is an action that Christ calls us to imitate. But for us, this is a source of encouragement because if we follow Christ to the Cross, we will also follow him to eternal glory.

Brian Ching, C.S.C.

March 18

Let us not forget that the development of the work entrusted to us depends upon our acceptance of the inspirations of grace and our fidelity in seconding the designs of Divine Providence. We should not count on individual talents to assure the successful cultivation of the portion of his vineyard to which he has visibly called us, but rather on the religious spirit.

—Blessed Basil Moreau

IN MY YEARS as a parish priest, I have had my fair share of duties filling my calendar. But I have found that my busiest days tend to be when I have the fewest things scheduled. For example, one day I was hoping to reorganize a program and to get an early start on my Sunday homily, but Providence had other ideas. First, a woman dropped by whose marriage was falling apart. Then a call came to anoint someone in the emergency room. After that a parishioner arrived, scared that she might be evicted from her home. I truly felt God calling me to accept his plans and to work with his designs for me that day.

Other days I am delayed as I try to do something "important" only to find myself bumping into a person at the door of the church or coming out of a school classroom whose first words are, "Thank God you're here; I really needed to see you!" Often they do not need to see me, just someone who represents that God is here with us, by our side. Whenever this happens, I find myself saying, "So, God, this is why you delayed me," and praying that I can be the instrument of his grace.

Such experiences teach us about the need to accept the designs of Providence more than depend on our individual talents and plans. They challenge us to see that interruption, delay, and "coincidence" can sometimes truly be "God incidents," that is, events in which Divine Providence is guiding us in cultivating his vineyard.

Eric Schimmel, C.S.C.

March 19—Feast of St. Joseph

In the Savior's poverty and woe, St. Joseph accepted his guardianship, took care of his needs, showed him the affection of his heart, and fulfilled all the duties of a father toward him. It was Joseph who procured for Jesus the food that made his sacred body grow to its full strength and stature and that filled his veins with the precious blood which was shed for the salvation of the world. Thus, God the Father gave divinity to Jesus Christ. Mary furnished him his body, and our patron saint preserved his existence.

—Blessed Basil Moreau

BLESSED BASIL MOREAU'S sermon on the Feast of St. Joseph reminds me of the passage from the Gospel of Matthew in which the evangelist tells us that Joseph was an upright man unwilling to expose Mary to the Law. His intent was to divorce her quietly after she revealed her secret to him; however, with trusting confidence in the revelation of the angel Gabriel about the miraculous conception of Jesus through the Holy Spirit, Joseph took Mary "his wife into his home" (1:24).

Our *Constitutions* state, "For the kingdom to come in this world, disciples must have the competence to see and the courage to act." St. Joseph's faith-filled response to the stunning revelation of the angel Gabriel confirms for us the depth of his competence and the steadfastness of his courage. The fact that Joseph had established a home even before the Incarnation took place speaks to us of how competently he had prepared and committed himself to his calling to be the head of a household and the provider for a family. His taking of the pregnant Virgin Mary into his home was an act of sublime courage.

The establishment of a home is essential to the development of a loving, flourishing family. The reality of this particular home in the humble village of Nazareth is essential to our understanding of the mission of the child whom Joseph would name Jesus. The essential elements of Jesus' teaching about the kingdom of God could only have been introduced and nurtured by St. Joseph, the head of the household at Nazareth, during Jesus' formative years. Love of God, trust in God's plan and purpose, steadfast faith, humility, and self-sacrificing love—the virtues that were the bedrock of the Holy Family's home became the foundation of the teachings of Jesus.

St. Joseph is not a central figure in the Incarnation story simply because he happened to be betrothed to Mary. God does not build his plans for us around coincidence; God does not entrust his plans for us to happenstance. God chose St. Joseph to teach Jesus more than a trade through which he could support himself. God chose St. Joseph to form Jesus for the mission that was to be his. As St. Joseph had learned to conform his heart to God's will, so he would teach Jesus to do likewise. Jesus' confident prayer in Gethsemane, "Not my will, but yours be done," mirrors the competence to see and the courage to act of the man who took Mary into his home as his wife.

In his sermon on the Feast of St. Joseph, Blessed Moreau said that Joseph showed Jesus the affection of his heart. That affection planted the seed that resulted in our redemption. As we celebrate St. Joseph today, may we confidently and lovingly open ourselves to the affection of his heart as Jesus did, so that Joseph might teach us, too.

George Schmitz, C.S.C.

March 20

How sweet it is to abandon ourselves to the love of our Father who is in heaven and to seek his holy will.
—Blessed Basil Moreau

SEVERAL YEARS AGO, at the end of a spring-break visit with my family, I checked my e-mail account as I prepared to go to bed before an early flight. As I reviewed the subject lines of my e-mail, one caught my attention. It read, "Sit down before you read this." As I opened the e-mail I quickly felt my face going pale. It was from my provincial superior, asking me to accept a new role of leadership in our province. This new role would require me to leave the University of Portland, a Holy Cross apostolate of which, at the time, I had been a part for over a decade. I turned to God in prayer, trying to discern what he was asking of me. Could I truly abandon a place that had become home? I was torn. On the one hand, I loved Holy Cross, so how could I say no? But on the other hand, I loved the University of Portland and our ministry there as Holy Cross, so how could I say yes? What was God's holy will? What was my holy will?

When all of us are asked to consider major or even small decisions in our lives, we are faced with the question of how we ensure that our needs, wants, and desires do not cloud the will of God's grace. We have to examine what it will require to abandon ourselves completely to the love of God. For if we are not seeking God's holy will in our lives day in and day out, we will never know how to seek it when the unexpected invitation, e-mail, letter, or phone call comes asking us to abandon ourselves to something possibly much greater, something maybe only God can see in us.

Edwin H. Obermiller, C.S.C.

March 21

We shall have most to share with others by dwelling together as brothers in unity.
—Holy Cross *Constitutions*

IN HOLY CROSS, we learn to share ministries as well as to come together to share our ministerial experiences. These experiences help to strengthen the bond between us as brothers and help us to continue reaching out generously in mission.

I remember first experiencing this communal spirit while in the novitiate. I was working in the Referral Hospital in western

Uganda when I attended to a girl whose parents were waiting for her to die. It had been four days since she last spoke. I prayed with them. After I had moved on to the next bed, the mother called me back, surprised that her daughter was speaking. The girl took my hands and said, "Thank you so much." She breathed her last while still holding my hands. The mother told me, "She was waiting for your prayers to leave us in peace." I was touched by her words, but at the same time, I was scared to death. Back at the novitiate, I shared the experience with my brothers. They said that my presence was important for that family and for other patients. Their encouragement and our community together empowered me to continue a meaningful ministry of presence at the hospital.

As St. Paul's letter to the Philippians invites us to embrace one another in our daily living (2:1–11), we are called to make a community that, within our wider society, is present to each individual's needs. We need to be present to the sick, lonely, abandoned, and homeless. Our word, smile, or prayerful presence might brighten their hearts and help them live with hope and gratitude. The community we form in this way will itself renew us to continue reaching out. Being present for one another strengthens the bonds of friendship and fulfills Jesus' desire for us to be one.

Tumwine Patrick, C.S.C.

*We shall accomplish very imperfectly the designs of
Providence on each of us, if to the love of retreat and
prayer, we do not apply ourselves at the same time, as
did St. Basil, to cultivating our intellects and enriching
our minds with the knowledge proper to our state.*
—Blessed Basil Moreau

OUR CULTURE VERY much values the intellect. Yet the dominance of reason in our secular as well as religious discourse has led to a crisis of faith for many. In looking at the tradition of our great Church, however, we find that while we frequently need to remind ourselves to develop our hearts, we must never neglect our minds. We desire to develop both fully so that they may work in harmony for the greater glory of God. Perhaps the disharmony in our culture's relationship to reason is not our use of reason, but our overuse. Ideally, our reason, our intellect properly oriented, gives us greater faith and brings us closer to God.

The grace of Providence speaks silently without the ear of reason to hear it. How can we know God's will if our senses, working with our intellects, are not tuned enough to experience it? How do we know where God draws us if we cannot feel the movement of his gentle, guiding hand? We develop our intellect not as an end in itself but as a means to a greater understanding of how God, especially as Providence, is present in our lives and in the lives of others. Whether it be through culture, language, history, science, or even our everyday experiences, God speaks to us and through us as his human children. The beauty of our intellects fulfills Providence and allows us to participate in the conversation God so desperately desires to have with us.

Gregory Haake, C.S.C.

March 23

The first means of perseverance in our vocation is prayer. Without it, our soul will soon become lazy and will quickly die. We are made of body and soul, and each part needs its food. The food of the soul is grace, and God does not ordinarily give grace except through prayer.

—Blessed Basil Moreau

AFTER ALL THESE years I still feel like a beginner at prayer. And yet a high school student requests, "Bless my hands, Father, so that I'll catch a pass during our football game tonight." I want to bless the hands of this hopeful youth, hands that someday may be extended to consecrate bread and wine at Mass. We've talked about a vocation to the priesthood, he and I. A colleague at work sends an e-mail plea to pray for her soldier son in Iraq. I hit "reply" with a promise to pray each morning until he returns home. I want to pray for his courageous heart ready to give all for a peaceful world. In sunrise solitude, I pray for this young man, his mom, and me, that we may courageously seek the peace that only God gives. Our superior general sends the obituary card of my brother in Holy Cross, requesting prayers for the repose of his soul. With gratitude for his life and ministry in Holy Cross, I am happy to offer Mass and pray for this man who has gone before me in religious life: Grant him eternal life for his labors in this passing world, O Lord.

Blessed Moreau understood that God's grace is food for the soul, food that sustains each of us in our vocation to do his will. This nourishing banquet is provided for us in prayer. To this conversation with God, who loves us more than we will ever know, we bring our hopes and fears, our weaknesses and strengths, our living and our dead. We bring ourselves. As a beginner or as one who is well seasoned, let us pray.

Tom Zurcher, C.S.C.

March 24

By our vows we are committed to single-hearted inti-macy with God, to trusting dependence upon God and to willing surrender to God. We wish thus to live in the image of Jesus, who was sent in love to announce God's rule and who beckons to us to follow him. We profess vows for the sake of this same mission of Jesus.
—Holy Cross *Constitutions*

FROM HIS TERRIBLE deathbed, Jesus cried out, "I thirst." This impassioned cry speaks to each of our hearts because it expresses more than the thirst for water; it voices the very human longing for union with God. We thirst for him. But this cry also speaks of a thirst for other people. Christ was alone on the Cross in death, and he cried out to those around him. We also thirst for communion with each other.

In my life, God opened the path of religious vows to help me quench and deepen evermore my own thirst for union with him and communion with his people. These three vows—chastity, poverty, and obedience—have called me to single-hearted intimacy with God, a trusting dependence on him, and a willing surrender to him. Supported in my thirst for God and his people by my superiors and fellow religious, I have gone in many directions in my ministry as a Holy Cross priest and religious. I recall, in particular, working with the poor in Latin America. In the suffering faces of the children, the peasants, the aged, and the prisoners there, the image of Christ became clearer to me. It was the image of the Crucified calling out in love for all of his children.

The plaintive cry from the Cross draws all people into the Heart of Jesus. Whatever our vocations might be, they are gifts through which we both fulfill and deepen our love and commitment to him. For ever deeper union with God and communion with each other, each of us must say, "I thirst."

Robert Pelton, C.S.C.

March 25

Our mission sends us across borders of every sort. Often we must make ourselves at home among more than one people or culture, reminding us again that the farther we go in giving the more we stand to receive.

*Our broader experience allows both the appreciation
and the critique of every culture and the disclosure
that no culture of this world can be our abiding home.*
—Holy Cross *Constitutions*

In his Incarnation, Jesus crosses borders of every sort to meet us where we are. He empties himself in order to take on our humanity and give us his life.

Since the moment of the Incarnation, a crossing of borders has been essential to the mission of Jesus' disciples. In the parable of the Good Samaritan, the priest and the Levite remain on their side of the road, but the Samaritan crosses over to meet the wounded man where he is and to care for him. As followers of Jesus, we, too, cross over to meet people where they are, to embrace and understand their realities, their cultures. In the crossing over, there is a dying to self. We imitate the One who crossed over first out of love for us. Paul calls us to have the same attitude as Jesus, who "emptied himself, taking the form of a slave, coming in human likeness" (Phil 2:6–8).

Sometimes the crossing over is a short but demanding journey into the life of a friend, a spouse, a son or daughter, a parishioner, a neighbor. At other times, the journey is longer and farther, and takes us literally across many borders into a world and a culture that is not our own. Whatever the case, there will be dying to do on our way to the Father, but we are heartened because we know that the farther we go in giving, the more we stand to receive.

Arthur J. Colgan, C.S.C.

*You, on the contrary, are united to your Divine Master
by habitual grace. The least of your acts, even as small
a thing as a sigh, enjoys the influence of that union
and will take on an infinite value. It will merit for you
paradise or a higher degree of eternal glory. The reason for this is quite simple. It will not be you who are
acting all alone but Jesus Christ acting along with you.*
—Blessed Basil Moreau

"**THE SPIRIT INTERCEDES** for us in sighs too deep for words.
Let us join in the prayers of the Spirit for . . ." For Dolores,
for Eugene, for Joseph, . . . the list goes on. Whenever I lead a
Rosary as part of a wake service, I use the Glorious Mysteries,
the reminders of the path of glory Christ marked out for us, as
we bid the beloved deceased to stride boldly along that path into
the Father's everlasting embrace. I introduce the third mystery,
the Descent of the Holy Spirit, with those words, drawn from
St. Paul, that I believe Blessed Moreau must have had in mind
when he picked a sigh as an iconic "small thing" through which
we encounter our union with God.

Sometimes all we can do is sigh. I think of a family I visited
about to be evicted from their home. I could make referrals,
bring food, listen, and pray, but maybe the most important
thing I could do was sigh with them. I've sighed at hospital
beds and gravesides. I've sighed because I can't fix everything.
Sometimes I've had to resign myself to the fact that all I can do

at some crosses is to sigh. But I know the infinite value of that sigh because I know that Christ sent his Spirit to sigh with us.

And I think of one triumphant sigh, the exultant exhalation of Bishop Kevin Rhoades at the annual Chrism Mass, when he breathed upon the oil that became the sacred chrism that two weeks later anointed my hands for priestly service. It is chrism that first conforms us all to Christ in Baptism and then strengthens us in the gift of the Spirit in Confirmation—chrism that thus shows us all quite how gracious a sigh can be.

Adam Booth, C.S.C.

March 27

Human judgments are only wind and smoke, which give us nothing and take nothing from us, which make us neither better nor worse. The purpose of our creation, on the other hand, is for the glory of God and for the praise and esteem he alone can rightly bestow because he alone can appreciate matters truly. If we can only win this precious esteem, if our great master will proclaim us one day in the assembly of the saints, it will not matter if the world ignore us or despise us.
—Blessed Basil Moreau

PALM SUNDAY MARKED the end of Portland's 40 Days for Life spring campaign. That afternoon, six students from the University of Portland's Voice for Life club and I drove to the Northwest District to pray outside the surgical abortion clinic. I hadn't known until we arrived that we would be the only ones praying during that hour. Never before had our club stood without the 40 Days for Life's leadership and volunteers by our side. I was a little nervous for us.

At the corner of the busy intersection, we huddled on the sidewalk—careful not to block any pedestrian's path and to stay just outside the red lines we could not legally cross—and we began to pray the Rosary aloud. We hadn't yet completed the first three Hail Marys when a twenty-something man scooted past and barked at us with two pretty nasty expletives. I glanced at the faces of our students. They looked startled and upset, and I felt bad. We continued simply to pray.

As we began the third decade, a couple pushing a baby stroller rounded a corner a few blocks away and headed toward us. About a block behind them, the man who had insulted us was returning with a bag of groceries. The couple passed us without uttering a word, but just the presence of mother, father, and baby made us smile. Soon after, the young man advanced and growled the same curse words. But this time, two of our women began to giggle, and right in the middle of the fifth Joyful Mystery, we all began to smirk or chuckle. Prayer had filled us with peace. Providence had favored us with a sign. Our fellowship had strengthened us. With all these graces from God, in the face of man's hatred, all we could do was laugh.

Charles McCoy, C.S.C.

March 28

On Calvary we see how much Mary loved us. She was standing even at the foot of the Cross, among the executioners and soldiers, so close to her dying son that not a single detail of his death escaped her. What was in her heart at this sorrowful time? While Jesus Christ offered himself to the Father for our salvation, Mary offered him herself for the same end.

—Blessed Basil Moreau

IT WAS NOT easy for Mary to stay there, to stand there, watching her son die a brutal death. But she did stay. Because of her love for Jesus, she could be no place other than the foot of the Cross. Yet as powerful as a mother's love for a child is, Blessed Moreau indicates that God's love for all of humanity was at work in Mary. For her, the events of Good Friday were not merely the result of Jewish and Roman political machinations. Her son was completing God's will for the good of others, for us. Mary chose to be a part of that, and so she stayed.

Mary could not have known that her assent to God's will, years before, would lead to this day. And so, too, it is with us. If we decide to follow God's will for our lives, we cannot know the pathways down which it will lead us. But wherever it may lead, Mary's example is a challenging reminder that our lives, struggles, experiences, and gifts are for the good of others. That is their true nature, and we must decide to live for others.

Our everyday activities, the way we greet others, the care we take in completing tasks, the help we extend, the inconveniences we accept—these and so many other little things, all within our reach, provide us with ample opportunities to live for others. Such a life is the way for us to stay, like Mary, and deal with whatever we confront. Such a life is the way for us to take up the graced adventure of completing God's will.

Joel Giallanza, C.S.C.

March 29

We asked how we might follow, and we found many footprints on the road. A great band of men had passed this way, men who had made and lived by their vows, men who had walked side by side in their following of the Lord. They beckoned us to fall in step with them. We wanted to be part of the family they formed in order to share in their life and work.

—Holy Cross Constitutions

THERE WERE MANY things that impressed me about Holy Cross when I first met them while I lived in Phoenix, Arizona. They performed great apostolic work, they lived their charism faithfully, and they dedicated themselves to the common life. But as much as I admired all of these things, what finally compelled me to cast my lot with these men and join their community was pretty subjective. The parish priests I knew were joyful men, and their joy seemed to be directly connected to their priesthood. The religious I encountered at Andre House exuded this same type of joy even though they worked among the poor and homeless in seemingly hopeless circumstances. I saw the peace that their religious consecration had given them, and I longed to have that same peace in my own life. This is a large part of the reason that I joined Holy Cross, and it has continued to be a source of strength in my own vowed life.

There are countless ways in which all of us show each other how to follow the Lord. Sometimes this happens through the work we do, but often it has just as much to do with how deeply we love. We are attracted to Christ through the lives of those who have found their greatest joy by offering their lives to him. Our hope must be that our lives will demonstrate that same level of Christian witness to all those who encounter us.

Steve Lacroix, C.S.C.

March 30

Especially in the sacrament of Reconciliation do we prove in a most remarkable way the mercy of the Lord. In it are united many precious advantages: assurance of pardon for sin through the priestly absolution; repose and tranquility of conscience in the happy impressions of grace that God makes us feel deep in our hearts; nourishment and support for our weakness in the advice given us by the priest.

—Blessed Basil Moreau

A FEW YEARS ago, a good friend listened intently, but secretly, to the conversation among his three children as he drove them to school one morning. It was Lent, and the family had a tradition of celebrating the sacrament of Reconciliation during the season. They were deliberating among themselves as to which priest they might go to for confession. Discarding one option after another for a variety of reasons, the middle son suddenly exclaimed, "I know who I'm going to! I am going to Fr. Scully because he won't care what I did!" The father chuckled quietly to himself, appreciating the honesty and youthful perspective.

I smile every time I hear this story. Some may interpret the young boy's selection as the easy way out. He chose a priest he knew might be more lenient. On a deeper level, however, this young boy expressed a profound insight. He chose a priest who, representing the presence of God in a tangible way, would not dwell on what the boy had done. Instead, the priest would only care about offering forgiveness and extending the kind of freedom that comes with knowing that nothing we can ever say or do will lead God to love us less.

The real invitation of the sacrament of Reconciliation is for each of us to let go of ourselves, especially of all the sins and mistakes that prevent us from experiencing fully the love of God. The healing words of absolution invite us into a deeper relationship with God, and once we realize this gift, we become freer to forgive others. We reach out in love because we have been loved first.

Sean McGraw, C.S.C.

Sorrows and afflictions are never separated from our joys here below.

—Fr. Edward Sorin, C.S.C.

AS AN ADVISOR at the University of Notre Dame to students interested in pursuing medicine and the healing professions, I find my attention can focus on the grades, MCAT scores, and résumés of the students approaching the application process. But all of these are thin criteria by which professional schools evaluate applicants. While they tell us something of the applicant's knowledge and motivation, they don't get to the heart of the healing encounter and the qualities required by physicians and embodied by the "good doctor."

Abraham Heschel once wrote, "To heal a person, one must first be a person." To know how to respond to the sufferings of others, to be able to walk with them as they confront the most difficult moments in life, healers must have faced these moments in their own lives or grappled with questions of their own vulnerability and finitude. How do I cope with my own suffering? Is there anything of value in me that will last as my abilities decrease? How have I learned to face the reality of death of loved ones? My own death?

Fr. Sorin knew the presence of pain in this life, not just physical pain but spiritual, emotional, psychological, and relational pain. But he also knew that to be a minister of God's healing, he had to be open to the healing power of God in his own life, bringing his suffering to the foot of the Cross and allowing

Christ to take it up and transform it. Only then is the mystery of human healing revealed—the power of the Great Physician to whom belongs the glory.

James Foster, C.S.C.

April 1

Our deliberations will include the pragmatic concerns of daily life, but they must also be a way for men of faith to explore the life of the spirit with one another, lest we should speak least about what means most to us.

—Holy Cross *Constitutions*

BLESSED MOREAU ONCE wrote, "Where all the members of a house are humble, there can be few sins against charity. Where charity is not violated, a religious house is a foretaste of heaven on earth." Humility is the most essential virtue, as St. Thomas Aquinas noted eight centuries ago, and we never suffer from returning to basics. We in Holy Cross have *Constitutions* to guide us and superiors to challenge us, but we govern our own attitudes. Ultimately, those attitudes shape who we become more than admonitions or written directives.

We have open seating in our refectory where we gather for meals. It is smaller than but nevertheless similar to our student dining halls on campus. In a community of sixty, as we are at Notre Dame, it is easier to gravitate toward tables where we feel most comfortable than to risk conversation with people we don't know as well—or those who grate on our nerves. But a religious community that becomes a compilation of friendship groups degenerates into a group of cliques. We have to talk to one another even when we don't want to, or we cannot work together effectively. Anyone who has ever been on a team understands that. Unity comes not only from participation in a common labor but by breaking through barriers to the honest communication needed to achieve it.

If we were skilled at speaking about important things, there would be no need for this line in our *Constitutions*. It is as difficult for us as for anyone to utter hard words charitably. But Blessed Moreau was right to call us to be humble. There is no "I" in family if its members wish to be friends of Jesus, the charity of the Father.

James B. King, C.S.C.

April 2

As virtues are greater, the occasion of practicing them becomes rare. So, giving up all one's goods, sacrificing self for an enemy, or confessing Jesus Christ before tyrants are virtues we rarely get to practice. But doing everything out of the motive of divine love, putting up with the failings of our neighbors and adjusting to their moods, never speaking evil of others nor in praise of self—these demand a constant self-denial.

—Blessed Basil Moreau

IMMEDIATELY AFTER MY ordination to the priesthood, I spied Fr. Jerry Wilson, C.S.C., a mentor and hero of mine in Holy Cross. I ran up to him and said, "Isn't this awesome? Now all I need to do is to die a martyr's death!" The smile left his face, and he said, "No, that would be too easy. Your martyrdom will be giving over your life day after day as a priest, putting up with the difficulties, trials, and tragedies in your life and in the lives of the people whom you will serve."

Many years later, I am beginning to understand the wisdom behind those words. While I still from time to time imagine being a great martyr like St. Stephen, St. Lucy, or St. Maximillian Kolbe, I have found it much more realistic to see in my daily tasks and responsibilities a communion with Christ's self-sacrifice on the Cross. For all of us, there will be dying to do on our way to the Father.

The gift that most of us are called to give is not something that happens in a single dramatic moment; it is a life dedicated to God amid all of the uncertainties and challenges of this world. These challenges can be momentous, like the death of a loved one, or they can be simple—even mundane—like being misunderstood or experiencing loneliness or discouragement. No matter what we face in our daily lives, we can all certainly pray for the grace to imitate the martyrs and saints who had their eyes constantly fixed on Christ above all things.

Bill Wack, C.S.C.

April 3

From the moment our blessed Lord came down into the immaculate bosom of his Virgin Mother to his last breath on the Cross, his whole life was, above all, an incessant prayer; not only for his devoted disciples, but even for his cruel murderers.

—Fr. Edward Sorin, C.S.C.

ON TUESDAYS AT Christ the King Parish, our third- and fourth-graders came to Mass. One week, as they were walking by me after Mass, I kept repeating to the third-graders, "Be good, and love God." But then a young girl turned to me and said, "Fr. Neil, I know all about that. I'm in the fourth grade!" And hopefully she did.

It's a constant challenge to keep grade-school children focused—on their schoolwork, on their conduct, and most especially on God. At every opportunity, we tell them to look at things through the eyes of Jesus so that they can live as he asks them to live. It's a lesson for us adults as well. It's easier for some than for others, but it's impossible to live well without prayer. If prayer is just something else we have to do, it will be the first thing we don't have time for in our lives. But if our lives are a prayer, then we will live as Jesus asks us to live.

Jesus' life was one of prayer, not only in those explicit moments when he went into the desert for forty days, went up the mountain with his disciples, or retreated to a deserted place, but in every moment of his life. We are called to follow his example and live a life of prayer as well. It isn't enough to be people who pray; we must be people of prayer. For then we are constantly in relationship with God, living the grace that comes from making our lives an incessant prayer.

Neil F. Wack, C.S.C.

April 4

People who live according to the will of God, even though they do only the most ordinary things, things with no attraction in the eyes of people, they are the people who will enter the kingdom of heaven and will receive a full reward.

—Blessed Basil Moreau

SUNRISE. HE WAKES slowly to the alarm. She is already out of bed, her body moving to the familiar rhythm of the early morning: make the coffee, hang his clothes by the bathroom door, leave his medication on the table. The smell of toast fills the air. She quickly kisses him goodbye and closes the door against the cold. Next, the children.

At 5:30 p.m., she hears the whine from his car as he backs it up the driveway, already pointing toward tomorrow. He washes, checks the headlines in the afternoon newspaper, and seats himself for supper. The children, as if responding to a silent summons, take their assigned places around the table. She makes each plate individually, careful not to waste food, sitting only after she checks to make sure that nothing—and no one—is missing.

Thus passed a "normal" day in my home—in most homes. Same picture, different wall.

My father worked for forty years as a quality-control inspector in a red-brick building like so many others that filled our industrial New England cities. My mother was "stay-at-home" long before it became a luxury. Their lives were "ordinary." Yet how many of us aspire to be "average" or "predictable"? Doesn't this go against our cultural bias towards exceptionalism?

Routine provided the stability upon which my parents raised our family and upon which I learned invaluable lessons: that you can count on others, that "forever" does not have an end, and that there is great joy to be found in doing small things with love. Daily prayer, community, service—my parents taught me the essentials of religious life long before I ever met my first Holy Cross brother. Mary and Joseph did nothing less for their Son.

Sunrise, sunset. The beauty of the ordinary. Every day.

Jonathan Beebe, C.S.C.

April 5

In the fullness of time the Lord Jesus came among us anointed by the Spirit to inaugurate a kingdom of justice, love, and peace. His rule would be no mere earthly regime: it would initiate a new creation in every land. His power would be within and without, rescuing us from the injustice we suffer and also from the injustice we inflict.

—Holy Cross *Constitutions*

THERE IS A huge gap between the values of this world, so firmly rooted, and the values of Jesus spoken in the Beatitudes, the charter of the kingdom. Both sets of values pull at our hearts although they stand in such contrast—competition and loving care, sophistication and childlikeness, revenge and forgiveness, dominance and humility, self-centeredness and service, individualism and community. Uprooting the first and tending the second can be excruciating. Yet scripture tells us never to grow tired of trying to do good, of trying to be part of that new creation.

Then I meet people here in Bangladesh—good people, usually poor and uneducated—who have so little and suffer so much but are clearly children of that new creation. These are people who daily carry heavy loads but continue to love, to smile, and to be generous and peaceful. Their lives quietly proclaim that the kingdom of God is among us, close at hand. They are the children of the Lord, who does not trample on the bent reed or extinguish the flickering wick.

I have seen the kingdom in them, and I am often in awe. The kingdom of God is not a place; it is people. My experience here is that when we share the lot of the people, they bring us to the faith. We can all think of those special graces of God, the people who have shown us the new creation—through a smile, a kind word, a gentle touch—beautiful glimpses of the kingdom among us.

Frank Quinlivan, C.S.C.

The aspirations of a Christian soul should lead to the further imitation of him who never turns his eyes from even the forgetful heart.

—Fr. Edward Sorin, C.S.C.

WHEN I SPEAK with others, I feel more at ease if we make eye contact. I get a better appreciation for the person, and I feel more connected to him or her. Conversely, I feel on edge if a person looks away while we speak. For me, the eyes make all the difference.

Fr. Sorin reminds us to keep our eyes on Jesus Christ our Savior. Just as the Savior looks upon us with love, healing, and forgiveness, so we are encouraged to focus our eyes on him in order to imitate him. This is not always an easy task; it is much too easy to forget. After all, plenty of distractions in our material culture can take our eyes off of Jesus—newer clothes, sportier cars, bigger houses, better cuisine, sleeker computers, and a more perfect physique. Even we priests aren't immune. There's the latest workshop on ministry in the sunniest resort, more luxurious vestments, and that ideal putter for the perfect golf game.

Yes, we are all human. Our eyes can go in all different directions at once, dragging our minds with them to everything but the Lord. On these occasions, we must renew our trust and belief that there's more to life than anything that this world alone can offer. We do this by looking once again into the eyes of Jesus. We turn our eyes to the One who never forgets us, the One to whom we've committed our lives, the Lord who comes to each of us in the Eucharist. And he draws us into closer union with himself.

Michael Belinsky, C.S.C.

April 7

Holy Cross is not our work, but God's very own. If each member continues to carry out his own particular obedience in a spirit of loyalty and simplicity and with the spirit of union which is inspiring all the members of the association, God will bless our whole Congregation.

—Blessed Basil Moreau

THE BEGINNING OF golf season each year is an opportunity for me to get reacquainted not only with my golf swing but also with my buddies whom I only know through the links. On our first round of the season, we bring each other up to date on what happened in our lives over the winter.

One year, one of these friends, Jimmy, shared an experience with his daughter. His daughter, who had a number of false starts at college, was now flourishing as a computer science major. This was Jimmy's major and is his career. Over the winter, he and his daughter worked together on a number of computer-related projects, and at one point, his daughter asked, "Dad, how do you know all this stuff?" For Jimmy this was a breakthrough since, in his words, "for years she thought the old man was the dumbest human being on planet Earth."

Jimmy and his daughter had grown close over the winter and rediscovered their respect for each other; their love, although perhaps not always overt, had always been present.

Jimmy's story is a familiar one among parents and so many other vocations: long periods where our faith, hope, and love seem to bear little fruit, and where the present is all duty and no delight. I've certainly experienced it as a college priest, professor, and president. Daily prayer, daily testimony like Jimmy's, and daily stories from hope bearers affirm for us that God will in time bless our efforts of simple loyalty in our own particular obedience to God's work. After all, our lives are God's work.

Jack Ryan, C.S.C.

April 8

The more we humble ourselves before God, the more God will raise us up and favor us.

—Blessed Basil Moreau

AT THE LAST SUPPER, the night before he laid down his life for us, Jesus gave his disciples a lasting memory of humble service as he washed their feet. In this simple yet deliberate action, Jesus gives us a model of mutual love and service to follow. Called by him to do likewise, we make Christ present today by washing one another's feet.

Over my many years in Holy Cross, I have watched my brothers embody that loving service by responding generously to the needs of the community, the Church, and the world.

As educators in the faith, they have accepted the call to serve as pastors, teachers, writers, artists, and chaplains. Whatever ministries they have fulfilled, they have gone about the work of making Christ present in the lives of those in need.

The realization that we are called to serve the people of God by washing feet and by saying yes to bear Christ in a variety of ways is both overwhelming and humbling. I remember the first time after ordination that I was assigned to hear confessions. I was scared and hardly slept the night before because I did not want to do it wrongly or make a mistake. I spoke with a wise priest in the community who gave me advice that I have never forgotten. This holy priest told me to remember that the sacrament of Reconciliation, as well as all other ministries, is about being an instrument of love. Through grace we humbly step out of the way and let God's love be alive and well in the world, raising us and those we serve into his embrace.

Joe Carey, C.S.C.

April 9

Zealous teachers know that all students are equally important to God and that their duty is to work for each with the same devotion, watchfulness, and perseverance.

—Blessed Basil Moreau

BLESSED MOREAU'S ULTIMATE vision for his Congregation was that we be educators in the faith. In our history, this charge has been interpreted quite broadly to include the many and varied ways that we as vowed apostolic religious attend to educating for faith. One of the more direct ways that we do this is as teachers in the classroom. There is in our ministry—apart from the context within which each of us teaches, and regardless of our respective disciplines—the demand to see in each of our students his or her cherished nature. Continued scholarship and professional development inform our ministry on every level. But even more than our attempts to keep abreast of the latest research methods and most effective pedagogy, we seek to root our learning, and that of our students, in an incarnational paradigm—one in which we know and appreciate the power and presence of a living God in and through one another.

Blessed Moreau teaches that education is a balance between the heart and mind, between faith and reason. The story is told in the community of a high school teacher released from his contract at midyear because he could not manage a classroom. Afterward, the department chair remarked, "I don't understand it. In the past, he taught math at the college level." The superior quickly responded, "Ah, therein lies the rub. Here we teach *students*." Like for many of us, it is often easier for teachers to deal with matters of the head than with matters of the heart. As Holy Cross religious, we strive to do both and invite others to do the same.

Jim Lies, C.S.C.

April 10

The footsteps of those men who called us to walk in their company left deep prints, as of men carrying heavy burdens. But they did not trudge; they strode. For they had the hope.

—Holy Cross *Constitutions*

ONE OF THE most vivid memories from my ordination was the laying on of hands. With a bishop and well over one hundred concelebrants, this process lasted quite a while. I was kneeling at the edge of the sanctuary. My eyes were closed at first, but I opened them eventually. Since I was looking down, I could only see the feet of the men walking by. I was struck by all of the different shoes that stopped in front of me, paused for a moment, and then walked off. It is an image that has remained with me.

There is a wide diversity of men in Holy Cross. We come from all parts of the country and serve in a variety of ministries. We have different senses of humor and interests, but we support and encourage each other in our vocations. After a hard day in the office, I love going to evening prayer and dinner with the community. Spending time with my brothers strengthens me to do my ministry and to live most fully my call from God.

Beginning with the first disciples, the band of women and men who have followed Jesus has been incredibly diverse. Although this diversity can at times produce tension, it can also be a great source of strength. Each set of footprints left by those who have gone before us in the faith reveals men and women who did not trudge but strode, for they followed Jesus in hope. Their examples serve as inspirations to us.

Every once in a while, I think back to my ordination and to that great band of men who laid their hands on my head. After the last one walked off, I stood up and joined them, strengthened by their witness of living a good and holy life.

Gerard Olinger, C.S.C.

April 11

If I could have foreseen the development of the Congregation of Holy Cross at the outset, I could then have regulated and coordinated everything in advance. If such were the case, however, the congregation would have been a merely human combination and not the work of Divine Providence.

—Blessed Basil Moreau

FOR THOSE LIKE me, we plan and prepare and like to think that we are somewhat in control of things. But thanks be to God, he is really the one in charge. When I began my life in Holy Cross, I felt that I was called to the ministry of teaching, and so I planned and prepared to enter the high school classroom one day. Even with all the things I have done as a Holy Cross religious in more than two decades in the community, I have never once set foot in a high school classroom. God's plan for me was to teach in other ways. Whether it has been guiding a college retreat, hearing a confession, serving as chaplain for a college sports team, serving as rector in a university residence hall, offering counsel to a student, or preaching at Mass, the Lord has provided me with countless ways of "teaching" that have been far greater than any for which I could have planned.

In our lives, it is good to have plans and dreams and aspirations, and it is good always to bear in mind that these dreams find their origin in the One who gives us all. And the One who gives us these great dreams and aspirations will be the One to bring them to fulfillment. So we continue to plan and dream and prepare. But in the end, we surrender it all to our loving God, who will fashion our hopes into the most life-giving gifts possible.

Tom Gaughan, C.S.C.

April 12

Let us disregard the suggestions of self-love and forget ourselves to see only God and the Congregation. For the future, let us heed nothing but the spirit of obedience.

—Blessed Basil Moreau

WHEN I WAS a new seminarian, an elderly priest surprised me by claiming that obedience was the hardest of the vows to embrace. Chastity, he said, dulled in intensity over time, and poverty was easy since we all lived it together. Obedience, however, was always ready to jump up and bite you when you least expected it. I doubted that he could possibly be right.

Father was right. Now, almost thirty years later, I can affirm that it is obedience, the ongoing call to surrender the exercise of my own will, that proves to be a daily challenge. It is a radical leap of faith to trust that I hear God's will for my life through the voice of my superiors and the works of the Congregation. Religious life militates against the spirit of individualism that drives the culture in which we live. Heeding the spirit of obedience is not only socially odd but must, at times, be borne as a cross. The question is whether we accept that cross with hope.

Religious are not alone in heeding the call of obedience. Married couples also take vows in a moment and live them through a lifetime, subsuming their own wants and desires in the needs of the other. Embracing God's will, as found in our commitments and responsibilities, is a true dying to self. In seeking only God, living our commitments, and heeding the spirit of obedience, we come to know our true selves. In making this effort, we learn the profound depths of God's love.

Gary S. Chamberland, C.S.C.

April 13

Has not Holy Communion made us many times more sacred receptacles of Jesus Christ than the consecrated vessels which contain his flesh and blood in our churches? Unlike the sacred vessels, we do not merely contain this flesh and blood; we really make it part of ourselves.

—Blessed Basil Moreau

MASS ON HOLY THURSDAY has always been one of my favorite celebrations of the Church year. As an altar boy, I had to sign up early and attend two practices to have the honor of serving at this Mass. Our pastor always told us that Holy Thursday was special because it commemorated the institution of both the Eucharist and the priesthood.

The procession around our parish church with the Blessed Sacrament led by incense and candles expressed the solemnity of the celebration. When I was old enough to carry the incense, our pastor told me, "Remember that you are giving honor to Jesus present in the Eucharist. Be slow and deliberate as you bless with incense." As moving as the procession was, the washing of the feet also stands out in my memory of Holy Thursday. Each year twelve men would take a seat in the sanctuary, and each year there was some uneasiness among them as the ritual began. Like St. Peter, they weren't sure about why their leader would wash their feet. But each year our pastor was "slow and deliberate" as he carefully and tenderly washed and dried the feet.

In our Holy Cross communities, parishes, and institutions, we still celebrate the sacredness of the Eucharist with processions and adoration throughout the year. We, like Blessed Moreau, believe in God's real presence in the Eucharist—body, blood, soul, and divinity. In its transformative power, we slowly yet deliberately become more like him whom we receive; we become Christ's sacred vessels, blessing with his presence all those we encounter, slowly and deliberately.

Kevin Russeau, C.S.C.

April 14

Try, then, to become perfect copies of the Divine Model, and nothing will ever shake your vocation. Not only will you carry whatever crosses you encounter in accomplishing the duties of your holy state, but you will love these crosses. Yes, you will even desire them and, after the example of the Lord, will choose them in preference to anything else.

—Blessed Basil Moreau

ON GOOD FRIDAY at Saint Mary's College in Indiana, the Sisters of the Holy Cross place a large wooden cross in the middle of the Church of Our Lady of Loretto. When the time comes for veneration, members of the congregation stream toward it from four directions. They show their love for Christ's Cross in many ways. Some genuflect or bow; others kiss the cross or grasp it with their hands or touch their foreheads to the wood. I have never been so inspired on Good Friday as I was when I experienced this rite with the sisters.

While the act of veneration is both simple and powerful, loving the Cross, and one's crosses, is a process that takes years. As I grow older, I realize that every cross that I am asked to bear, no matter how burdensome, might be borne as a gift. Each time I have fallen beneath the weight of failure and disappointment, I have risen with God's help as someone who more intimately knows Christ.

As we imitate the Divine Model when we bear the weight of our burdens, we are reassured by the fact that there is no such thing as a perfect copy. Whether we are painstakingly replicating the work of an Old Master or simply photocopying a document, there will always be telling differences between the copy and the original. We will never be perfect. We strive nevertheless to become ever more like Christ, especially in our love of his Cross, and our crosses.

George Piggford, C.S.C.

April 15

We do not imagine that those who commit themselves in other ways to the following of Jesus are thereby hindered in their service of their neighbor. On the contrary, we find in them willing and complementary partners in shared mission. We want our vows, faithfully lived, to be witness and call to them as their commitments, faithfully lived, are witness and call to us.
—Holy Cross *Constitutions*

I REMEMBER MY first Easter Vigil as a priest. Newly appointed as Director of Campus Ministry at the University of Portland, I wanted everything to go smoothly. We gathered outside of the Chapel of Christ the Teacher around the blazing Easter fire. Then, as we entered the chapel in procession, I lowered the Paschal Candle to share the light of Christ. Not following directions, one of the servers removed the glass windscreen from the candle. Immediately, a gust of wind blew out the flame. The server froze. I looked around in a panic. Then, from behind me, a ninety-two-year old Holy Cross priest calmly reached into his pocket and pulled out a cigarette lighter. "Light of Christ, kid," he said with a grin as he relit the Paschal Candle and the light began to spread through the church.

After Mass, I readied myself for some good-natured teasing. After all, the "baby priest" had let the Light of Christ go out! What I heard instead was the joy the people had experienced in seeing us—the oldest and youngest religious in the Holy Cross community at the university—working together.

Togetherness is the Holy Cross way. We belong to one another. We religious strive to model it for others. We are inspired as we witness it in the families of those with whom we work and to whom we minister. As a family of sisters, brothers, priests, and lay collaborators, our lives are bound up together—at the Chapel of Christ the Teacher, at the University of Portland, and around the world. Without each other and our unique gifts, our ministry—even our capacity to dwell with God—falters. Working together makes it possible for the light to spread through the Church.

Mark DeMott, C.S.C.

April 16

There is in our eyes of faith nothing that merits our respect and our adoration more than the Sacred Heart. If we contemplate it as it is, it is a part of the flesh of our Lord, the center of a life that was consecrated wholly to the salvation of the world, and the source of the precious blood that purchased us for God.

—Blessed Basil Moreau

TO REALIZE THAT a human heart contained the fullness of God's love is a truly astounding thing. This beauty of the Sacred Heart of Jesus is not manifested solely in the intensity of the love that it contained—this one Heart so full of love that it is literally aflame with passion. The wonder includes the reality that humanity and divinity were united in it—in the Heart itself and as a result of it being pierced and poured out for us all. The mystery of this Heart also encompasses the reality that it did not cease to be at the Crucifixion. Rather, through Jesus' bodily Resurrection and Ascension, he continues to carry this Heart still beating and burning with love for all.

Contemplation of this wondrous Heart leads to the realization that we are invited to enter into it. To enter into this love involves not only the sheer joy of knowing that we are loved, but also the potential of being set ablaze. Truly letting go and being consumed by this love is daunting, for who knows where it will take us? It is intimidating to step forward into that vast love, yet how can we not? That we may live in that love is the very reason that fleshly Heart was formed and pierced. To be enveloped in that love is the end for which we were created. It is meant for us, and we are meant for it.

James T. Gallagher, C.S.C.

April 17

The perfect life will be an interior life, elevated to God by the habitual practice of acts of faith, hope, and charity after the example of Jesus Christ, who is to be the particular model of our conduct. It is absolutely essential for us to lead with our Lord a life hidden in God.

—Blessed Basil Moreau

THE PERFECT LIFE will be an interior life. To be honest, I'm not really too sure about that. After all, we don't live only in the interior; we live in the world—a world of work and play, a world of struggle and joy, a marvelous world filled with the splendor of nature and the blessing of human relationships. And so, my practice of faith, hope, and charity must somehow or other express itself in this complex world. At the same time, this world expresses itself in my life. The secret of this interchange is Jesus himself, the creative Word made flesh.

In the midst of the daily hustle and bustle of everyday life, I have often thought of the restful consolation of a "hidden" life with our Lord. But then the doubts come. Can there ever be a life that is "hidden" in God? How could that be if God is indeed everywhere? As Jesus said, I have to go into my interior room, close the door, and there, in prayerful silence, converse with him.

I can't help thinking that the purpose of developing a deeper interior life, along with the practice of faith, hope, and charity, is to live out what we sing very often during Communion in our school Masses at our schools in Santiago, Chile: "To love, as you love; to feel, as you feel; to see things through your eyes, Jesus."

Robert Simon, C.S.C.

April 18

Sometimes you meet people whose thoughts, feelings, sense of taste, tone of voice, and mannerisms all resemble one another. How is that? It is just because the custom they have of living familiarly with one another, the close friendship that unites them, intermingles them, and unites them in such a way that they have but one heart and one soul. Therefore, love Jesus Christ, and before long his thoughts, his feelings, and his way of living will be your own.

—Blessed Basil Moreau

In the Acts of the Apostles, we read that the community of believers was of one heart and soul (4:32). The successes of the early preaching of Peter and the others—as well as the signs and wonders that accompanied that preaching—were miraculous. Thousands embraced Jesus and each other in a community of friends. John Robertson, a gifted preacher and Greek scholar, once translated Acts 4:32 as "one heart and soul was in the believers." Perhaps the greater miracle was not so much that these new converts embraced Jesus but that they allowed Jesus' heart and soul to enter into their lives. This would be the source of the Church's unity and the glue that held them together, despite differences and disagreements. This, too, was Blessed Moreau's prayer for his Holy Cross family: that the heart and soul of Jesus may be in each one of us.

I live in a large, diverse Holy Cross community of priests and brothers. We are teachers, administrators, seminary formation staff, hall rectors, hospital chaplains, pastors, and retired—with ages that vary between twenty-seven and ninety-four. Yet no single ministry is as important as the overall mission of the Congregation of Holy Cross to make God known, loved, and served. While engaged in different works, we share common prayer, a common purse, and a common table. However, in keeping with the spirit of Blessed Moreau, our true unity comes from loving with the heart of Christ, thinking with the mind of Christ, and serving with the passion of Christ. To do this is to allow the heart and soul of Jesus to be in each one of us. What is central is not so much to be successful in what we do, but to be faithful to Jesus in the doing.

Tom Jones, C.S.C.

April 19

Let us continue to remain thus united in our Lord, and let us often come together in spirit despite our distance which separates us. By these relationships of mutual friendship and dependence we shall help one another correspond with the designs of Providence in our regard.

—Blessed Basil Moreau

As a North American, the opportunity to live and work with postulants at St. André Formation House in Uganda has been a privilege and adventure. At the same time, there has been a sense of being "off the grid" when it comes to relationships with family, friends, and confreres in Holy Cross. It is easy to feel isolated, alone, and even abandoned by those who know and love me in the United States.

Despite the physical distance, multiple time zones, and the reality of being on a different continent, there is one sure and certain thing that connects me with those I left behind: prayer. If I cannot be face-to-face with my loved ones, prayer allows me to be heart-to-heart with them. My daily exercise of prayer is an opportunity to hear the voices and see the faces of those who are dear to me. During morning meditation, I deliberately pray for specific people and ask God to bless them. As I walk to the college seminary where I teach, I pray the Rosary and ask Mother Mary to intercede for a particular person in need. My daily Mass intention is frequently for someone back in the United States who asked for prayers. My prayer for others unites me with them in a bond of love that cannot be broken.

Just as Blessed Moreau prayed for his fledgling religious community as it grew beyond the boundaries of France, we can pray for our brothers and sisters in Christ who live miles away. Prayer weaves us together in a beautiful tapestry of spiritual support and encouragement that keeps us close, despite the distance. Unlike the Internet, Skype, and cell-phone networks, prayer never fails—no matter how far away we or they are.

Michael C. Mathews, C.S.C.

April 20

Resurrection for us is a daily event. We have stood watch with persons dying in peace; we have witnessed wonderful reconciliations; we have known the forgiveness of those who misuse their neighbor; we have seen heartbreak and defeat lead to a transformed life; we have heard the conscience of an entire church stir; we have marveled at the insurrection of justice. We know that we walk by Easter's first light, and it makes us long for its fullness.

—Holy Cross *Constitutions*

OUR SCRIPTURES, LIKE our lives in discipleship, are tested frequently by seemingly hopeless situations. From Abraham walking alongside Isaac, the heir of the covenant who carries upon his shoulders the wood on which he will be sacrificed, to the anonymous friends of a paralyzed man who carry him day after day on his stretcher, to the courageous yet terrified women who stand at the foot of Jesus' Cross. Several of us in Holy Cross walked with these ancestors in faith as we approached the casket of a young student, taken by leukemia soon after his college graduation, and greeted his parents, who kept vigil by his body.

And then, almost confoundingly, Abraham spots a ram in the thistle. The men carrying the paralyzed friend hear of a healer, climb a roof, and begin pulling up tile. The women prepare burial spices and venture vulnerably into the Sunday dawn where angels await. And, almost utterly unexplainably, the mother by the casket, even while tears ran down both cheeks, consoled us with the words of Psalm 118: "Somehow this, too, is the day the Lord has made; so we must find a way to give thanks and rejoice in it."

What can explain such relentless boldness—what but the gift of hope, what our *Constitutions* name our "longing for Easter's fullness"? Thankfully, this hope is neither self-generated nor the logical response to the facts of any desperate situation. We persevere in longing for the Resurrection, even in the face of death, because we are recipients of a divine gift that compels us to believe that the darkness and suffering we encounter is not the final fact. In Jesus Christ, to whom we have consecrated our lives in Baptism and in Holy Cross, God has blessed us with a stirring in our hearts, which swells into a conviction, and then bursts forth into the darkness. Today, Easter Light will shine!

Lou DelFra, C.S.C.

April 21

We know to us are addressed those words of Jesus Christ: "Suffer the little children to come to me," etc., "for it is to them, and to those that resemble them, belongs the kingdom of heaven."

—Fr. Edward Sorin, C.S.C.

As a young religious, I often wondered what in the world these words of Jesus might mean for me as an adult. Wasn't I to put aside the things of childhood, eat the food of adults, and live the life of a mature religious? A lifetime of experience, though, has brought me to a new understanding of Jesus' words.

I travel quite a bit and spend a good deal of time sitting in airports where I enjoy people watching. Very small children, if they are not fussing, are wonderful to watch. They have a bright, welcoming smile for everyone. Everything they see is filled with wonder and joy, and they accept it with a welcoming heart. On one overseas trip, I sat in a row behind a seven-year-old who was sitting with his mom. As the plane was taking off, he grew excited: "We're taking off, we're taking off. We're flying, Mom, we're flying!" His joyful shouts filled the whole cabin with smiles.

As we grow up, we can lose our sense of wonder in the seemingly ordinary. Jesus teaches us how to rediscover the simple joys of our youth, how to enter into his kingdom. In living out our ordinary, humdrum existence, Jesus blessed it. Even in his last years, Jesus could still find beauty and delight in the ordinary—the lilies of the field, the birds of the air. Everything speaks of awe, of God. Perhaps the kingdom is for those who, like little children, can still find wonder and joy disguised in the ordinary—the face of a stranger or the taking off of an airplane.

Raymond Papenfuss, C.S.C.

April 22

We must be contented to be treated as poor. Should we gain nothing else by this new general effort but to conform ourselves to the spirit of poverty, we might

well congratulate one another; for the spirit of poverty is the greatest riches of a community.
—Fr. Edward Sorin, C.S.C.

THE GREAT DANGER of riches is that they can fool us into believing that we can make it on our own, that we don't need to depend upon others, let alone on God. Conversely, by our vow of poverty we in Holy Cross pledge dependence upon one another as we hold all our goods in common and share them as brothers. This disposition requires and thus expresses a true confidence in one another. For our poverty is not merely our own; by its very nature it draws us closer together and binds us into community.

Our renunciation of the independent use and enjoyment of the goods of the land causes us to acquire riches not of this world. They are the riches of a deeper connection with and dependence on one another—riches of a deeper connection with and dependence on God.

Yet for all Christian believers, our spirit of poverty should not express or exhibit a disdain or even contempt for the material riches and the blessings of the earth. Rather, it should express a yearning and eagerness to share the bounty that the Lord has placed in the world. It is this sharing of the earth's abundance that draws us together and binds us as the human family. We liberate our very hearts in order that they might be possessed entirely by each other and by God. Our graciousness, then, is an imitation of the abundant love with which the God of the universe created us—the love that is truly the greatest of riches.

Fermin Donoso, C.S.C.

It follows that your whole novitiate, rather your whole life, must have as its purpose to assimilate so well the thoughts, judgments, desires, words, and actions of Jesus Christ, so that you can say with the great apostle: "I live, rather no, I live no more, it is Christ who lives in me."

—Blessed Basil Moreau

IN MY THIRD year of temporary vows in Holy Cross, I was sent to teach in Holy Cross High School, Tuikarmaw, in the state of Tripura in northeast India. I was one of the organizers of the school's sports day, and I put together a twenty-five-meter running race for the kindergarteners. After explaining to them the rules and how to win, I blew the whistle, and they began to run.

Suddenly, one child fell, and immediately, all the other children stopped. Some walked toward the one who fell as if to help. When I asked them why they stopped running, they answered, "Because she fell, we stopped." Fortunately, she did not have any injury and was ready to run again. I explained once again the competition and insisted that they not stop until they crossed the finish line. Again, the race started after the blow of the whistle. To our surprise, another boy fell, and all the children stopped running. We laughed and worried about how to complete the competition. My superior then came over to me and said, "Alexander, these children are already living the Gospel values, and you are trying to spoil them by teaching these competitions."

Our upbringings and backgrounds with their powerful cultural and social influences have conditioned—and still condition—our thoughts, judgments, desires, words, and actions. Though intellectually we know the thoughts, judgments, desires, words, and actions of Jesus Christ, they have not been assimilated or incarnated enough in our lives. We must become aware of those conditionings that block this process of conforming ourselves to Christ and internalizing the Gospel so that we can say with the great apostle St. Paul, "I live, rather no, I live no more; it is Christ who lives in me."

Alexander Susai, C.S.C.

April 24

It does one good to see the wisdom of those great champions of the faith "who chose the better part." They passed from a momentary tribulation into endless joy.

—Fr. Edward Sorin, C.S.C.

ONE OF THE many highlights of the ordination liturgy to the priesthood is the litany of saints. Just before the litany begins, all those assembled kneel, while those to be ordained lie prostrate on the ground. Once people are in place, the litany begins, and for the next five minutes the choir intones the names of saints throughout history, with the assembly chanting in response, "Pray for us."

The litany of saints is a wonderful reminder of God's love for us. From the very beginning of time, God has shed his love upon the earth, and we are reminded of that love through the service of so many faithful men and women. These holy disciples of the Lord were no different from us. Throughout the course of their earthly lives, they experienced difficulty, but they kept their focus on what mattered most—the love of God and his fidelity to his children.

Today, in a world that seems to reject the presence of God, we can be tempted to despair. Yet it is precisely at these moments that we must seek the wisdom and strength of those who have gone before us. The litany of saints is not reserved solely for the ordination of priests or even liturgy in general. It is a prayer that can and should be used in our daily lives. There is no reason that we should act alone on our journeys to discover the Lord, for through the intercession of so many faithful people we already have access to our loving God in so many wonderful ways.

Holy Mary, Mother of God, pray for us. St. Joseph, pray for us. St. André Bessette, pray for us. Blessed Basil Moreau, pray for us.

Peter McCormick, C.S.C.

April 25

There will not be a single member of our association who will not make his own personal contribution to the progress, according to his strength, intellectual ability, and particular aptitudes. One will do intellectual work and another, manual labor; this one will teach, that one will administer the sacraments; and all the while this activity of the individual will help the community; and the activity of the community will, in turn, help each individual.

—Blessed Basil Moreau

SOMETIMES I WONDER what my life would be like if I'd chosen a different path. I'd like to think I could be a good husband and father and that I might even make some money, but something tells me I would be a lot poorer in other ways. I think so because I tend to be cautious in how I define my abilities, and it is entirely possible that, left to my own devices, my life might be defined as safe and predictable. No such life exists in Holy Cross.

Since joining the Congregation, I have been asked to do things I never thought myself capable of doing. For the sake of the mission, the community has time and time again called me beyond myself, helping develop gifts I'd never seen. In those times when I have fallen short, when tasks have been beyond my talents, the community was there to pick me up, dust me off, and fill that gap with hope and grace.

So it is with all of us. If we see our lives and work as being in and for Jesus, then what we do is not what ultimately matters. God will use us and call out from us what his people need in a given time and place. Sometimes we are most effective when we are doing what we least expected to do. It is not what we do that makes us who we are. Instead, who we are and how we allow others to call us forth makes a big difference in what we do.

Peter Jarret, C.S.C.

We pronounce our vows in a moment, but living them for the sake of the kingdom is the work of a lifetime. That fulfillment demands of us more than the mere wish, more even than the firm decision. It demands the conversion of our habits, our character, our attitudes, our desires.

—Holy Cross *Constitutions*

HAVING HAD THE privilege of working with several hundred couples preparing for the sacrament of Marriage, I have experienced one inspiring constant in the great majority of cases. Aware of the increasing percentage of divorces and oftentimes having felt its effects personally, most couples express a sincere, even passionate, commitment to "making this marriage work." I want always to affirm the inherent rightness of this desire. At the same time, I challenge the couples to place this desire in the context of grace. I speak about the reality that any genuine vocation breaks those who are called to it. I share my firm conviction that marriage, like religious or dedicated single life, demands every ounce of their energy; once they have expended this effort, there will come a time when they discover it just isn't enough. At that point, they can either give up, or give themselves up to God.

In Holy Cross, we believe that all vows to God are tried and refined through formation and transformation. Whether preparing for religious life or marriage, we owe it to each other to form ourselves in the great wisdom of these vocations as they are handed on to us in our Catholic tradition. Yet, in the end, the living of vows—in religious community or in marriage—will always depend on the grace of ongoing conversion. Conversion is transformation. It demands consent of the will, and then it demands a surrender of the will. Formation is what we can do; transformation is what only God can do in us.

Don Dilg, C.S.C.

April 27

When our expressions of thanks are offered together, they will more fully satisfy the debt of the family of Holy Cross. Our homage, rendered in this way more agreeable to our Lord, will be the source of new blessings, because, as St. Bernard says, ingratitude is like a burning wind which dries up the channels of the waters of grace.

—Blessed Basil Moreau

AT THE VERY core of the Christian faith is the attitude of thanksgiving. Indeed, followers of Jesus might well be defined by their desire to render thanks unto God at every moment of every day. To celebrate the Eucharist, the communal prayer that the Church calls the source and summit of our faith life, is to give thanks through the perfect offering of Jesus' self-sacrifice on the Cross. This is not just what we do but who we are.

The daily struggle for each of us is how to live a life of thanksgiving. How do we continue in our everyday actions and words the thanksgiving that we celebrate together in the

Eucharist? We may, in fact, be tempted to dismiss the need to maintain a thankful heart in our daily routines since the fruit might seem inconsequential and the results unnoticeable. Whether or not anyone notices, our thankfulness truly matters.

Blessed Moreau founded Holy Cross as a family united in heart. The first seal of the Congregation was an anchor with three hearts for Jesus, Mary, and Joseph—depicting the intimate relationship of Holy Cross priests, sisters, and brothers. Blessed Moreau trusted deeply in the power of prayer generated by hearts united in faith and love. He knew that all of our expressions of thanks are most powerfully offered together. If the grace of thanksgiving fills our individual hearts and links us closer to the thanksgiving of our sisters and brothers, then surely the waters of grace will flow from our lives and will help to revitalize the world we touch. Such thanksgiving makes a difference.

Steve Wilbricht, C.S.C.

April 28

For the kingdom to come in this world, disciples must have the competence to see and the courage to act.
—Holy Cross *Constitutions*

I STILL REMEMBER that great day when I rode my bicycle for the first time without training wheels. I was elated and proud of my mastery of the task. It was even better than learning to tie my shoes!

We spend much of our lives striving to be competent in many ways. We work to have those competencies certified with diplomas, degrees, promotions, professional certifications, trophies, medals, and so on. We are a competency-based culture.

Our Holy Cross *Constitutions* speak of a much more important competency—even the most important competency—because it deals with the building of God's kingdom. It is a competency of the heart that is supported by grace, nurtured by hope, and rooted in faith. It is an effective and successful skill that enables us to "see" the events of the world and the signs of the times with the eyes of a faith-filled heart. At Baptism, we begin to hone this competency. We learn to see God's grace and activity in the world. We also see the world's impoverishments; we see the brokenhearted, the poor, the hungry and sick, the oppressed and abused. Yet this competency of the heart allows us to see the transformation of the Cross of Christ as our hope and a sign of the coming kingdom.

Gaining this competency, however, is not sufficient. Competence without action is ability misspent and can lead to a life of indifference. This competency is to rouse us to action—to fill us with zeal to bring relief to God's children and to be heralds of the kingdom. It can take a wellspring of courage to bring the relief so essential to the world. For us disciples, then, courage is a crucial habit to develop. It leads to a life of fortitude, the very virtue that sustains the acts of courage necessary to establish the kingdom of God.

David T. Tyson, C.S.C.

April 29

What a source of interior consolations it is to be able to give oneself this glorious testimony: I love my God, and I am loved by him.

—Blessed Basil Moreau

AT MY ORDINATION, I was instructed "to live with the smell of [my] sheep." Serving in a men's residence hall at the University of Notre Dame, I can tell you that's a dangerous proposition. So many smells, so many combinations of smells. Hot dogs wrapped in pepperoni and jalapenos. Two-by-fours sanded for chariot racing. Body spray, both Axe and Old Spice. Socks, lots of socks. Root beer mixed with vanilla ice cream. Popcorn that didn't need seven minutes in the microwave. And the occasional, economical fermented beverage, imported from Milwaukee and St. Louis and Golden, Colorado.

So many smells—not all of which are bad. When my guys smell "excited" after a first date, when they smell "confident" before an exam, when they smell "pumped" during an interhall game, I don't mind smelling like my sheep. In fact, it's fun to smell like them—to share life with them so abundantly that I can't avoid the scent of their laughter and joy. The challenge comes when their lives don't smell so rosy: when they don't feel loveable, when they make a mistake, when they're embarrassed, when things break.

In those moments, it helps to remember what I really smell like: not socks or body spray or sadness or shame but Christ, the Good Shepherd. It helps to remember his smell, to recall the sweet-smelling chrism that anoints our heads and hands and hearts as Christ's disciples with his joy. Every time we celebrate Eucharist, we become what we receive. We become anew God's consecration. And through that mystery, we all come to reek of Resurrection.

Patrick Reidy, C.S.C.

April 30

In Baptism, we received the seed of spiritual life which must grow and be strengthened until Jesus Christ is formed in us. In this way, we become other Christs and his life is made manifest in ours.

—Blessed Basil Moreau

DURING MY TERM as pastor at Christ the King Parish in South Bend, Indiana, a seventh-grade student in our elementary school was suffering from a rare form of leukemia. Numerous radiation and chemotherapy treatments left him so weak that he was unable to attend classes. To the boy's surprise, his uncle asked him to be the godfather for his first son. The young cancer patient was excited to be chosen for this honor and responsibility. He sincerely said, "I hope that I can be as good a godparent as my uncle was a Confirmation sponsor for me."

That young seventh-grader clearly understood the importance of Baptism and growth in the life of Christ. Baptism is important because we are who God says we are: beloved sons and daughters of the Father, beloved brothers and sisters in

Christ who share in his mission. What God does for us in this sacrament has unique and cosmic significance. It is more than a naming ceremony because through Baptism the tiny seed of God's love is forever planted in our souls.

This seed, however, requires nurturing and cultivation if it is to grow and bear fruit. The examples of others living lives in Christ—sponsors, godparents, parents, teachers, and mentors—teach us what it means to be people of faith, gratitude, and service. We in turn, like the young student with leukemia, are then called to model Christ to others. For by Baptism we are forever changed in a way that summons us to be agents of hope for others who live in the little acre of the world that we call home.

Tom Jones, C.S.C.

May 1

St. Joseph, who was so noble by reason of his ancestry and so eminent because of the mission entrusted to him, lived a humble life, earning his bread in the sweat of his brow, following the plans of Divine Providence, obeying the powers of earth, and resigning himself to the most difficult trials. Behold our model and the model for all the faithful.

—Blessed Basil Moreau

I DON'T REMEMBER when I first met St. Joseph, but I know that I was still a boy. The pictures in my children's Bible showed him either walking beside a donkey or working in his carpenter's shop. My own father had a workbench and would often help me use the tools. I remember thinking that Jesus and Joseph were very lucky always to be able to smell sawdust.

My appreciation for Joseph didn't develop until later in my life when I was a young adult and relearning that we don't always get what we want. Pouting and dejected, I ran to Jesus for comfort and met Joseph along the way. As I again read his story, I realized that Joseph had to keep revising his expectations for his life. Imagine being told, "Your fiancée is pregnant, but it's not yours." Or, "There is no room in this inn." Or how about dreaming of angels who always give life-changing commands? "Marry the woman." "Flee to Egypt." "Return to Nazareth."

St. Joseph, without complaint, took the bumps in the road, the changes to the plan. He didn't need to understand everything, nor did he bargain to do things his way. In the grand drama of our salvation, he was just a supporting actor—without even one line. Silent, steadfast, and reliable, Joseph shows us when our plans disintegrate that God still has a plan—one that includes a role for us. Trustworthy, loyal, and just, Joseph shows us how to carry on despite initial disappointment, believing that God will finish the good work that he has begun in us.

Brent Kruger, C.S.C.

May 2

While Jesus Christ offered himself to his Father for our salvation, Mary offered him also for the same end, and

*we were then so much the sole object of the thoughts
of the son and the mother that the Savior, turning upon
her his dying eyes still filled with love, addressed her
a last word, which was not of himself or of her, but of
us. Christ saw at his feet, below the Cross, one of his
disciples, whom he made represent all the others and
the whole world. Thus, enfolding us all in the person
of St. John, he presented us to Mary, saying, "Woman,
behold your son."*

—Blessed Basil Moreau

THERE'S A SPECIAL grace some people possess that makes others feel valued, respected, and loved. These special people usually have a certain dignity and warmth—a radiance—that attracts others just as bright light attracts moths. That's how I remember Mama.

My very earliest childhood memory is of her praying the words of the Hail Mary in French. After dinner each night, Mama invited my father and their twelve children and any guests present to kneel and pray the Rosary together.

The Little Flower once asked a schoolmate, "Have you ever seen a saint praying?" She answered her own question, "I have. My father, when he says his night prayers." When I read that line of St. Thérèse of Lisieux, my memory immediately leapt back to my mother praying the Rosary. My siblings and I all believed that we were watching a saint pray when we prayed with her.

At the conclusion of the vigil the evening before her funeral Mass, as my seven brothers, four sisters, and I reminisced about the impact of our mother on us, we made a startling discovery.

Somehow, she had left each one of us with the conviction that we were her favorite. It was quite a feat of grace.

Her life was not about herself; it was about offering all to God for the salvation of her family, her children, her neighbors. When the dying Jesus says, "Woman, behold your son," he and Mary offer everything to the Father for the sake of the beloved disciple. The beauty of that scene radiates the great love of God for each of us. I have seen that beauty beginning at home, praying the Rosary with Mama.

Willy Raymond, C.S.C.

May 3

It seems to me I hear the voice of God, saying to us as formerly to his people: Salvabo te, noli timere—*"I will save you, do not fear."*

—Fr. Edward Sorin, C.S.C.

AS THE ISRAELITES stood at the far end of the Red Sea, having just crossed over dry land and witnessed the destruction of Pharaoh's army, they were abundantly aware of God's power to save. They now knew that they did not need to fear their enemies, for God was with them.

We Christians stand at the other side of the Cross of Christ, and so we, too, are abundantly aware of our Lord's power to save. We have witnessed the love of the Father made manifest in the Son: in his actions, in his preaching, in his suffering, indeed in his very person. We have witnessed the reign of sin and death torn asunder by the passion, death, and Resurrection of Jesus. In this we now know that there is nothing we need to fear. We need not fear our enemies; they can do no worse to us than they did to our Master. Indeed, we now know that we can even love them.

There is nothing left to fear in being full-hearted in living out our Christian vocation: to proclaim the Good News, to assist those in need, to witness to the call to love, and to invite others to follow. As we unite ourselves to Christ, to his life and to his death, we become one in his way of living and in the salvation he offers us all. To live in Christ is to know of his power to save and to live fearlessly in light of it.

James T. Gallagher, C.S.C.

May 4

The Holy Spirit alone can form and reform religious congregations as he formed the Church, after first forming the humanity of Our Lord in the womb of the Queen of Virgins, the masterpiece of his influence and love. Hence, I beg you to invoke him frequently.
—Blessed Basil Moreau

THE HOLY SPIRIT moving among us is an amazing, even down-to-earth, phenomenon. In the beginning, the Spirit hovered over the waters and life began, creating human beings whom God called "very good." Then, in the fullness of time, the Spirit overshadowed the Virgin Mary, and God's Son took on our same human flesh. Ever since, the Spirit has continued to fill our world and our Church with divine grace.

Men and women fall in love, families take shape, and children are born and raised into a relationship with the loving God. The Church grows, the sacraments are celebrated, and its members show forth God's love to the world by the example of their lives. Religious communities are formed and re-formed to carry the Gospel to the ends of the earth. Come, Holy Spirit.

Parents find support to bring up children even in difficult circumstances. Teachers feel strength to challenge their students to reach their fullest potential. Preachers stand up with courage to face the injustices of their times. Believers are amazed at what they can accomplish through the power of faith. Come, Holy Spirit.

We've all seen the smiling faces of the poor, ready to hope and believe that they can overcome. We've watched the energy of the young, ready to conquer the world. We've marveled at the fortitude of the bereaved, the sick, the abandoned, and the abused as they continue to pursue their dreams. Nothing moves us quite like the Holy Spirit, and his presence is everlasting. Come, Holy Spirit.

David E. Schlaver, C.S.C.

May 5

Study well the Divine Model. Imitate him in your chosen vocation by your poverty, obedience, and chastity. Imagine him saying to you now, as he once said to

*the disciple who asked leave to go first and bury his
father, of whose death he had just been informed:
"Follow me."*

—Blessed Basil Moreau

THE VOICE ON the phone message sounded pained and urgent.
Jen, a former student, whose wedding with Mike I had celebrated, left the curt request: "Father G., please call me when you
can." The hesitancy in Jen's message told the story: she knew it
was exam week. I returned the call immediately.

"It's my sister, Vicky," Jen answered. "She died suddenly last
night. She was forty-seven." I could feel the crushing weight of
that reality, which brought back the pain of my own brother's
death. "She wasn't feeling well lately but waved it off as just
being tired. My mom is a wreck." Jen hoped I could preside
at the burial. She was sounding apologetic again because of
the timing. "Jen," I reassured, "grading can wait. Let's work on
the service for Vicky." Friday was to be the day. I had no exam
scheduled, but someone else could have proctored it if I had.
The service, simple yet moving, touched us all.

God's time cannot wait for our priorities. My own tendency
to fret was challenged in this request. While we are consumed
with the tasks that often preoccupy us, the Lord continually calls
us to be willing to drop everything as he beckons: "Follow me."
The commitment to discipleship isn't ruled by plans or sched-
ules but is rooted in the example of the Christ who was available
constantly to those whom he encountered. It's not a matter of
convenience but of covenant—a relationship that requires us
to respond without hesitation and with deep compassion to
the people and needs before us. Our priority is to make God
known, loved, and served. What we have planned for the day

can wait; furthering God's loving and compassionate presence should not have to wait. It is our priority always.

Anthony Grasso, C.S.C.

May 6

You will prove to the world that there flows in your veins the same blood that coursed in those of the early martyrs of zeal and Christian charity. You will also show that people who are in the habit of dying daily to the world and themselves in the spirit of evangelical renunciation do not fear death when their lives can be useful to their neighbors.

—Blessed Basil Moreau

SEVERAL MONTHS AFTER the main killings of the Rwandan genocide, I visited our Holy Cross parish there and our Canadian priest who was pastor. He had worked in Rwanda for several decades, but on that day he was still reeling from the recent bloodbath. We listened to a tape he had made of machine-gun fire and anguished screams as the mobs attacked the Tutsi refugees he had tried to shelter at the parish. "I made this tape," he said, "because I was afraid no one would believe the terrible story we would tell." Now he was worried about revenge because the new army had arrived and new scores were being settled. He had already given an interview to the foreign press, and the authorities were angered by the unhappy publicity. A certain colonel had told me clearly, "You tell him he better be careful and keep quiet."

On that day he was just glad to talk and to laugh about Holy Cross. We ate and drank and said a few prayers. He said he was pleased that the people were returning some of the furniture that had been looted from the clinic. He seemed somehow to have a glimmer of hope. Four nights later they came to his house during dinner—his dessert plate was still on the table. The soldiers led him into his bedroom and let him kneel in front of the crucifix for a while. Then they broke his skull open with a hammer and left him in a pool of martyr's blood.

Our passion is to be God's servant. Our peace is in his will.

Thomas McDermott, C.S.C.

May 7

It is essential to our mission that we strive to abide so attentively together that people will observe: "See how they love one another." We will then be a sign in an alienated world: men who have, for love of their Lord, become closest neighbors, trustworthy friends, brothers.

—Holy Cross *Constitutions*

IN OUR RELIGIOUS life in Holy Cross we do not choose those with whom we live and work. There is a danger in that. We could treat our brothers in community with civility, yet remain aloof. And indeed, the work may get done and the life may get lived, but by not truly loving one another, we run the risk of disliking our life and work together, even of compromising our very mission. People would observe nothing extraordinary here.

Our Holy Cross mission is more demanding than a job; it requires that we do more than tolerate each other. Mission requires attentive abiding. A respectful, loving group is more effective in ministry and certainly less tense than a bickering crowd. But there is an even greater fruit than this. When we abide attentively together, we not only work together for the Lord but we witness the Lord's very presence in our midst through our love for one another.

We all have a mission in this alienated world in which we often divide ourselves into different groups of them and us. Even as our societies struggle to become more integrated, we can still tend to associate only with those people who are like ourselves, distancing ourselves from those different from us. Striving to abide as closest neighbors, trustworthy friends, and brothers and sisters with all people, therefore, is a prophetic sign that our modern world sorely needs. And so we all share the call along with Holy Cross to be hopeful signs in an alienated world, willing to cross borders of every sort to love one another.

John Paige, C.S.C.

May 8

The Savior greatly rebuked his apostles for being so slow in believing in the Resurrection. He then opened to them a vast field for their zealous efforts.

*He promised them he was going to remain with them
and with all of his future disciples until the end of time.*
—Blessed Basil Moreau

IN THE AFTERMATH of World War II in a German town, the people were devastated to see the terrible destruction of not just everything they had built but, more importantly, all their hopes and aspirations. Picking up the pieces left by the bombs in one village, the people collected what they could, including a broken crucifix. After reconstruction, the villagers were divided about whether to keep the old crucifix or to get a new one. Finally, they agreed to place the old crucifix with its broken limbs above the altar, along with the following inscription: "I have no hands but yours; I have no legs but yours, to continue the mission and usher in the kingdom of God." Jesus continues to remain with us, even in the challenges, through the hands and feet of one another.

Within ten years of founding a new congregation, Blessed Moreau sent missionaries to Algeria, Poland, the United States, and Canada despite the Congregation's relatively small number and the ever-increasing need of the dioceses of France. His trust in Divine Providence coupled with his zeal for God's mission led Holy Cross out of France and around the world with very few vocations and meager resources. Blessed Moreau trusted that God would use the hands and feet of his religious to usher in the Resurrection in ordinary people's lives.

The Resurrection can be an elusive experience for us today, as it was for the first disciples. While it takes the eyes of faith to see the Resurrection, it also takes the concrete hands and feet of those willing to walk with Jesus in faith through all of life's challenges and difficulties, its hardships and uncertainties. But then, as our *Constitutions* promise, the Resurrection can become for us—for all—a daily event.

Gaspar Selvaraj, C.S.C.

May 9

Divine Providence has blessed us with a spirit of devotedness and energy that will remain, I trust, as the characteristic feature of all the children of Holy Cross.
—Fr. Edward Sorin, C.S.C.

ALMOST FIFTY YEARS of my life in Holy Cross have been devoted to working with youth. Yet from time to time I have wondered what good, if any, I was accomplishing. I suspect this is true of most of us regardless of our vocations in life. "Why do you expect so much from me?" "Come on, Brother, give me a break." Similar questions or pleas were common reactions when I tried to bring out the best in my students. Believing they had much more talent and potential than they could see in themselves, I would find the energy and wherewithal to challenge and stretch them beyond what they could imagine for themselves. Such single-hearted devotion to educating the mind and the heart is essential for the success of our mission as educators in the faith.

When I served as provincial superior, I visited with many of our alumni and heard their stories about brothers who taught them. So many said in different ways that the Holy Cross brothers, or one brother in particular, made them who they are today. Others recounted how the brothers believed in them, giving them the confidence to make something of themselves. These inspiring and life-changing stories are repeated by all those whom Divine Providence has blessed with a Holy Cross education.

We all want to make a difference in the lives of others. Believing in Divine Providence gives us the assurance that God puts us in the right place, at the right time, and with the right people. We will make a difference if we have the devotion, the generosity, and the faith to respond to God's grace at those moments in our lives.

Robert Fillmore, C.S.C.

May 10

Visits from above are not always of gladness and of joy, but much more often of pain and sorrow; we must be prepared to receive them all with faith and merit. Children never turn more quickly to their mothers than when in danger or in suffering. When does she receive and press them to her loving heart more tenderly than in their fright and pain?

—Fr. Edward Sorin, C.S.C.

MY TWENTY-FIFTH ANNIVERSARY celebration as a priest was approaching, and I was not feeling very spiritual. God, however, provided me with just the visitation from above that I needed. While visiting Chile, one of our Holy Cross Associates invited me to accompany her as she brought Communion to a blind woman named Lucia, whose apartment was in a poor area of Santiago. When I entered her home, Lucia proclaimed, "Thank you, God, for the blessing of this spiritual priest visiting me." We had an engaging visit. Before leaving, I asked for her blessing.

I returned to Lucia's apartment for many more visitations before leaving Chile. Through her challenging persistence, I shared with her deep feelings about the death of my mother six years prior after an eight-year struggle with Alzheimer's disease. I was able to express my pain to this blind woman of faith and see more clearly why it was that I was not feeling spiritual. Years later, her daily prayers and our other visits and phone calls continued to be graced and joyful moments in my life.

In addition to Lucia, my ministry and spiritual life have been nourished by countless women, from Holy Cross sisters to women faculty, staff, alumnae, and students at the University of Notre Dame. Like Fr. Sorin, I have discovered that the mystery of God's unconditional and compassionate love can be likened to the love of a mother for her child, tenderly embracing us in all moments of our lives.

Don McNeill, C.S.C.

May 11

May our hearts catch on fire as we walk along with him, just as it happened to the disciples on the way to Emmaus. May we, in turn, be able to say with them:

"Were not our hearts burning inside us as he was talking to us?"

—Blessed Basil Moreau

WHILE IN THE seminary at Notre Dame, I accepted a placement for two semesters as a team member at Fatima Retreat House for the diocesan-sponsored Cursillo retreats. As a team member, I participated fully with both laity and clergy to help renew and instruct men and women from the area. As part of my training, the team leaders asked that I first participate in one of the Cursillos myself. After the weekend retreat experience, I was "hooked on Jesus." The Lord gave me a new sense of purpose and love within the Church. As I walked back to the seminary on that late fall Sunday night, I wanted to greet anyone that I met on the road. And not only that—I felt like I was walking on air. Having experienced Jesus speaking to me, I then understood what the Emmaus gospel passage was for me. Blessed Moreau's monition is true: my heart was burning inside as I walked home because Jesus had spoken to me through faith-filled believers, and I, in turn, was able to share my faith, too.

The same Jesus of Emmaus that Blessed Moreau writes about and that I experienced on my Cursillo is prepared to touch all of our lives and situations. He wants to draw near and walk with each of us so that we can encounter him anew today. Perhaps it will be through a scripture study, taking on an outside activity that is service-oriented, or making an effort to pray and worship with full-throated participation. The key is to take a step and find the intention and action that will provide a new possibility of a closer walk with the Lord.

James T. Preskenis, C.S.C.

May 12

I shall have no fears for the Congregation, and even if all of you had abandoned me on hearing of our catastrophes, I should have begun all over again as soon as I could, so convinced am I that what I have undertaken is the will of God.

—Blessed Basil Moreau

WHEN FR. SORIN returned to Notre Dame from one of his trips to Montreal, he arrived to find the Main Building burned to the ground with bricks still smoldering. The small university that he and his brothers in Holy Cross had founded was destroyed. His reaction was to gather the community together in Sacred Heart Church. He exhorted and challenged the discouraged religious. They had to rebuild but even bigger than the previous time, for the fire could only be a sign that Mary had even greater designs for the university consecrated to her name. And they did rebuild. The brothers began pulling the still-hot bricks from the rubble. They made more bricks and rebuilt the Main Building, topping it with a glorious golden dome and a statue of Our Lady.

We might think about how much would have been lost if Fr. Sorin and the Holy Cross community had given up that day. They had no way of knowing how different the world would be because of their resolve. So many lives have been touched, including not only students, faculty, alumni, employees, and supporters but also people who are simply proud of the most famous Catholic university in the United States.

We all want to be careful in claiming to know and do the will of God. We know there have been cases of people who imposed things on others claiming it to be God's will. But we mustn't be slow to reflect on his will and to be firm in challenging ourselves to be faithful and committed to it. We don't know how much good may be depending upon it.

John S. Korcsmar, C.S.C.

May 13

If the tree of the Cross has been planted in the vast field which is ours to cultivate; even if, more often than not, its fruits have seemed bitter; we must recognize that it has become a tree of life and that we are now reaping from its fruit which is as "pleasing to the eye as it is good to the taste."

—Blessed Basil Moreau

THE CROSS SPEAKS to me of my journey to a vocation in Holy Cross. I did my high school in the minor seminary, yet when I finished, I was indecisive about continuing or going to study civil law. One of my friends then gave me a booklet that had addresses of different religious congregations in East Africa. When I went through the booklet, I landed on two congregations: I liked the Dominicans because they were described as preachers, and I liked Holy Cross because of its name. I applied and was accepted to both congregations, but I chose to enter formation in Jinja, Uganda, with Holy Cross because I had a burning zeal to be a member of the Congregation that bears the name of the Cross of Christ.

I faced many challenges in my years in formation. To give but one example, one classmate died of an unknown infection that was thought to be Ebola. Given our close proximity, there was great concern that we were all infected. For some days, we were quarantined indoors. At that moment, zeal and love for the Cross seemed to bear bitter fruits. Thankfully, none of us became ill, but God was starting to teach me what it really means to bear not just the name of the Cross but the Cross itself. It was an important lesson for me—and for all of us who bear the name of the Crucified—because while the Cross is a tree of life, it can be very bitter at times. Yet when we bear our suffering in faith, love, and hope, God's grace is sufficient and able to transform the seemingly bitter fruits into good ones. I am blessed to have tasted it in my own life and in my ministry as a Holy Cross priest.

Leopold Temba, C.S.C.

May 14

Imagine hearing that divine babe saying to you, with an accent that cannot be described, while turning his eyes from you to the Blessed Virgin: "Here is thy mother"; and then, looking to his mother: "Here is thy son."

—Fr. Edward Sorin, C.S.C.

I HAD A conversation with my mother in which I made the mistake of telling her that I had made it safely home from a trip. She quickly reminded me that home is where your mother is. After a lively debate about what defines "home," I received a coffee mug from her with the gentle reminder on it: "Home is where your mother is."

Like so many in our increasingly shrinking world, I have already lived in many places and realized that part of life, especially as a religious priest, requires the freedom to move wherever one is called to serve. In such a world, what does it mean to call one place home? One of the essential things I have learned from my mom is that home is not so much a place as it is a relationship. Even more so, my parents have taught me that a true loving relationship is one that both gives a sense of stability, love, and support and also sets us free to do the same for others.

In John's gospel, when the disciples ask Jesus where his home is, he never shows them a place. Instead, he invites them into a relationship with him as he says, "Come and see" (1:46). This relationship with Christ becomes their true home. Even until his last moment on the Cross, Jesus continues to teach that it is through relationships—relationships rooted in him—that we find meaning and grace in our lives. As Jesus invites the beloved disciple and his faithful mother into this relationship, he offers a way for God's home to endure among us.

Sean McGraw, C.S.C.

May 15

Grace is a participation in divine nature, a created gift, a divine principle which gives us the life of God, divine childhood, and the right to a heavenly inheritance, so that the Holy Spirit really lives in us with the Father and Son to whom he is united always. He produces godlike actions in us.

—Blessed Basil Moreau

ONE OF THE greatest gifts God gives to creation is a participation in his life. The very human lives we live are a gift from God; this very world is a gift from God and is filled with his holy presence. Throughout history God has called people to be his very own, to live lives in relationship with him. The spectacular culmination of that call came through the Son. Through his Incarnation, ministry, passion, death, Resurrection, and sending of the Holy Spirit, the Son filled the world with the invitation to participate in God's life.

The world has been filled with grace—allowing us to participate in the life of God and giving us the help we need to live in the divine presence. To help us remember this call and this grace, Christ founded the Church and gave us the sacraments—real, tangible, and reliable encounters with that grace. The very first sacrament we receive, Baptism, makes us God's sons and daughters; it draws us into the divine life. The remaining sacraments enrich that life and, when we fail in that life, repair it.

Most of us live grace-filled lives. In a sense, we cannot help it because we live in a grace-filled world. The challenge for followers of Christ is to be conscious of living that life. God has given us the gift; God has given us the grace. But as with all gifts, it must be accepted. It must be remembered. It must be lived in grateful response to God's action in our lives.

Jeffrey Allison, C.S.C.

May 16

It is only in recollected souls that the Lord makes his voice heard. That is why he leads into solitude the soul he wants to favor with his wordless conversations, according to these words: "I will lead her into the wilderness and will speak to her heart." Why into the solitary wilderness? It fosters peace, inner calm, and recollection.

—Blessed Basil Moreau

ONE OF THE first lessons that we religious of Holy Cross learn is the need for a period of silent meditation each day, a time when we withdraw from our daily activities to sit, be quiet, and listen to God speaking to us. At first, this can be very foreign given the fast-paced and hectic lives that we often come from when entering religious life. Particularly in the novitiate year, silence is emphasized to a level of solitude and meditation that we will never again experience in our active ministries. This lesson must be engrained in us early if we are to be effective in our work with people.

This lesson of setting aside time every day to be quiet and listen to God has been reinforced for me time and again over more than fifty busy years of religious life. There is nothing more fulfilling than to stop, to go over the day's many activities, to think about those whom we have helped or perhaps not helped, and to pray for them. Otherwise, the very people we are trying to love in God will take us from God. A spiritual director advised that, rather than spending time worrying about individuals who bother us, we would better spend that time praying for them and us. Another director counseled that it is important to remember that God also made those who irritate and bother us. With that background, a regular period for meditation, recollection, or just quietness brings all things into a perspective that doesn't happen without setting aside time. So if we long to hear God's voice and love others as he loves them, we must take time to be quiet and recollected.

Donald J. Stabrowski, C.S.C.

May 17

Mary, Jesus, and Joseph, who represent so visibly the invisible Trinity, represent also the unity of God, but one heart and one soul.

—Blessed Basil Moreau

UNITY WAS DEAR to the heart of Blessed Moreau. As a young boy, he experienced the unity of family and community in the small French farming village of Laigné-en-Belin. As a disciple, he longed for union with God in Christ. As a priest, he labored for unity in the Church. As a founder, he counseled unity for the members of Holy Cross. The unity of the Holy Family of Nazareth and the unity of the Triune God motivate and inspire us to live and minister in like manner: in love and communion with one another and with those whom we serve.

Where hearts dwell together in harmony and peace, burdens are shared, bonds of affection are strengthened, and joy is found. When we religious of Holy Cross collaborate with lay staff and volunteers—in church, in the classroom, in the residence hall, in pastoral ministry, in administration—we put into practice and further the spirit of unity commended by our founder and by the Gospel we serve.

Disagreements are bound to arise. Differences of opinion are normal. Unity doesn't mean that we are all the same or that we never experience conflict or tension. Nevertheless, the unity to which we aspire obliges us to seek to resolve our differences according to the spirit of our common Baptism as adopted sons and daughters of one and the same Father. The path of reconciliation is often not easy, but it is always worth the effort. For unity, while good for the mission, is even better for the soul.

John DeRiso, C.S.C.

May 18

*Our mutual respect and shared undertaking should
be a hopeful sign of the kingdom, and they are when
others can behold how we love one another.*
—Holy Cross *Constitutions*

WHEN ANOTHER BROTHER and I were visiting our Holy Cross
high schools to assess the effectiveness of our mission there, we
set up meetings with randomly selected groups of students. We
asked them to tell us what was special about their school. At one
of the sessions, a young woman spoke up, saying that at some
schools one only gets respect if he or she is smart, athletic, or
popular. She then added, "What I like about our school is that
we are respected the minute we walk in the door on the very
first day."

Jesus came among us preaching about a kingdom where
mutual respect and understanding are central. And indeed, these
qualities are indispensable elements in spreading the kingdom
of peace and justice in which everyone will have life and have it
to the full. Mutual respect and understanding only come about
when we do what Jesus did—that is, when we look at the world
around us through the loving eyes of the Father.

I've thought often of the young woman's remark. It spoke
so well about that school and made me proud of our mission
as Holy Cross educators. But the reason that it has really stuck
with me is because it challenges me to love ever more deeply.
For if any of us are to help extend God's kingdom on earth, we
can't size up a situation and then act. We have to be open to

giving every person respect and understanding when they come through the door for the very first time.

George C. Schmitz, C.S.C.

May 19

Whatever they may be, let us not forget that the heaviest crosses contribute most to the general good of our work and to the welfare of each one of us.
—Blessed Basil Moreau

PREACHING AT MY grandfather's funeral is still one of the hardest things that I have done. He taught me how to garden, fish, play cards, pitch horseshoes, catch night crawlers, and cheer for all the Detroit teams—whether winning or losing.

I was able to say goodbye to Grandpa although I didn't know it at the time. He was the first person to whom I showed the chalice that my parents had bought for my ordination. Because of his stroke, Grandpa didn't say many words, but as he lifted up the chalice, he did so purposefully, as a priest would. He said, "Good, good," and gave it back to me with a tear in his eye.

My tears came in preaching the funeral. It was, for me, a powerful experience that has helped me to realize the Cross as a precious treasure. Like the Cross of Christ, our crosses lead to something; they are not the end for us. Our pain, hurt, suffering, and losses lead to Resurrection experiences just as Jesus' did. My grandfather's death taught me deeper compassion and empathy, which have helped me to walk with others in their times of grief. His death also led me to trust in his eternal life. To this day when I hear the clink of the horseshoe or watch the bobber go down while fishing, I remember Grandpa—both as he was to me then and as he is to me now. The crosses in our lives are certainly painful, but my grandpa has taught me that they are not all bad. In fact, for the Christian, they become "good, good."

Kevin Russeau, C.S.C.

May 20

The feast of Pentecost has this special quality: the mystery we celebrate now is renewed, in fact, every day. It is not only to the disciples gathered together in the Cenacle that our Savior promised the Holy Spirit, but to all who over the centuries will be found worthy of this glorious promise. This same Spirit still truly comes down to souls well-disposed, no longer in a visible way as on the apostles, but in a way no less real for being invisible.

—Blessed Basil Moreau

THE HOLY SPIRIT'S presence with us and within us shows his strength in his subtlety. While the scriptures use the rich image of fire to speak to us about the Spirit, Blessed Moreau speaks about the Spirit in a way that is perhaps closer to how we experience the Spirit's movements. In other words, he leaves out the fire and reminds us that the Spirit is no less visible for being invisible. Is the fragrance of fresh flowers dulled in any way just because we cannot see them? On the contrary, the fragrance of lilies evokes innumerable and vivid memories of Easters past, of the renewal of springtime, or of St. Joseph's Day before we ever lay our eyes on their visual beauty. The presence of the Spirit works similarly, recalling to our minds those moments in the past where we were sure he was there, guiding us, pushing us, consoling us. We have known the fire; we have known its burning; we have known its fragrance; we have known the wind.

When we celebrate Pentecost, however, we celebrate the birth of the Church in the upper room long ago, but we are also beckoned toward the future. We open our souls and our hearts to where its sweetness will lead us. This future is no less real because we have yet to experience it. Pentecost calls us once again to embody it as we commit ourselves to being consumed by it. Indeed, the Spirit is no less strong for being so subtle, and we anticipate with wonder our next celebration of this great mystery, if only to bear witness to how the Spirit's power will have shaped us yet again.

Gregory Haake, C.S.C.

May 21

In consecrated celibacy we wish to love with the freedom, openness, and availability that can be recognized as a sign of the kingdom.

—Holy Cross *Constitutions*

THE MAN POUNDING on my rectory door looked crazed. Often homeless folks would call on Sunday afternoons. I wondered, "Do I open the door?" Tired from a weekend of Masses, a wedding, and several Baptisms, I knew I had to make a choice. I turned the lock, opened the door, and invited this man and his chaos into my life. The first thing that came out of his mouth was, "Father, I need a priest."

Soon we were telling his four-year-old daughter that Mommy had gone to live with the angels so she could be her guardian angel. Her mother's death had been sudden and violent, but we had mediated an annunciation that was peaceful and prayerful.

Divine Providence had placed me in their lives. My witness to God's faithfulness had to be called forth, shaken from me by the insistent pounding of a stranger. Yet the decision was a free and conscious one. The decision to love can never be recognized in the abstract; otherwise it would be only the desire to love. Authentic love, true love, only exists in the concrete reality of our lives. To love freely, openly, and with availability is a sign of the kingdom, to which not only religious but all of God's children can witness. Yet the gift of consecrated celibacy flowers in due season when the self-possessed divest. When it blooms in selfless love, it enriches and inspires all who love. For only if we are truly free can we decide to love, to be open, and to be available. This decision to give ourselves radically to others is our prayer, our worship, and our consecration.

John Donato, C.S.C.

This is not enough, you must identify yourselves with your model, not only in order to become a faithful copy, but to become somewhat another Christ, according to his request to the Father for his followers: that they become one with me as I am one with you, Father, and that they be in me as I am in them.

—Blessed Basil Moreau

IN MY CHILDHOOD, while at the Holy Eucharist, I used to wonder and think very deeply about what the priest drinks from the chalice. I had a deep desire to drink one day from the chalice like the priests do, for in Bangladesh the crowds at Mass are too big to distribute the Precious Blood to all. I have always believed that this was the first realization of my vocation. Now, after joining the seminary and becoming priest, I have drunk so many times from the chalice, and still, the desire remains the same.

I remember that in my youth I used to imitate my favorite hero. The way he spoke or walked or smiled or laughed, I tried to imitate in my daily life. I wanted to become like him. Very often—consciously or unconsciously—I imitated him, and it affected my life. Something similar happened after joining the seminary: I was very impressed by my first director, who was very calm and quiet in nature, simple in his lifestyle, and humble in behavior. He loved each one of us so much. The way he formed us inspired me to become like him in the future.

It is very true that we need models in our lives, and imitating others can help us to become good and mature people. But it is not enough to imitate blindly. Jesus Christ is the model for us. He was always united with his Father because he and his Father are one. And through a personal encounter with him, Christ invites us to unite with him as well as with one another. In this loving relationship, as we try to imitate him, we become our real selves—we become another Christ.

Ashim Theotonius Gonsalves, C.S.C.

May 23

Prayer must come from the heart. It consists less in the words than in the longings or in the aspirations, these pulses of the soul that need neither long formulas nor an abundance of words. Prayer is an ardent and continual longing.

—Blessed Basil Moreau

CANCER. IT'S THE dreaded word no one wants to hear. My doctor knew that when he told me that I would need surgery to remove a mysterious lump on one of my glands. "After a biopsy," he said, "we will then know how to proceed."

I lived three long weeks with the uncertainty of not knowing whether or not this dreaded word would take my life in a direction I had never previously expected. During that time, I would frequently retreat to the chapel hoping to find comfort, consolation, and understanding. Ironically, just when I felt I needed God most, I found I could no longer pray, at least not in the way that I was accustomed. Nothing felt right. Nothing worked. I would sit there, and then my mind would just wander with the various "what-ifs" that would confront anyone in my situation.

This was more than twenty years ago. God was good to me. The lump was benign, and the gland was removed. While prayer was strangely uncomfortable for me during this time, I was still drawn to it. Often we focus more on the end product of our prayer as opposed to what simply brought us there to begin with—a heart longing for God's loving presence and unconditional love. Prayer is not just about the words we say as much as it is about our presence, fidelity, gratitude, and need. As difficult as prayer may be for us, no matter what the circumstances, sometimes we need to be content and satisfied that our ardent desire for God is simply enough and the best that we can give. If we accept this, then we have accepted the grace of our prayer. Blessed Teresa of Calcutta once said, "God does not require that we be successful, only that we be faithful." Such wisdom, such insight, such consolation.

Paul Bednarczyk, C.S.C.

May 24

We form a community as did those who first believed in Christ's Resurrection and were possessed by his Spirit. The whole group of believers was united, heart and soul. No one claimed as private any possession as everything they owned was held in common. With

one mind they shared the same teaching, a common
life, the breaking of the bread, and prayer.
—Holy Cross *Constitutions*

THE *CONSTITUTIONS* OF our Congregation articulate an ideal of community living rooted in the example of the earliest Christians, who "devoted themselves to the teaching of the apostles and to the communal life, to the breaking of the bread and to the prayers" (Acts 2:42). The touchstone of this vision is the unity made possible by the workings of the Spirit. We serve others because the same Spirit motivates and encourages us all. Though we are "many minds," as we say at Stonehill College where I teach, we gather for "one purpose"—that is, to educate our students' minds and hearts for lives that will make a positive difference in the world. To declare a single purpose is not to say that we are automatons but that we place our gifts at the service of one another, our ministry, and the world in order to allow the Spirit to do the work of transforming our lives and the lives of those to whom we minister.

We can pursue this mission only if we are inspired by the same Word and strengthened by each other's sustaining presence, especially during gatherings for prayer, meals, and celebration. We must come to know and trust each other if we are to continue to strive for an authentic union that is both emotional and spiritual. This is the goal of all Christian communities, as it was the vision of Blessed Moreau, inspired by the prayer of Jesus for his friends: "That they may be one" (Jn 17:11).

George Piggford, C.S.C.

Place yourself under the gaze of the Divine Savior. He is the heavenly original of which you need to become a living copy.

—Blessed Basil Moreau

STUDYING FILM IN Los Angeles where residents boast of sunny, seventy-degree weather, I decided on a routine to place myself under the sun for ten to fifteen minutes per day. After all, studies confirm a little direct sunlight each day helps boost levels of vitamin D. Most days, I would research the weather: tracking the angle and intensity of the sun, knowing exactly the times of sunrise and sunset, and avoiding the few times of the day where clouds would obscure the otherwise bleached out city. By getting "to know" the sun, so to speak, I found myself becoming a better filmmaker. Since the time of Caravaggio, most art forms, film chief among these, have required a manipulation of natural light sources. Acquiring knowledge and fashioning light to create a professional-looking image gives life both to my art and to my very essence as a budding filmmaker.

Placing oneself under the gaze of the Divine Savior sounds, at first blush, like a passive endeavor. I, however, interpret this insight from Blessed Moreau as a very active pursuit. To become a living copy of Jesus Christ, an *alter Christus* for our world, we must know a good amount about our Lord and then incorporate him into our very being. We must seek out more knowledge about him through our study of scripture, partaking of the sacraments, reading the lives of saints, and doing daily meditations such as those in this book. This active and continuous mystagogy of learning more about the Savior whom we are to emulate ensures us of staying under his gaze and becoming more like him.

Vince Kuna, C.S.C.

May 26

In order to be a foreign missionary, one must know the mystery of the Cross. From the mystery of the Cross, the missionary must draw the apostolic strength of those generous imitators of Jesus Christ, whose life below was but a continuous martyrdom.
—Blessed Basil Moreau

THE PEOPLE OF Holy Cross Parish Dandora in Nairobi, Kenya, know suffering up close. Persistent poverty, job scarcity, hunger, violence, and disease threaten the dreams of every family there. And so it didn't surprise me that they wanted the roof of their new church to feature the cross prominently.

The original design had a large, heavy cross at the top of the church, held up at a thirty-degree angle by iron supports fashioned to look like the arms of people. It was to represent our parishioners' everyday struggle to carry their crosses together. But it was not to be. "The proposed design makes it appear that the cross is defeating us, is too heavy for us," the parishioners said, "but that is not true. With Jesus, we can lift it high. The cross is not just a sign of struggle with suffering. It is our sign of victory, even in the midst of suffering. It should stand tall!" And so it does today, stretching upward from the peak of the new church, straight and tall into the African sky.

Victory even in the midst of suffering, the very mystery of the Cross, is so often taught to the missionary—and to all of us—by the faithful poor. It is this mystery, fully embraced, that keeps us from fleeing suffering and enables us to sacrifice willingly on behalf of those who suffer most. Yes, like the first disciples, we are tempted to run from the Cross. But in the end there is no other place in which salvation might be found.

Tom Smith, C.S.C.

May 27

Let us be one, just as our Lord Jesus Christ asked this unity for us of his Father. It is only on this condition that God will give us his own strength. This strength is that which flows from charity, mutual harmony, oneness of mind, and the sweet bonds of brotherly love.
—Blessed Basil Moreau

IN MY MORE than fifty years of working in Holy Cross education, I have been blessed to witness so many miracles in the lives of young people. Through these years as a teacher, counselor, coach, principal, president, and administrator, I have seen truly extraordinary happenings. Graduation day seems to bring it all to light. That day is always a testament that God's miracles find their way into youthful lives through the attention and care given by so many colleagues in our shared ministry of forming minds and hearts for Christian life.

No matter what ministry I've been doing, I have often had to confront the temptation to go solo in my efforts, thinking I have the strength and wherewithal to do it all myself—as if the miracles were mine to perform. As I reflect back on the numerous circumstances where I have tried to play "superman," they become laughable at best and pathetic at worst. Thankfully, a sizeable number of my colleagues in ministry have had the care to challenge me in my foolishness. Since the day I first stepped into the classroom, my brothers in Holy Cross, alongside numerous lay men and women, have empowered me to be all that I have been able to be for so many youngsters. More importantly, however, they have taught me the great truth that being one in mind and heart, united together in the sweet bonds of charity and mutual harmony, is the way to miracle. It is only in this condition that God will give us his strength.

Jim Branigan, C.S.C.

May 28

Instead of acting like a royal personage before whom we must abase ourselves and from whom we must keep a respectful distance, Jesus even wishes to let our hands touch him, our hearts melt into his own, our whole being be filled with his. When we think that he actually gives us his body to eat, his blood to drink, that he communicates his own virtues to us

*and applies to us his own merits, we shall begin to see
how he loves us.*

—Blessed Basil Moreau

WHILE VISITING THE sick in the villages, I remember coming
to an elderly lady who looked pretty beat up by life and its
challenges. I administered the sacrament of the Anointing of
the Sick and gave her Holy Communion. The way she received
the Eucharist brought me utter amazement: she received the
Body of Christ with a big smile, and I could see her relishing
the experience as tears rolled from her eyes. After consuming
Holy Communion, she turned and asked me, "What took you
so long to bring me Christ?" I did not have a proper answer, but
I promised to check on her regularly.

I receive Christ daily, yet sometimes I don't pay as much
attention as this lady did. As she experienced it, she touched
Jesus, her heart melted into his own, and her whole being was
filled with Jesus. This was manifested in the eagerness and longing she had for Holy Communion. Her genuine example of
simplicity stirred within me a desire to yearn for Jesus in the
Eucharist—to long to touch, taste, and feel him, so that I may
draw from him the lessons of life.

Jesus in Holy Communion is our friend, victim, and food.
As friend, he is truly there for us to share in our burdens and
sorrows. As victim, he died on the Cross to set us free from the
bondage of sin and our human frailties. As food, he is the bread
that strengthens us and brings a smile and amazement. When we
receive Jesus in the Eucharist as that lady did, we come to know
how he loves us. Then, through us and our words and deeds,

Jesus can touch others—even to the point that they, too, may in utter amazement feel his touch and taste his love.

Christopher Letikirich, C.S.C.

May 29

I beg you to walk more and more perfectly in the path of obedience, tightening the bonds of fraternal charity, and meditating frequently on your individual responsibility in the work of Holy Cross.
—Blessed Basil Moreau

ON OCCASION, MY students ask me about the life of a Holy Cross brother. After I explain a bit about our life of prayer, ministry, and the religious vows of poverty, chastity, and obedience that bind us to each other in community, a typical student asks, "But do you really have to do what they tell you?"

The vow of obedience can be difficult to understand in a society and culture that exalts individual freedom. I think of the path of obedience as freely and willingly trying to live a "mediated" life. In other words, to know and to follow God's will in my life, I must discern with the help of faith-filled others. My individual actions as a member of a religious community are not isolated; what I do or do not do affects the rest of the community. And my invitation to others with whom I live to help me to discern God's desire for my life tightens our bonds of fraternal charity.

Perhaps this concept of obedience as living a mediated life is not so strange when we consider other life contexts. In marriage, do I have to consult my spouse? At work, do I have to consult my colleagues? At home, do I have to consider my family's needs? Thus, to some extent, we all live mediated lives. The more we open ourselves to each other and to God in the decisions of our daily lives, the more we can fulfill our individual responsibilities with joy and enthusiasm, resulting in tightened bonds of love and respect among us.

John Paige, C.S.C.

May 30

Jesus Christ is faithful, and he will not permit you to be tempted beyond your strength. If we but know how to awaken him from his seeming sleep by our prayers, he will command the winds and the storm, and we shall have once more the calm of bygone days.

—Blessed Basil Moreau

FOLLOWING IN A long line of Holy Cross priests who served as military chaplains, beginning with Fr. William Corby, C.S.C., in the Civil War, I have done two stints as a Navy chaplain. One early assignment was aboard the *USS Midway*. One night, as howling winds and raging waters muscled waves across the flight deck eighty feet above the sea's surface, I stood above it all on the bridge of the carrier—warm, dry, confident, and unafraid. Among the largest of ocean-going vessels, created and mobilized by the most powerful navy in history, the ship in its eminence insulated me from the tempest below, from all harm. I was immune.

The storm grew in intensity. The nearby captain called out orders, asked for information, and considered his options. With one stark sigh—"This is not good"—he instantly sent a chill through me, washing away all of my confidence. His humility confronted my counterfeit calm. His judgment displaced fascination with fear. The truth he uttered roused me: "This is not good."

Seduced by the loftiness that had conditioned me and lulled by the shell that had cushioned me, I had permitted temptation to take up residence. In such times, when we are distracted by accomplishment and wheedled by privilege, a wake-up call may be warranted. Standing on the bridge, vulnerable and trembling, I called upon the Lord, who seemed aloof and unaware. "Where have you been?" came his reply. "Who's really been asleep here, anyway? Welcome home."

William D. Dorwart, C.S.C.

May 31

Let the doors of our houses, and still more the doors of our hearts, be ever open to the pallid countenances of the poor. Should we even be poorer ourselves than they, still let none be ever turned away from us hungry.
–Fr. Edward Sorin, C.S.C.

MY RATIONAL SIDE wants to ask Fr. Sorin, Should we even be poorer ourselves, then how can we help them in their hunger? Yet experience teaches me that giving and satisfying hungers is possible, even if we are poor.

For several years, I was blessed to work at André House of Arizona, a Holy Cross ministry to people experiencing homelessness. I witnessed tremendous generosity from benefactors. More touching were moments where I was privileged to experience a reenactment of the poor widow in the gospel offering all she had (Mk 12:41–44). I have seen people literally give the shirt off their back or their only blanket to someone who really needs it. Such witness truly uplifts.

Still, the temptation remains for each of us to hold on to what we have. The struggle persists not to allow our possessions to possess us. Though personally I know that what I do to the least of these I do to Christ, I struggle with individualism and materialism that make it difficult to help others who do not seem to help themselves. I know that I have to see Christ in others and to help them; however, this sometimes seems a trite platitude. Then I reflect on Jesus' life. How did he support himself and the apostles? As an itinerant preacher, where did they get food, lodging, and so on? Twice he multiplied loaves and fishes, but what of the other days?

As we depend upon God for all that we need to survive, Jesus and his disciples depended upon the generosity of others for their needs. Though rich, God entered into a relationship of interdependence by becoming poor, just like the person hungering before you and me.

Eric Schimmel, C.S.C.

June 1

Christianity, and with still greater reason the religious life, is nothing else than the life of Jesus Christ reproduced in our conduct.

—Blessed Basil Moreau

OF ALL THE surprises that Jesus' Incarnation unleashed—the revelation of the Beatitudes, the awesome power of the miracles, the scandal of the Cross, and the ultimate triumph of the Resurrection—there is one mystery, easy to miss, that in a sense startles me more than all the others. One day Jesus beheld the crowds "like sheep without a shepherd" and so asked his disciples to "ask the master of the harvest to send out laborers for his harvest" (Mt 9:36–38). Is it not at least puzzling, if not downright shocking, that the self-proclaimed Good Shepherd should suddenly see the crowd as "shepherd-less"? Though, just as he did so, Jesus cast a longing, inviting eye toward his disciples as if to ask, "Perhaps you will help me?"

Here lies a great mystery. God performs the miracle of miracles—allowing his own Son to take on human flesh so that we might be saved. Then his Son, in the midst of his public ministry, announces that his own mission must continue in us, his followers. In hearing this summons, do we realize the deep mystery of cooperation into which God calls us? Do we dare accept this invitation to become, as Blessed Moreau bids, "reproductions" of Christ in the world?

For religious—certainly for all the faithful—it is an invitation into joy, a life of the Beatitudes, miracles, and, yes, the

Cross and the Resurrection, too. And yet it is by reproducing the life of Jesus Christ that we draw not only ourselves but also others into the same saving mystery of the God who came to share in our lives so that we might share in his.

Lou DelFra, C.S.C.

June 2

May you have but one heart and one soul. May you show complete disregard for whatever differences of talent or occupation could prevent or weaken this perfect union. Let us all strive after the same goal by constantly using the means which our rules point out to us for its attainment.

—Blessed Basil Moreau

ALL THAT MARKS the graves of the men in Holy Cross who have laid down their lives in service of the Lord are silent rows of crosses. If these simple crosses could speak, we would hear an interesting and colorful accounting of saints and sinners, of master builders and humble servants. Yet beyond personal talents, abilities, or occupations, these crosses would speak of men whose ultimate goal was to know, love, and serve God and, in turn, to make God known, loved, and served. In seeking to conform their lives to Christ, these men were of one heart and one mind.

Like those who have gone before us, there will be some among us recognized for their great talents and accomplishments. But that will not be the case for the vast majority of us. Most of us lead lives of steady faithfulness. For each of us, whatever our journey in life, our road to greatness is to walk the path of holiness that is set before us each day. It is to accept and live each moment mindful of God's presence. It is to trust in God's grace, generous in our love for others. It is to remain faithful to who we are and what we are called to be. Through this fidelity, we are drawn ever more fully into the mystery of God's love at work within us, opening us to God's transforming grace wherein we, too, are then able to say that it is no longer we who live, but Christ who lives in us.

Ken Molinaro, C.S.C.

☧

June 3—Solemnity of the Sacred Heart of Jesus*

No matter what the cost, let us remain united with our superiors through obedience and united among ourselves by the bonds of that love of which the Sacred Heart of Jesus is the burning center, and which, so to speak, should form a chain linking together all the members of Holy Cross. This, moreover, is the recommendation of our Divine Lord to his apostles. It was the object of his touching prayer to his heavenly Father for us when he said: "Holy Father, I pray that they may be one, in the unity of one spirit, one faith and one love, and that just as thou art in me and I in thee, so also they may be one in us."

—Blessed Basil Moreau

EVERY TIME I pray the Our Father, I am acutely aware that the line about forgiving those who trespass against me is probably one of the hardest things that I will ever pray. It seems that, despite my best efforts, the slights and failings of others accumulate in my mind in an accounting system that I hope is never used against me. Gossip, lies, pettiness, selfishness, and plain old grumpiness stand in stark contrast to all that the love of God calls forth in us—and I am as guilty of these faults as everyone else. Would that accounting ledger be revealed, who could stand before the Lord? Yet on the Solemnity of the Sacred Heart of Jesus, we celebrate that the Lord's gaze is not an accusatory one, counting up our sins. Instead, the Lord gazes on us with affection and deep, deep love, welling up from the depth of his Sacred Heart. This, then, is the remedy for our sinfulness and preoccupation with self: the very Heart of Jesus.

One of the most comforting things about following Jesus is that he never asks us to do what he has not already done. So when he tells his disciples to love one another, he adds, "as I have loved you" (Jn 13:34). His love was strong and passionate for them, even though he knew that Judas was betraying him, Peter would deny him, and they would all run away when he needed them the most. Despite his knowledge of their failings and weakness, he never stopped loving them with a firm, steady love capable of changing lives. Indeed, his love forgave the disciples and made them stronger people—people who, in turn, would be able to show that same love to others.

When Jesus speaks to his disciples, he is speaking to us. This love of Jesus, poured into our own hearts, links us to him and to one another. Christ has given us a command that carries with it the pattern and energy for carrying it out. When we must forgive our brother and sister—when we are supposed to show them love—we are able to do so because of that ardent desire that Christ expressed: that we be one. It is his love at work in our own hearts that is able to transform our feeble feelings for one another into a robust caring.

It is this love that we celebrate in devotion to the Sacred Heart: Christ's love that not only binds us to him but is also capable of binding us to one another. In the furnace of his Sacred Heart, the weak links of our relationships are forged into a strong chain. We find that we are connected in his love and his desire becomes ours. We want the best for one another—to the point of sacrificing ourselves, of forgiving others.

And as for that accounting ledger that keeps track of our neighbor's sins? Jesus' fiery love burns up that wretched register and, at the same time, consumes our own sins as well.

Brent Kruger, C.S.C.

* The Solemnity of the Sacred Heart of Jesus moves each year based on the date of Easter. It is celebrated on the Friday nineteen days after Pentecost. June 3 is the date of the celebration in the year 2016. It will be celebrated on June 23 in 2017, June 8 in 2018, June 28 in 2019, and June 19 in 2020.

June 4

If we are not animated by the spirit of the saints, the important work of Holy Cross will come to naught, and our efforts for the sanctification of youth will be vain and useless.

—Blessed Basil Moreau

THE SPIRIT CHANGES everything. Water becomes the wellspring of everlasting life. Oil becomes the bearer of the seal of God's abiding presence. Bread and wine become the body and blood of Christ. The Spirit indeed changes everything.

The Spirit changes everyone. Immersed in the waters of Baptism, consecrated with the oil of gladness, and nourished with the Eucharistic bread and wine, we are invited into the life of the Father, Son, and Holy Spirit. In these sacred mysteries of love's extravagance, we are conformed to Christ and drawn into the fellowship of his Body, the Church, the Communion of Saints.

The Spirit changes every work. Re-created by the grace of the sacraments and animated by the spirit of the saints, we no longer live merely ordinary lives. For our ordinary labors become extraordinary as the Spirit enables us in the way of God's own, self-emptying love. All our works, imbued with God's love, become a prayer—a prayer that calls forth the Spirit who lives in us and beyond us. Thus, enlivened by this same Spirit, our human work becomes the means of the sanctification of youth and of all for whom and with whom we labor.

The Spirit changes everything, everyone, every work. Both the work of Holy Cross and the work of all God's children depend on this sanctifying power of the Spirit. If truly we are grounded, transformed, and sent in his life-giving Spirit, our efforts will never be in vain.

Thomas P. Looney, C.S.C.

June 5

"I have chosen," says the Lord, "and have sanctified this place, that my name may be there forever, and my eyes and my heart may remain there perpetually." Oh, how fervently each of us should wish these words should apply to our own hearts.

—Fr. Edward Sorin, C.S.C.

ONE DAY WHILE I was flipping quickly through the local paper at lunch, a name in the obituary section caught my startled eye. "It cannot be," I thought. But it was. There before me lay the condensed life story of a man I had thought long dead. He had been my father's one-time employer, and he had passed away at age ninety-five.

More than fifty years before, when I was a Holy Cross novice, my young father suffered a fatal heart attack, leaving my mother with nine children still at home. She was without a job or money, without insurance, and with mortgage payments due. Quietly, my father's boss took over the mortgage payments and arranged for the firm to continue sending my father's salary checks to my mother for years afterward. His heroic action rescued my mother and saved my family. "He was my friend. What else could I do?" the man explained.

This man's goodness had a permanent effect on my life in so many ways, providing material care and comfort that could be felt and tasted. It takes a lot of reflection for me, or for any of us, to understand even a small measure of the gifts that God has given to us because many are not tangible. We need a great deal of prayer to ask for the strength in order to bring those gifts to others, to be a continuous source of nourishment, and to act with the same selfless love that has been etched in our hearts.

James Kane, C.S.C.

June 6

The sacrifice of the Cross is again offered to his Father for the salvation of the world. He renews it, not just on one day, but every day, every moment of every day, in the thousands of different places among all people willing to receive him. The heart of our God at the altar is a blazing heart where a sacred fire always burns to receive our souls.

—Blessed Basil Moreau

When I was growing up, I was fortunate enough to go to a Catholic school with daily Mass. I can't say that I was always the most attentive person in the church each day, but one image has always stuck with me. As I sometimes zoned out during the homily or the Eucharistic Prayer, I always found my eyes drawn to the gigantic crucifix that hung directly above the altar. For me that image made real the love of our God, a love so strong that he was willing to become one of us, to suffer and die on the Cross so that we would have the promise of eternal life. So even though I didn't necessarily understand the theology of the Eucharist, I knew that it flowed from the sacrifice of Jesus on the Cross and that this sacrifice wasn't in vain. The Cross led somewhere—to heaven. And so did the Eucharist.

Even today, when I am at Mass, that early image of the Eucharist flowing from the Cross still inspires me. In times when I feel the weight of the Cross on me, it is the Eucharist that gives me the strength to bear it and go on. For I know that, through Jesus, the Cross leads somewhere, and the Eucharist is the food that gives me the strength to get there.

Anthony Szakaly, C.S.C.

June 7

The face of every human being who suffers is for us the face of Jesus who mounted the cross to take the sting out of death. Ours must be the same cross and the same hope.

—Holy Cross *Constitutions*

"HONGO," THEY CALLED him. "Fungus." He was nine or ten, short, with messy hair and a dirty face. The kids teased and played with him, but not mercilessly, despite the nickname. When I met him on a hot summer day in our poor, urban parish in Guadalupe, Mexico, he sat astride an old, rusty bicycle. The paint was chipped, and it was surely a hand-me-down. He was wobbly on it, mostly because his right arm was twisted and misshapen. What stood out, though, was that he kept smiling. When he couldn't steer the bike as he wanted, when kids played and he couldn't keep up, he smiled. He knew that many in his neighborhood went hungry. He also knew the fear of living with screaming and gunshots, with adults who got drunk and angry. But on that day, and whenever I saw him with his friends, he smiled. He was a kid, trying his best to be a kid.

When we suffer—both in ways this extreme and in ways not as enormous but just as overwhelming—we can remember that smile, that determination to be a kid. Why? Because we are all kids. We are all children of a loving God. We ache as we, too, are nailed to the heavy, rough wood of the suffering in our lives. But people with an indomitable joy remind us that, in the end, we can only be children of a loving God who will raise us up on the third day. And so the best thing we can do is join our hearts with those who suffer, with Christ who suffered, and thus strengthened by him who mounted the Cross for us, we can try to smile and live with the hope that we will all rise with him as well.

Matt Kuczora, C.S.C.

June 8

Everyone must show his gratitude by ever-increasing generosity. Let us then renew our zeal; and the better to ensure success in our efforts, let us sanctify ourselves constantly by fidelity to chastity, poverty, and obedience.

—Blessed Basil Moreau

THE HOLY CROSS *CONSTITUTIONS,* the rule of life for those of us in Holy Cross, speak of our vows as an act of love for the God who first loved us. For all of the many mysteries that may surround living the vows of poverty, chastity, and obedience, that simple phrase has always answered for me the question of why men and women would seemingly forsake so much of the world to live the religious life. In the depths of our own hearts, we hear a voice that recalls for us the abundance of grace and love that each of us has known in our lives.

Although now an ancient way of life, the vows are renewed in every age by men and women who hear that specific call to religious life as a way of giving back to God for all that we have been given. The surest sign of a true vocation to the vows we profess is the freedom and joy present in our lives because we give ourselves back to God in gratitude. While my vocation may be to live out this gratitude as a professed religious in Holy Cross, are not all men and women of faith called to make of their lives an offering of thanksgiving to God? The life of any faithful Christian, well lived, is a free and generous act of love for the God who first loved us.

Walter E. Jenkins, C.S.C.

June 9

Great abilities, unless supported by virtues, are in danger, and seldom prove a blessing.
—Fr. Edward Sorin, C.S.C.

USE IT OR lose it. We probably have all heard this saying and perhaps even used it ourselves. It expresses our need to take full and responsible advantage of the talents and opportunities with which God has blessed us. For if we neglect our gifts we will lose what we already have been given. At the same time, in taking advantage of our God-given talents, we must be careful to use them properly because our strengths and gifts can easily become harmful to ourselves and others when used irresponsibly. If we are too strong and confrontational, we may become less compassionate. Our penchant for organization, taken too far, may make us overbearing. In these cases, our great abilities cease to be blessings.

Fr. Sorin thus reminds us that we must clothe our talents in virtue so that we can effectively use these special gifts to support the common good. Through virtues—such as humility, generosity, and charity—we can direct our academic acumen, organizational skill, pulpit eloquence, indeed all of our God-given abilities, in ways that are welcoming, helpful, and empowering to others. For it is ultimately in uniting our gifts and our talents with Jesus' efforts to build the kingdom of God in our world that they become the blessings they are truly meant to be—for ourselves and for others. Only in such faithful service to God in small matters will we be given greater responsibilities and ultimately be invited to share in our master's joy.

Richard Gribble, C.S.C.

June 10

*The Trinity is totally taken up, so to speak, with raising
us up to the godhead. Our creation is the work of the
Father, our redemption the work of the Son, and our
sanctification the fruit of the working of the Spirit.*
—Blessed Basil Moreau

MY FIRST CONFUSION about the Trinity arose on June 10, 1990.
Until then, I had never thought much about the three persons
of God, but this was Trinity Sunday, the day of my first Mass as
a priest, and I felt that I should be able to say something profound about the mystery of faith that grounded my vocation.
I have no idea what I said that emotional day at the Chapel
of Mary at Stonehill College, and I might well have preached
some heresy, but for the family, friends, community members,
and parishioners that gathered with me that morning, it didn't
matter. A first Mass is pure joy!

Twenty-five years later, I now realize that my inability to find
words to express God that Trinity Sunday was a grand silence
akin to Moses before the burning bush of the Ancient One. Surrounded by love, the theology and liturgy of priestly ordination
had caught up with me, and my heart knew—despite my ego's
desire to say impressive words—that silent tears of joy were the
best that could be said amid such sacrament and Communion.
A true self emerged, forever seeking union with God.

My prayer at the time of ordination was one I learned from
Moses: If I am your friend, let me see your glory (see Ex 33:17–
18). It's my experience that God answers this remarkable prayer,

for the Father is so totally taken up with raising us up to himself that he sent his Son, so that through the Spirit we would learn love of God and neighbor: the birthplace and home of the true self.

Daniel J. Issing, C.S.C.

June 11

Everyone should be zealous for the preservation of that unity of mind, heart, and conduct which is the principle, not only of peace, but of the very existence of the community. This should not be difficult where all have the same God, the same faith, the same sacraments, the same rules to observe, the same establishments to maintain—where the good of one must be the good of all, and the evil of one must be the evil of all.

—Blessed Basil Moreau

As I looked out into the congregation and made the announcement to the parish that I had just completed my fourth year as pastor and was ready to begin my fifth, I did so with great joy—and, to my surprise, tears of joy. St. John Vianney Parish and School in Goodyear, Arizona, is an incredible and incredibly diverse place. We never know what a given day will have in store for us. We might find ourselves speaking Spanish more than we speak English. We might both baptize a newborn infant into the community of faith and anoint a beloved matriarch of a family as she's called to join the Communion of Saints. We can be surrounded by hundreds of energetic schoolchildren and their families at morning drop-off and then be seated with a solitary person seeking counsel regarding a difficult relationship. As diverse as the people and our experiences with them might be, we are drawn together at St. John Vianney as one family, one body, one community.

Blessed Moreau understood that, though many and diverse, we are united. It is this community spirit that enabled our founder to gather priests, brothers, and sisters together in service of God's people. We are to live and serve zealously for the preservation of that unity of mind, heart, and conduct. At St. John Vianney, this is not a lofty goal but a blessing that we experience every day. It is a blessing that God wants to share with us wherever he draws us together to be his Church, to be a diverse and united community of faith. And with God, we can make it happen.

Tom Eckert, C.S.C.

June 12

I am not the least bit surprised by all these trials. Thanks be to God. They have only increased my confidence in him who alone has founded and maintained this Congregation. He it is who will expand it more and more.

—Blessed Basil Moreau

At Kenyatta National Hospital in Nairobi, Kenya, I visited a woman with a very serious condition on her face and in her eyes. I was serving as a chaplain at the hospital with one of my brothers in Holy Cross from Tanzania. Each week, we visited and prayed with the sick. To do this, I had to learn Kiswahili, the local language of many of the patients. Yet even with my newly acquired language skills, I was at a loss for words in conversation with this particular woman. She explained, "I yearn to cry, but I have no tears. I endure the pain." Given the severity of her condition and the anguish of her words, I felt helpless. At first I got caught up in what I could say or do in order to lessen her pain. Then I realized that what really mattered was that I simply was there for her and could share my tears. Breaking through the silence, she said, "Your being with me speaks volumes. Thank you."

To endure pain, disillusionment, and setback in our lives can be trying, but it should not be surprising. These things are a part of all of our lives. The grace is to see these trials, as Blessed Moreau did, as opportunities to increase our confidence in the Lord. This is the grace that comes as we stop searching for what to say and what to do and begin simply to rest in God's presence with us.

Ronald M. Kawooya, C.S.C.

June 13

There is no looseness or indifference about a devoted religious; you see in his very countenance, in his bearing, in his every step that he is in earnest; that he means to be a doer and not a talker; that he feels an interest in the cause; that he feels happy in proportion as he devoted his energy to that cause.

—Fr. Edward Sorin, C.S.C.

AS AN UNDERGRADUATE in the 1940s, I did not personally know Fr. Peter Forrestal, C.S.C. To me, he was simply another old Holy Cross priest on the University of Notre Dame campus. I recognized him as rector of Sorin Hall and as a Spanish professor, but as far as I knew, those were his only duties.

How wrong I was. I learned later that this self-effacing Irish immigrant had been a man of boundless energy and pastoral zeal, the kind of man who spots a problem and then does something about it. As one of his brothers once said, "Pete does more ministry before breakfast than a lot of people do all day." Years before, Fr. Pete had discovered the large, Mexican American migrant camps around South Bend, Indiana. As if he didn't have enough to do on campus, he established a ministry to the Spanish-speaking peoples in the local area, administering the sacraments and becoming their friend and confidant.

Revered as a saint, Fr. Pete lived up to Fr. Sorin's description of someone who was earnest about what he believed, someone who was a doer and not a talker. In my life in Holy Cross, I've met many whose unwavering commitment and zeal were a lot like Fr. Pete's. These men and women devoted themselves to helping the poor and the marginalized. And, as Fr. Sorin said, they were happy and fulfilled because they knew that they were doing the Lord's work. Their example has provided inspiration for me, and it shows the way for the rest of us to be doers, not just talkers, for Christ.

Thomas McNally, C.S.C.

June 14

How peaceful and happy we would be if, by putting this divine lesson into practice, we would come to snuff out at its origin the accursed passion of human respect that is ours by nature. Then, freed from human judgments, as calm and serene as a rock in the midst of the waves of opinions that come and go, we would let the world be stormy around us, let it exhaust its evil fury against us, but our happiness would not be disturbed by it all because we would have learned to value only what God put in us and to judge ourselves for what we really are.

—Blessed Basil Moreau

WHEN I TOLD my friends and family I was headed to the Holy Cross Novitiate in Colorado, they thought I was crazy. "Fifteen hours of silence a day?" was a common response. But it was there, on that holy mountain, unplugged from social media, free from distraction by television or radio or the Internet, unable even to leave the property without permission, that I came face-to-face with my God. It was there, at the base of Pike's Peak, surrounded by stillness, that my heart finally found the time and space to speak its burning desire for unity with Jesus Christ.

One of the ground rules at the novitiate is to do only one thing at a time. If you're pulling weeds in the yard, that's all you do. You don't listen to music, you don't sing to yourself, you don't let your mind wander to thoughts of not-pulling-weeds. You just focus on those weeds and your pulling. This is known as "practicing the presence of God." By making ourselves fully present to whatever task is at hand, we learn to find God even in the smallest and most mundane moments. And we come to realize that what matters most is that God loves us so much that he gave us life and calls us to life eternal.

Once we come face-to-face with this love, nothing else matters so much—certainly not the fickleness of those who inflict their wicked judgments on us. Practicing the presence of God—one weed, one task, one person, one moment at a time—we fall instead head over heels for the God who first loved us. We are then free to focus our energies on making God known, loved, and served wherever we go.

Dan Parrish, C.S.C.

June 15

Let us ask this good Savior for a humble heart which knows its origin in nothing, a gentle heart which knows how to contain itself, a loving heart which is compassionate to the sorrows of others and eager to relieve them. May we have a pure and faithful heart which will be faithful to its work and generous in fulfilling its obligations, obedient to the counsels of faith and the inspirations of grace.

—Blessed Basil Moreau

A STUDENT ONCE asked me if I found hearing confessions depressing, hearing of the worst of people's deeds. His idea was far from the reality. The penitent, in naming sins, confesses the faith and the desire for holiness against which those sins are measured. Many moving tales of the quest for holiness can never be told because they were heard in confession. There we see the truly humble heart. There we also see the heart full of hope. It is the hope that the quest for goodness will succeed, that sin may be left behind. And it is the hope—the sure and certain hope—that the Lord from whom we ask forgiveness will grant forgiveness. In this simple act of asking forgiveness, we experience our nothingness, our utter dependence on God, our dependence on a love that we do not deserve. We experience, too, the absolute dependability of that love.

The humility and faith expressed and experienced in confession are models for our way of life. In knowing the compassion of our Lord, we are all moved to compassion. In seeing our need for forgiveness answered, we are moved to forgive. In the reawakened hope that our lives may become holy, we embrace our lives, our work, our obligations. We seek the counsels of faith and the inspirations of grace, hoping that our lives may be schools of humility and hope.

Richard Bullene, C.S.C.

June 16

The Congregation began and developed in a manner so mysterious that I can claim for myself neither credit for its foundation nor merit for its progress. Therein lies the indubitable proof that God alone is the founder of this Congregation.

—Blessed Basil Moreau

BLESSED MOREAU'S WORDS speak of his faith in God, his trust in Divine Providence, and, in a very personal way, his humility. While all of these qualities resonate with my experiences of ministry, leadership, and community life in Holy Cross, the one that is most profound for me is humility. There is little that I can take credit for personally. While having some perceived successes, I know that none of them would have been possible without God's love and guidance. I also have learned—and not always easily—that at times everything doesn't go as I have hoped or striven. I have come to understand that God does not abandon us in those times, and that his plan for our lives continues to unfold—even when we might least expect—if we faithfully trust in him.

It is here that we see the need for faith and trust if we are to be humble. To live with deep humility, we must be able to have faith in God and trust in his guidance of our lives, personally and collectively. This is especially true because, as Pope Francis said, "God is not afraid of new things! That is why he is continually surprising us, opening our hearts, and guiding us in unexpected ways." Openness to the God of new things, the God of surprises, comes from a humility born of faith and trust.

And so, with deep gratitude for the gift of faith, and confident that God accompanies and guides us always, we pray that, like Blessed Moreau and Pope Francis, we may humbly let God move in mysterious and surprising ways in our lives so that together we can marvel at his great work—which is not yet complete!

Mike DeLaney, C.S.C.

June 17

May we learn how to rise above the joys of a day and secure everlasting enjoyments.
—Fr. Edward Sorin, C.S.C.

WHEN I FIRST entered the seminary, I had no clear idea of what I preferred to do as a priest. So many possibilities held attractions for me—parish assistance, retreat preaching, hospital ministry, and so on. But I gradually enrolled in several classes at the University of Notre Dame taught by outstanding Holy Cross priests. Following their example became especially attractive to me, and eventually my superiors sent me on to graduate studies and assigned me to university teaching. For more than fifty years, I have thoroughly enjoyed helping young men and women grow intellectually, researching and writing on my own, and being a small part of such an outstanding Catholic institution as that of Notre Dame.

This also poses an exciting challenge. Should not any occupation—teaching, growing crops, working in industry, managing a business, caring for a home—be more than a satisfying and enjoyable career? It can and should be if we view it with the eyes of faith. The classroom teacher is assisting young men and women to perfect their intellects, created in the image and likeness of God. The farmer and gardener are cooperating with God in renewing his creation year after year. Industrial workers can be making life happier and more comfortable for their brothers and sisters in the Lord. Parents and homemakers are assisting the young to grow and become ever more the persons God created them to be. This list could go on, but one goal of life is to choose a worthwhile career, to experience genuine joy and satisfaction in it, and to discover its true worth in the eyes of God.

Thomas Blantz, C.S.C.

June 18

In the Holy Eucharist, he is joined to matter; and by this wonderful act of his love, he left us his body and blood until the end of the world.

—Blessed Basil Moreau

"BEHOLD, I AM with you always, until then end of the age" (Mt 28:20). With these last words, Jesus promised that he would not leave us orphans. He would remain with us in his words and works. And so he instituted the seven sacraments as signs of permanence, as sources of strength, and as channels of grace. Indeed, they maintain his presence among us.

Primary among the sacraments is the Eucharist. In the Mass, in that simple ritual with a few spoken words, a tremendous transformation takes place. For when Jesus took bread and said it was his body and took wine and said it was his blood, he indicated that the immensity of the Divine is captured and contained in this now-consecrated bread and blessed wine. In other words, Jesus was telling the apostles and all of us that he will be with us, body, blood, soul, and divinity, in the blessed host and the sacred wine. Yes, through the words of consecration Jesus truly is present in our midst today. What a tremendous gift.

If we keep the Eucharist in mind, we don't have to look far when we hear Jesus summon us. "Come to me all you who are hungry, all you who are thirsty, and all you who are lonely," he says. We will know where to find him: on the altar during the Mass, in the sacred host in the tabernacle, in the monstrance during Exposition. There is Jesus the Son of God, the son of Mary; there is Jesus true God and true man; there is Jesus our teacher and friend, with us until the end of the world.

Alfred D'Alonzo, C.S.C.

June 19

These children who today attend your school are the parents of the future and the parents of future generations. Each one of them carries within him or her a family. Influence them, therefore, by all the means of instruction and sanctification.

—Blessed Basil Moreau

FATHERHOOD IS A beautiful and precarious thing. It involves a unique kind of loving, protecting, guiding, and forming that we learn from those who have raised us. In marriage, my father gave his love to my mother, that she might love him and honor him all the days of his life. In fatherhood, he gave his love to my siblings and me, that we might love and honor others. Husbands hold close; fathers give away.

Commencement reminds me of this precious charge each spring. Watching my seniors from Keough Hall process into Notre Dame Stadium for the last time, I'm reminded of my own father's emotion. These are my boys—and they always will be—but they're not mine to keep. Just as they were gifts to me, just as they were gifts to their parents, they've become gifts for the world. And as their father here at Notre Dame, it's my turn to give them away.

I love seeing them go. I also love having them back. I savor every moment sitting beside them on the couch, swapping duty stories and football statistics and dating sagas, wondering how long they will be mine before they're gone again.

To mentor young people is to know that longing for life shared. It's not just that they're funny or clever or true. It's that, in an indelible way, their stories have been written into our stories. Their hearts have shaped our hearts. For me, the men of Keough Hall have taught me how to be a father.

Patrick Reidy, C.S.C.

June 20

Faith, as well as reason and experience, demonstrates conclusively that "in union there is strength." Union gives rise to strength by blending all the parts into the whole, like mortar which holds the stones of a building together and unites them all with the keystone.

—Blessed Basil Moreau

BLESSED MOREAU KNEW the power of both unity and division. Nineteenth-century France was divided socially, politically, and religiously. Crises accompanied successive waves of revolution. In such times, Moreau realized what shared effort and unified hearts could achieve if they all cooperated with Divine Providence.

In our global culture, we are painfully aware of the divisions, needs, and struggles of peoples around the world. There is so much to be done. On one level, we feel called by the Gospel to have compassion and to serve the needs of the world. On the other, we know our personal limits. No one of us can do it all.

It is then that I find consolation in unity with Holy Cross, an international community that is part of the universal Catholic Church. I take comfort in the reality that my brothers and sisters are working around the world. I can imagine the thousands of people who will today deepen their faith, grow in knowledge, be fed and clothed, visited and comforted, gathered and mobilized by us, united sons and daughters of Blessed Moreau, united brothers and sisters in Christ.

For all people of faith, reflecting on our union as members of God's family reminds us that our prayers and labors as well as our attempts to form communities are part of something much bigger. Yet the consolation of knowing that we are united in our efforts does not diminish personal responsibility. The modest energy and limited efforts of any one of us when joined with the whole become a powerful force of hope for a world too often in crisis from forces of enmity and division.

David Guffey, C.S.C.

June 21

Our teaching leaves behind us all the aspirations of the world and fits our pupils for eternal life.
—Fr. Edward Sorin, C.S.C.

SPIRITUAL DIRECTION IS the graced accompaniment of one soul with another on the journey to God. In monthly, one-on-one meetings as a spiritual director, I have been blessed to listen to the faith journeys of many inspiring men and women as we together discover their God-given gifts.

Of all the graces I have witnessed, one example stands out. I directed a Hispanic woman who, by participating in an Old Testament course, indicated her interest in going deeper into her spiritual life. She did not at first understand the purpose of spiritual direction. But as we talked, she began to discover her own gifts and her calling from God. The call she uncovered through spiritual direction led her to leave her job at a jewelry store and become a director of religious education in a parish. This call continued to unfold as she sought further training, accepted a diocesan position as a faith educator, and completed a master's degree in theology. Now God works through her to train others at catechesis conferences across the country.

At the heart of her story, however, is her dedicated development of a life of daily prayer and meditation. It is this deep prayer life, refreshed and renewed by ongoing direction, that has sustained and guided her. And this is the end of spiritual direction, indeed of all forms of faith sharing and education in the faith: that people see God as their deepest longing and are able to see their worldly responsibilities in the light of their commitment to him.

John Connor, C.S.C.

June 22

His delights are to be with us; our greatest happiness is to live for him and with him, to follow him and obey his holy will.

—Fr. Edward Sorin, C.S.C.

ONE SUMMER, WHILE I was working as a seminarian at our camp in Maine, twelve of us were returning from a three-day canoe trip when a terrible storm came up on Lake Sebago. Thunder, lightning, and high waves threw us into a panic. I spotted a small island several hundred yards away, and we focused all of our attention on paddling to it. Two hours later, we reached it with our hands blistered and energy sapped, but we were eternally grateful for the ability God had given us to stay focused on our goal.

When I went to Holy Cross Parish in South Easton, Massachusetts, several years ago, I had already been a priest for more than three decades, yet this was the first time I would serve as pastor. When I took the job, I felt at first like I did that day on Lake Sebago. I suppose I could have allowed myself to be overcome with fear and uncertainty. Instead, I decided to take each day as it came, to stay close to God, and to do all in my power to help others to do the same. In all honesty, I was not always certain in my ministry there. But as long as I kept myself focused on doing what God had called me to do, I was filled with gratitude and happiness.

If we are going to be true to our God-given callings, the challenge for all of us lies in keeping our sights set on Christ, especially in times of fear and uncertainty. He will always live in us if we live in him. And, therein we will find our greatest happiness.

R. Bradley Beaupre, C.S.C.

June 23

Considered in relation to ourselves, the Heart of Jesus is of a friend, a brother, a father, and a Savior. It is a Heart of mystery, wherein justice and peace have given each other a kiss of union, and worked out those prodigies of power and mercy which have renewed the face of the earth.

—Blessed Basil Moreau

THE HEART OF Jesus Christ is one of the devotions that Blessed Moreau held near to his own heart. If we look at the Sacred Heart of Jesus, we discover a fundamental element of our faith: God became man in the person of Jesus Christ. Therefore, the Heart of Jesus is a heart that has experienced for us and with us joy, admiration, and thanksgiving but also disappointment, pain, and suffering. The Heart of Jesus is a symbol of the Incarnation of the Word; it manifests in the concrete the very closeness of God with his people.

Yet our turning our own minds and hearts to the Heart of Christ is neither a simple nor a nostalgic evocation of Jesus' life on earth—whether that be the inner life of the Lord in his time among us, his life on the roads of Judea and Samaria, or his life upon the shores of the Lake of Galilee. Far more, we are called to contemplate in our present time the Heart of the One risen from the dead, the Heart of One who assures us that victory is already acquired, since everything was renewed on the morning of Easter. Ultimately, then, to contemplate the Heart of Christ is to be invited to see further, beyond the appearances of a world still in the pains of childbirth. It is to contemplate God's plan for our humanity and gain a completely new perspective. In the Sacred Heart of Jesus, risen to die no more, justice and peace are definitively given; in him, power and mercy are ever dispensed by the gift of grace; in him, the Father calls us to become truly ourselves as the artisans of a world being made anew.

Romuald Fresnais, C.S.C.

June 24

Ingratitude, says a great saint, dries up even the source of divine favors. Common sense tells us the same, and daily experience proves it.

—Fr. Edward Sorin, C.S.C.

FR. TED HESBURGH, C.S.C., always maintained that his best day, the most important event in his life, and his greatest honor was his ordination. I, too, look upon my ordination as the ultimate defining moment in my life. It was the culmination of my years of study and formation, the fulfillment of my lifelong dream, and the beginning of my public ministry. Yet who I am today is a result not only of my ordination but of every day of my life. I draw strength from my family and my many experiences of growing up with their love. Over the years my friends have supported, encouraged, and challenged me. I am able to do what I do because of God and because of my family and friends. God has given me many talents and gifts. My family and friends have provided me with the vitality and richness that makes those gifts and talents radiate God's goodness.

To recognize our dependency on God and on many others is the beginning of gratitude. We do not accomplish great things independent of others or of God. Any attempt to isolate ourselves and our achievements from the influence of others is to isolate ourselves from the source of what makes us God's greatest creation. Instead, we express our thanks, we acknowledge our dependency, and we seek to strengthen ourselves so as to continue becoming a better and stronger reflection of the God in whose image we have been created. For everything that has been, thanks. For everything that is to come, yes.

Mark B. Thesing, C.S.C.

June 25

Jesus Christ ascended into heaven to teach us the road which leads there. Come and see the route I have taken to arrive in the place of eternal happiness. Walk after me, do not let my footsteps escape from your view.

—Blessed Basil Moreau

WHEN I WAS chaplain to the medical-care facility of the Sisters of the Holy Cross, I was honored to serve nearly two hundred sisters whose average age was eighty-six. They had been teachers, nurses, administrators, and pastoral-care ministers, but at this point in their lives, they served through the ministry of prayer for the needs of the Church and world. Shortly after I arrived, I was called upon to anoint Sr. Rita Estelle, C.S.C., who was more than one hundred years old and was dying. At her bedside, a number of her fellow sisters, as well as nieces and staff, gathered in prayer. As I went to pour holy water upon her, she said softly, "I want to follow Jesus now and forever." She then signed herself with the cross.

Those who knew Sr. Rita Estelle testified that she always lived her life with her eyes fixed intently on Jesus Christ. As a result, she knew to walk after him even in the last days as her earthly life was drawing to a close. For all of us who have patterned our lives on Christ through Baptism, we need courage, humility, and trust in order to keep our eyes fixed on him. This faithfulness requires the continual cultivation of good habits in us—prayer, Eucharist, retreat, and works of mercy. We can know, too, that we are sustained on this journey by the prayers of the faithful who have gone before us, the prayers of the Communion of Saints. Thus we, like Sr. Rita Estelle, are not alone as we follow the path that Christ has prepared for us into eternal glory.

Jim Bracke, C.S.C.

June 26

If at times you show preference to any young people, they should be the poor, those who have no one else to show them preference, those who have the least knowledge, those who lack skills and talent, and those who are not Catholic or Christian. If you show them greater care and concern it must be because their needs are greater and because it is only just to give more to those who have received less.

—Blessed Basil Moreau

MY PASSION FOR working with young people began in 1986, when Fr. Jim Fenstermaker, C.S.C., asked me to help with a youth group at St. Stephen Parish, which served a poorer, immigrant population on the west side of South Bend, Indiana.

Today, a collage of photographs of that first youth group hangs on my wall. A recent e-mail reminded me of those days. It said, "Remember us? We were in your youth group back in the 1980s. We just celebrated nineteen years of marriage, and we were thinking about you!—Felipe and Esther." Their simple message reminded me of one of the things I love most about Holy Cross: impacting the lives of young people.

Similar experiences continue for me today as a teacher and chaplain at Moreau Catholic High School, which serves a diverse population in Hayward, California. A student wrote me a note: "Thank you for being an amazing teacher. God through you has taught me to be more open-minded and really understand what it means to live the Gospel. I hope you continue to let God use you to touch children like me.—Kadija."

Not always do we hear from those whose lives we have impacted and changed. But when we do, it becomes a great moment of God's grace. It reminds us of that sacred baptismal call to make God known, loved, and served. When we help prepare the hearts of young people, especially those who are poor, disadvantaged, or marginalized, by sharing our love of Christ with them, God's love grows and spreads—through them, through their children, and through their children's children. The care and concern that we show them helps transform the world; it even helps transform us.

Bruce Cecil, C.S.C.

June 27

*The legitimate love of neighbor comes from love of
God and leads back to love of God.*
—Blessed Basil Moreau

I LIVE CLOSE to the fishing village of Moree in southern Ghana.
Like many typical fishing villages in Ghana, lack of basic infra-
structure makes life difficult and sometimes unbearable. Yet in
spite of these harsh realities, the villagers have an overwhelming
sense of joy that overshadows the poor living situation in which
they find themselves. The villagers' steadfast trust in God can
easily shame the rest of us. Never is this more apparent than
when groups of American students from Holy Cross College
visit Moree as part of their international study program. The village fascinates and disturbs them as they come face-to-face with
the deprivation and helplessness of the people, experiencing life
in a manner they have never known. The students cannot help
but think of their own vulnerability and dependence on God.

We are fragile creatures dependent on our Creator and
on one another. Like the students, whose Moree experience
changed their perspective on life, inspiring them to help the
people in their helplessness, we, too, can become instruments
of God's providential care. We only have to pray for an increase
of our faith and trust, the things often abundant in the lives
of the impoverished people whom we serve. For we, too, can
cultivate a deeper faith and trust in God that are not only the
product but also the source of our love and service. In doing so,
Divine Providence finds concrete expression in our hands and

feet as we serve the coming of God's kingdom on earth. And so it is in the midst of all the complex connections of life that we discover God is the One holding it all together.

Paul Kofi Mensah, C.S.C.

June 28

God so loved the world that he sent his only Son that we might have live and have it abundantly.
—Holy Cross *Constitutions*

I DON'T HAVE any children—as you might have guessed! When I think about people I know who do, the thought of losing a child is unbearable. After my twin brother and I were born, my mother gave birth to a stillborn child. She would later give birth to another child, my sister, but not before my father died very suddenly and very young of a heart attack. I remember as a young man being struck by something my mother would much later say about these events. Even as the death of my father left her widowed with nine children under the age of fourteen and another child on the way, my mother said that it was more difficult to lose that child than it was to lose my father. That revelation has always stayed with me. Parents and spouses die in the normal course, she explained. They might die young, but they lived. A mother gives birth to new life; parents aren't meant to outlive their own children. There was something unbearable about this loss—pun intended.

And so we can only begin to imagine the depth of the love that God has for us in sending his only Son to suffer and die for us so that we might have life. What resulted—the life, death, and Resurrection of our Lord Jesus Christ—blew wide the doors of heaven, and of hope, for all of us. Life has overcome death! My mother's conviction of this truth in the face of all loss was a model of faith for all who knew her, particularly for us, her children. It was a fitting preparation for my twin brother, also a Holy Cross priest, and me to live Blessed Moreau's motto for his Congregation: *Ave Crux, Spes Unica*—Hail the Cross, Our Only Hope!

Jim Lies, C.S.C.

June 29

We learn that formation and transformation are both the Lord's gifts which we as a community can help one another to receive.

—Holy Cross *Constitutions*

FORMATION IN THE Christian life never ends. We always can be transformed more fully into Christ. The person who rests satisfied has missed one of the deepest truths about human life—our hearts are restless until they rest in God. Even Fr. Sorin realized his need for help in this continued transformation, so he asked Br. Vincent Pieau, C.S.C., to be his spiritual monitor in Indiana. Each month, Br. Vincent would counsel Fr. Sorin, giving feedback, even constructive criticism, on his leadership of the nascent Notre Dame community.

It is not easy to accept correction, but if it comes from a trusted friend, it can be transformative. We cannot know ourselves well without the mirror of an outside commentator, someone who can point out to us the things that impede our transformation into godliness. In fact, we owe each other such simple admonitions. For if we are to progress together, whether as a family, community, school, or parish, we all have to grow in the same direction of faith. None of us can be exempt from continual formation.

The result of our opening up to others is a freshness of heart, a cleansing we cannot achieve in isolation. Among the greatest gifts we can give to our brothers and sisters is to look out for one another. We need each other, not only in good times, but also in times of sickness, spiritual wandering, and even darkness. For we build each other up in the light, coming to our full stature in the one Body of Christ. Together we are formed; together we are transformed.

George Klawitter, C.S.C.

June 30

It seems to me that no prayer can be sooner heeded than one addressed to the conquerors of the world, who laid down their life for their love of the Cross, on

behalf of their remote successors enrolled under the same soul-stirring, divine standard.
—Fr. Edward Sorin, C.S.C.

OUR HOLY PREDECESSORS in the faith, those valiant conquerors of the world, have all in some way laid down their lives for love of the Cross. For some, including some men of Holy Cross, this love has led to the ultimate sacrifice of martyrdom. For others, and most likely for us, love of the Cross demands taking up our own daily crosses and dying to ourselves in the little matters of life.

Fortunately, we are not alone on this path. Countless others have left their footprints on it before us, and they can serve as our guides. We have only to seek inspiration from our predecessors, the Communion of Saints, and, like them, strive to put on Christ. We follow their examples, we ask for their intercession, and we journey with them as companions. It is through praying in their company that we grow into deeper union with God and all those united in his Son's Cross.

Through our fellowship with the saints, God will accompany us with his grace. All of us who seek to live united with the will of our Heavenly Father will never be abandoned. It is when we accept in faith and in action our soul-stirring, divine standard of the Cross that we immediately see its benefits. Like those men and women before us who bore their crosses to the very end, we, too, can shoulder our crosses in love and without fear. For the Cross is not without hope.

Mario Lachapelle, C.S.C.

July 1

Our mission is the Lord's and so is the strength for it.
We turn to him in prayer that he will clasp us more
firmly to himself and use our hands and wits to do
the work that only he can do. Then our work itself
becomes a prayer: a service that speaks to the Lord
who works through us.

—Holy Cross *Constitutions*

CHANGE IS NEVER easy. The vow of obedience was very tangible for me as the Lord's mission beckoned me to pack up and transition from South Bend, Indiana, to Easton, Massachusetts. There were many quiet moments during the fifteen-hour car ride when prayer eased my sadness of letting go and quelled my anxiety about introducing myself to a new parish.

The parishioners at Holy Cross Parish have been very welcoming with their New England accents. There are many new names and faces, but in celebrating Masses, getting to know people in the office, and visiting parishioners in the hospital and in their homes, I'm strengthened by the Lord's same abiding presence in this place as in every other place I have lived and worked in my ministry in Holy Cross.

God's Spirit strengthens the faith and hope necessary to love anew. It is exciting to preach the Gospel and celebrate the Eucharist and other sacraments in a new place because, even though I am many miles from where I was baptized, confirmed, and ordained, the universality of the Catholic faith makes this new place a home away from home.

I often pray that fellow Catholics—but especially young adults who frequently move—take the necessary time to nurture an abiding faith since it is more and more common to be uprooted and move today than in years past. Moving as a religious is a bit easier because faith is at the heart of the reason to move. Yet it can be challenging for all of us not to give faith a backseat while other motives for a move ride up front. We ask that the Lord guide our hands and enlighten our faith on each move of life's very interesting and exciting journey.

Brad Metz, C.S.C.

July 2

The brothers shall remember always that the children in their charge are given to them by God himself to teach them to love and serve him; and by consequence, their principal care should be to form them in virtue.

—Fr. Jacques Dujarie

FOR MANY YEARS, I had the privilege of living with and caring for youth in the Hogar Santa Cruz, a home for abused children run by Holy Cross in Santiago, Chile. I don't know who profited more from our time together, them or me. They certainly helped me to learn a lot about myself through their open and frank observations. Although they still had a great deal of their lives ahead of them, these children came to our home laden with memories they did not willingly wish to examine. They carried the heavy burdens of abuse and neglect. Those of us who worked with these children had the responsibility of helping them gain positive experiences that would be more colorful and pleasant to recall.

Many of the children with whom I lived at the Hogar Santa Cruz have now grown to become young adults. When they come to visit me now, it is clear that it was not so much what I said to them that made a lasting impression but the manner in which I spoke. My tone of voice, my facial expressions, and my gestures are what left the more enduring mark on them.

For all of us who raise or work with children and young adults, it is critical that we welcome them into our hearts so that they can experience a true concern for their well-being. This loving care is the expression of the dignity that they deserve. In this way we can hope to make a lasting, positive impact on the young who are entrusted to our care.

Donald Kuchenmeister, C.S.C.

July 3

On poverty, as I see it, depends the blessing of heaven on the Congregation of Holy Cross, the progress of its individual members in the love of God, and each one's perseverance in the spirit of our holy vocation. Poverty is a supernatural virtue which is born of faith, feeds on hope, and grows to maturity in the love of him who said, "Blessed are the poor."

—Blessed Basil Moreau

"DID YOU SEE that priest's pictures from Europe on Facebook?" "No, but I did see a Holy Cross brother at that new restaurant." Comments—and actions—like these raise questions about our vow of poverty as religious. They also raise questions about the simplicity of life we are all called to live as disciples of the One who said, "Blessed are the poor." So what is the vow of poverty? How does such evangelical poverty fit in a world where people struggle to survive?

Poverty in itself is evil. It suppresses the dignity inherent in every person and is often caused by injustice. We do not seek to add to the poverty of this world. Instead, we as religious let go of the control over our resources so that they can be used for the good of all, especially the poor.

When a Holy Cross religious travels or eats out, we should question. Was the travel related to his ministry or the meal a way to celebrate a joyous occasion? Most of all, was this a worthwhile use of the resources at our disposal? A priest or brother's answer to these questions challenges all Christians to ask, How can I best use my resources?

The evangelical poverty and simplicity of life that Christ demands entail a difficult balance between what is necessary and what is selfish. This balance is so difficult that it's not humanly possible. It's something we work hard at, but it's also a supernatural gift from God, intimately intertwined with the faith, hope, and love that sustain and direct all we do.

By this vow, religious unlock a special witness, hopefully reminding all of us that the things of this world are passing away. What endure are our relationships with God, who is the source of all our wealth, and the same God's unbreakable love.

Matt Kuczora, C.S.C.

July 4

We wished to abandon all to follow Christ. We learned in time that we still had it within ourselves to hold back. We wish to be wholehearted yet we are hesitant. Still, like the first disciples we know that he will draw us along and reinforce our loyalties if we yield to him.
—Holy Cross *Constitutions*

HOW EASY IT is for us to create for ourselves a God we want, a God who, instead of being the ground of our existence and the center of our life, sanctions our life's choices after we have already made them. All who grow into the holiness God envisions for them—as priests, consecrated religious, or lay people of God—learn this truth in their strivings to remain faithful to their callings. Our sinfulness has a stubbornness not easily overcome, a clinging resilience not dissolved by even the most earnest choices made in the fullness of all the freedom possible in a given moment. In the face of sin's intractable nature, vows can be necessary but insufficient—pledges and promises desirable but fleeting. Instead, grace has to make and remake us, over and over again. In this divine refashioning, we learn just how dependent we are and how seductive are the ways in which we claim our independence from God and not through God.

Here the wisdom of the Church—the wisdom of truths proclaimed and lived, of generosity practiced and preached—becomes the indispensable plank of our salvation. For in the Church, all who seek to follow Christ are drawn together in his body. Then, from one another's strivings after faithfulness, from our regular, heartfelt worship and prayer, the Body of Christ draws us along and teaches us how to follow him from whom we receive the fullness of our identity.

Paul Kollman, C.S.C.

July 5

This pure, prompt, universal, constant fidelity to what is prescribed for us daily, weekly, monthly, yearly will make of us so many victims of divine love, so many living hosts.

—Blessed Basil Moreau

AN *ABUELA* ALL in white led the way down a dusty road in Monterrey, Mexico. She, Fr. Matt Kuczora, C.S.C., and I were making Communion visits to the homebound, and we were coming to the last address on our list. When we arrived at the house, however, something immediately felt . . . off. The front door was open. Inside, it was dark, and an odor hung on the air. In a back room, we found the woman we had come to visit, helplessly splayed out on the floor, moaning, uncomprehending, and amid evidence of having been there for some time.

Fr. Matt and I did what we could to bring stability to the situation, but this *abuela* did something that I will never forget. With compassion etched across her face, she simply bent down, held this soiled woman against her perfectly white dress, and, after changing her, got her into bed and let her rest. She didn't just give Jesus to this woman; she was Jesus for this woman.

It used to bother me that the Gospel of John leaves the words of institution out of its account of the Last Supper in favor of the story of Jesus washing the disciples' feet. Now I think I see why. The Eucharist isn't primarily something we receive; it's someone we become. In approaching the Eucharist faithfully, we ourselves are transformed into the Body of Christ. Jesus' life becomes our life, a sacrifice of praise to God and of service to our neighbor.

St. Paul once wrote, "It is no longer I who live, but Christ who lives in me" (Gal 2:20). I believe my *abuela* in white could say the same. In her life, Jesus' life takes on flesh again. In our lives, too, Jesus makes us into living hosts of eternal life.

Chase Pepper, C.S.C.

July 6

We never have enough of good hands. The humblest and most unpretending, if animated with a good will, will give glory to God.

—Fr. Edward Sorin, C.S.C.

WHEN MEETING SUCCESSFUL people, I tend to come away with one of two very general impressions. Some strike me as overbearing, carrying perhaps a prideful confidence stemming from their successes. Other individuals are unpretentious, seemingly more attentive to conflicting viewpoints and thus less imposing. By most standards, both types of people are equally intelligent, confident, and passionate about their work. Yet more often than not, the less pretentious people are those who leave the more lasting positive marks on us.

Successful people who exhibit humility and lack pretense are not necessarily meek or dispassionate. As talented and as important as they may actually be, they recognize that others could fulfill the same duties with equal proclivity. Thus, they bring a certain strength and honesty to daily interactions that communicate the conviction that their truest, most confident self abides in something greater than their work. Simply put, they recognize their transient place in the world.

We, too, are called to live with such humble conviction, always animated by a good will that seeks to do God's. Both our humility and our conviction deepen as we come to recognize God's omnipresent goodness. In seeking a greater good than our own, we allow God to transform our will into our most prominent, yet unpretentious, quality. In this way, we are given the blessed opportunity to be humble prophets heralding Jesus' message through the very work of our hands.

Jesus Alonso, C.S.C.

July 7

Oh, the folly of the world! Oh, the wisdom of the Cross! Here is our study, our hope.
—Fr. Edward Sorin, C.S.C.

IN MY FIRST parish assignment, one of the first home visits I ever made was to a woman with a degenerative disease that had liquefied her muscles. By the time of my visit, she had been reduced to unbearable pain as her spine compacted upon itself. She looked at me and said, "Deacon, Jesus did not suffer as I have suffered. Three hours on a cross is nothing compared to twenty years of intense pain. Why do I suffer so?"

Pious platitudes seemed empty and even cruel to speak, yet I sputtered them anyway, desperate for something to say. Watching me, she shook her head and said, "Oh, Deacon, stop. I suffer. I don't know why bad things happen in our world. But this I know—God didn't cause this suffering. He's the one who gets me through it." She then described how God's love had filled her through the years of her illness and how his abiding presence comforted her, even as she ranted at him.

In life, we will all face crosses of our own. The world tells us to avoid, sanitize, or eliminate them. But should we shirk our cross, we will miss the opportunity to encounter Love itself and experience God's gentle embrace. There is no need to romanticize human suffering or make of it a virtue. But when, in faith, we accept our suffering and shoulder the burdens of our lives, we open our hearts to God. Such is the hope of the Cross—the ultimate school of love.

Gary S. Chamberland, C.S.C.

July 8

We must be responsible—each of us—for the conformity of our lives to the Gospel and for the harmony of our ministries with the mission of Christ. The Spirit of the Lord may choose any of us to speak the truths we all need to hear. Our vow of obedience itself obliges each of us take appropriate responsibility for the common good.

—Holy Cross *Constitutions*

CONFORMITY, OBEDIENCE, OBLIGATION, common good—generally speaking, these are not popular words in today's Western culture. In order to make it in the world, we are trained at a young age to be self-reliant, ruggedly individualistic, and independent in our thoughts and actions. As a result, unfortunately, it is easy to be duped into believing that life and the world is all about me. Nothing, though, could be further from the gospel truth. A true follower of Jesus Christ knows that it cannot be just about me. It can only be about us, together.

From the beginning, Blessed Moreau aligned the mission of the Congregation of Holy Cross with that of Jesus Christ. For his mission to be successful, Blessed Moreau knew that he needed men and women united and rooted in their faith, so that they would have the courage to preach and to witness to the gospel truth. He realized early on that it had to be more than just about him. It had to be about everyone, together.

As we look at the dire needs of our world, our planet, and the human family, we cannot think just about "me" any longer. More so than ever, and for the sake of the Gospel, we must take appropriate responsibility for the common good so that together we can ensure our future.

Paul Bednarczyk, C.S.C.

We live our consecration in many lands and cultures. Our commitment is the same wherever we are, but we seek to express it in a manner rooted in and enriched by the varying contexts and cultures in which we live. In this way, we hope to make our witness and service more effective for the kingdom.

—Holy Cross *Constitutions*

IN HER BOOK *Out of Africa*, Karen Blixen wrote, "I had a farm in Africa." If I were to begin my own book, I would write, "I have a family in Africa."

That, however, was not the first thought that crossed my mind when, over lunch, the provincial asked me to consider something "out of left field," as he described it. "We need someone with seminary experience to run our formation house in Nairobi, Kenya." There were so many reasons why it seemed crazy to entertain the idea. I had no experience of the culture. I had only spent ten days in East Africa. Most likely, I would have to learn Swahili. Yet after much conversation, prayer, and reflection, I said yes.

Although there is plenty that I have found in Africa to be foreign to me, there is much more I have found to be familiar, common, shared. There is no greater example than the Holy Cross community. Although our skin color, English accents, and tastes in food—let alone in football teams—are different, we share the same consecration of our lives to God and the same zeal to serve God's people. They and I are clearly family—family in Holy Cross and family in God.

One of the greatest gifts we in Holy Cross and we in the Church can give our fractured world is precisely this sense of family that transcends the undeniable differences of nation, race, and culture. When we cross cultural, linguistic, and other barriers to work together out of our common faith in a common mission, we become the first rays, as one lifelong missionary put it, "of the dawning of a new age, where diverse people live and work side by side, where the lion and lamb lie down together."

Patrick Neary, C.S.C.

July 10

Certainly we celebrate the love and affection of the people we love. Even greater is our joy and love toward Jesus who has loved us so much more.
—Blessed Basil Moreau

YES, WE ARE loved by those who love us, but it is in experiencing this love from others that we also experience a greater love, the love of God that surrounds us and challenges us to go beyond what we are content to do.

As a Holy Cross priest, I have found love from others and from God present at every step of my ministry. This was certainly the case at my very first funeral, when I was unsure of how to minister to the family and the larger community. Just how do we reach out to many different people who are all suffering from the aftershocks of a double murder? I had to rely on the love that I had received from others and trust that Jesus would guide me. I do not remember what I said, but I do know that the love of Jesus did embrace all of us during the tragedy.

Love was also present when I later moved to Mexico to minister among the people there. Just how do we reach out to people with a language, culture, and way of living so different from our own? It was the love that I had received and given in my previous ministries that helped me to move on to this next challenge in my faith journey, and it was the love I encountered there that helped me to fulfill it.

Jesus continuously provides all of us with opportunities to walk in his steps, to face the unknown, and to share the love that we have received from him and from others in new and unexpected ways. It's when we have shared this love—his love—with others that we realize just how much love Jesus shares with us.

Joseph Moyer, C.S.C.

July 11

You can appreciate the beauty and glory of your calling if you but know how to make yourselves worthy of it by faithfully imitating the hidden and public life of our Lord.

—Blessed Basil Moreau

IN THE SIXTH century, St. Benedict wrote his timeless rule with its motto *Ora et Labora*—Pray and Work. This phrase sums up the totality of the life of Jesus. We know from the gospels that he spent long periods in prayer from which he emerged to be about his Father's work of teaching, healing, and sharing the good news of God's unconditional love.

It is rather easy to imitate the public life of Jesus, at least in the working aspect. No matter what our vocational calling, there will always be ample work to be done. The problem is that the work can be grueling and demanding, and it can get in the way of our appreciating the beauty and the glory of our vocations. It's only when we step back as Jesus did and enter into conversation with our loving God that we can gain the true perspective of our callings.

The true beauty and glory of our callings is that they come from God. Therefore, we can look upon our quiet, hidden time with him as an opportunity to report back on what we are doing during our public works. This quiet time of reporting back is very important for our spiritual growth. In the quiet of prayer, we will find God waiting with joy and with love to hear of our best and most successful undertakings. In the quiet of prayer, we will also find God with his hands open to receive all of the burdens of our most challenging and discouraging endeavors.

George Schmitz, C.S.C.

Adore, praise, and bless the God of generosity who dispenses his graces so abundantly. Lose not a moment that God has given you to work out your salvation.
—Fr. Jacques Dujarie

I VISITED EAST Africa one summer with a group of Holy Cross priests and several of our lay collaborators. After Sunday Mass at the parish in Bugembe, Uganda, we were led on a walking tour of the neighborhood. Several families welcomed us into their homes and gave us food, cool drinks, and a place to sit for a while. We made whatever conversation we could muster in their broken English or through an interpreter. One elderly gentleman, who lived alone, had only the shade from a single banana tree to offer us. But his wide, toothless smile and gracious manner made us feel like royal dignitaries.

The generosity of the poor is one of the most humbling things I have experienced. Time and again, in spite of our limitations and failures, people who know the God of generosity open their hearts and homes to us. When I was a new seminarian for Holy Cross, our class went on a retreat led by the late Sr. Kathy Reichert, C.S.C. The frame for the retreat was Jesus' comment on the Widow's Mite. Sr. Kathy spoke of the call all of us receive in the shade of the Cross to give not from our surplus, but from our want.

Fr. Dujarie and Blessed Moreau began an ambitious work with very little at hand. Something impelled them to forsake comfortable lives and take up the urgent needs around them.

The flip side of Blessed Moreau's confidence in Divine Providence was a deep, sustaining gratitude to the God who provides. Gratitude is the foundational disposition of Jews and Christians, the fountain from which all virtue and all authentic progress in the spiritual life springs. All depends upon God's generosity. All is gift.

Mike Connors, C.S.C.

July 13

At the foot of the cross, we were so much the object of thought of both mother and Son that the Savior looking down on her with love as he was dying spoke to her a last time. He spoke, not of himself, nor of her, but of us only. He presented us to Mary in the person of John as he said to her: "Woman, behold your son."
—Blessed Basil Moreau

WITHIN MY FIRST months of priesthood, I was called on several times to baptize infants facing serious health problems. To say these are heartbreaking moments is a huge understatement. Of course, the one person in the chapel or hospital room most intensely focused on the health—bodily and spiritual—of her newborn is that little one's mom.

One night, I was called to the children's hospital to baptize a little boy, the son of longtime parishioners, who had been born with a critical condition. I hurried over and arrived just ahead of his surgery. Without much time, we began the rite, and I asked one of the young doctors, who happened to be Catholic, to stand as godmother. Mom and Dad never took their eyes off their son. There were no dry eyes during the prayer: "We now ask God to give this child new life in abundance through water and the Holy Spirit." He was baptized, and the Church welcomed her newest member. What could have been a terrible moment of despair was really a moment of profound grace, attested to, above all, by the strength and hope of the little boy's parents. His mother would never have thought of leaving his side, and every thought in her world disappeared in the light of her baby's soul.

My own mom, one of the strongest and most loving women I know, has taught me that such single-hearted devotion to her children is just how a mother's heart is hard-wired. Mary would never have thought of leaving her Son's Cross. Her heart broke for her boy, but she was with him. Her eyes remained on Jesus until the end—just as his remained on us.

David Halm, C.S.C.

July 14

May we all, more than ever, find in each other's edifying example an efficient means of sanctification to the last.

—Fr. Edward Sorin, C.S.C.

AS A BROTHER of Holy Cross for more than fifty years, I have found that Fr. Sorin's words about edifying examples bring back memories of many people who, by the grace of God, helped me along the path to sanctification.

I have only to reflect back on my early assignments in houses with forty or more religious. As I think back now, it was the retired brothers who had spent many days and years on the missions or in the classroom who gave us younger religious the greatest example—how they were devoted to personal and communal prayer, how they were faithful to our community life, and how thoughtful and kind they were with everyone living with them. These older religious were saints in our midst. I only wish that we would have taken the time then to look and follow their examples of living the vows a little bit more.

Then, through the years, there were so many lay men and women living with burdens often unknown to us religious. They labored in silence with children who were handicapped and parents who needed their care while living with wages that barely covered their expenses. Many times these laypersons showed much greater dedication to our mission than we did. These people often saw the brothers and priests as examples to be followed, but if the truth be known, they were the examples we had to follow in reaching our own personal sanctification.

We just have to sit down and reflect for a while, and we will all find a multitude of edifying examples, both in the past and present, to follow along our own roads to sanctification.

Charles P. McBride, C.S.C.

July 15

At the sight of regions so much in want of evangelical laborers and so widely open to their zeal, who would not address our Heavenly Father in the words of the Lord himself: "Pray to the Lord of the harvest that he send forth laborers into his harvest"?

—Fr. Edward Sorin, C.S.C.

"FATHER," HE SAID, "remember the retreats you used to give us? They really helped me to pray and find God in my life." I was touched by the young man's memory of those retreats because I had not worked at the Holy Cross parish in Nairobi, Kenya, for over a decade. He continued, "Now I belong to a prayer group we have just formed to pray for the needs of others. They made me the leader, but we don't know how to begin. I was thinking, Father, that you might come and teach us to pray as you did years ago. How can we pray for others if we are not praying for ourselves?"

His experience of God had given his life meaning and hope. Now, in faith and zeal, he wanted to share with others what God had given him. That is how we become laborers in God's harvest: we get a taste of God's love and mercy, and it drives us to satisfy the hunger for God we see all around us. It drives us to labor with Jesus.

As this young man learned, praying for God to send out laborers is not enough. We need to pray that we ourselves may hear God's call to labor with him. We are all called. Whether this call is to join a prayer group, raise a family, or be a priest or religious, we can join Jesus in bringing in the harvest. There is nothing more satisfying than when our hunger for God meets the hunger of another.

Frank Murphy, C.S.C.

July 16

The merit of the small virtues—and I would even say their superiority to more dazzling actions—lies in their requiring a more constant mortification and a more solid charity and humility.

—Blessed Basil Moreau

WHEN I ARRIVED at my first assignment as a priest, I rang and rang the doorbell of the rectory, and then I rang it again. Finally, one of our priests answered the door. He really seemed put out that I had disturbed him. He gave me my room number and walked away. I figured he was just having a bad day and didn't think much more of it. Much to my surprise, almost twenty years later, when I was elected provincial, that same priest congratulated me and apologized for the way he had treated me that first day. I wondered if that small action had been bothering him all those years.

I myself must confess that, coming out of the seminary, I was a type A personality: everything had to be done yesterday. After ordination, while working in the African American community in the South and later while serving in Mexico, the people of God taught me that it is the people who matter. I started to slow down. The person you are with, whomever he or she might be, is the person who really counts at that moment.

Like so many in Holy Cross, I have traveled far and wide doing our apostolic work. I have crossed many borders and experienced many cultures. Yet wherever I have been, small virtues have left fond memories: "see how they love one another." A simple thank you for a gift received, a helping hand extended in need, a shoulder to lean on, the offer of a prayer, a smile—all these are little things that make a big difference. "Amazing grace, how sweet the sound" leads to "precious Lord, take my hand" and "just a closer walk with thee." We can indeed "reach out and touch somebody's hand" to walk together as brothers and sisters in Christ Jesus.

Leonard J. Collins, C.S.C.

July 17

To spend ourselves and be spent for the needs of neighbors; to be available and cheerful as a friend in Holy Cross and to give witness while others hesitate; to stand by duty when it has become all burden and no delight . . . community too can draw us nearer Calvary.

—Holy Cross *Constitutions*

A LEGENDARY HOLY CROSS priest, Fr. Charles Sheedy, C.S.C., left a legacy of many witty and deeply spiritual one-liners. One of his best went like this: "Community life is all about just showing up." Family life is not so different. To come to meals on time and disposed to enter into conversation, to be well dressed and ready to leave for Sunday church, to show up at weddings, funerals, birthdays, and anniversaries speaks volumes about our love for our families.

If, in addition to simply showing up, we can help out with community tasks and carry the burdens of others, it is a bonus. If we are able to show up, forgetting the grudges and wounds of the past, and be polite and interested with even our unfriendly neighbor, this graciousness will recall the kind of unconditional acceptance God gives each of us every day. Just to do our jobs, completing what is required even if it is not done quite perfectly, remains a mighty contribution.

Our world would grow in peace and love if we all just did our jobs, and it would be all the better if we did them humbly and kindly. For indeed, none of us stands alone. We support one another by our very presence and by our fidelity to what is asked of us. And that will mean, at times, that we will find ourselves at the foot of the crosses of others. But we need hardly speak. Just to stand alongside will be enough.

Nicholas Ayo, C.S.C.

July 18

There stood by the Cross of Jesus his mother Mary, who knew grief and was a Lady of Sorrows. She is our special patroness, a woman who bore much she could not understand and who stood fast. To her many sons and daughters, whose devotions ought to bring them often to her side, she tells much of this daily cross and its daily hope.

—Holy Cross *Constitutions*

SHE WAS A twenty-three-year-old mother, and this was her firstborn. The child was fine his first two days of life, but within hours of going home he had to return to the hospital not as a newborn but as a life-or-death patient. For seven months he continued on the edge of life, and every day his mother was there. On the eleventh day of the seventh month, it became obvious that he would not survive. His mother was distraught. Within moments, the doctor came into the room and advised that she withdraw the many tubes that were keeping her beloved son alive.

She looked to me for an answer, but all I could do was grasp her hand and put my arm around her. She wailed, moving back and forth. My heart ached for her. Then, with the calm that only grace and faith can give, she looked at me and then at the doctor and said, "I have had him these seven wonderful months. It is time to give him back to God." I could hardly control my tears. I walked her to the crib of her firstborn, arms around her shoulders. She reached down, kissed her beloved son, held his hand, and began a slow prayer, silent but more sincere and profound than any prayer I had experienced. Then, as if to confound all who were present, this woman of sorrows quietly uttered, "Into your hands I commend him." As if previously orchestrated, the tiny body with a full head of hair and tubes protruding looked directly at his mother, smiled, and breathed himself into the arms of God.

John Gleason, C.S.C.

We must prove by our behavior that the Savior does nourish us by his Word, just as we must prove by our actions, after having received Holy Communion, that he has nourished us with his body and his blood. It is not enough just to gather from his heavenly teachings some vague longings or weak feelings, even strong but fleeting ones, or phlegmatic emotions. Just staying put and enjoying these sentiments is no proof that the Lord has spoken to us.

—Blessed Basil Moreau

I STILL REMEMBER my first day in accounting as part of my MBA. As I sat in the back of class, I quickly wondered, "How did this become my new normal?" Soon, I was questioning, "Do I have what it takes to complete this program?"

Just two days later, I met with the religious superior at Notre Dame, Fr. Jim King, C.S.C., to seek permission to leave the program. Fr. Jim listened and let me voice my concerns and grapple with my fears. He then looked over and assured me that I had what it would take to succeed. Fr. Jim reminded me that this type of training would ultimately help me serve the people of God in new and unexpected ways. In the end, he said no to my fear-laden request because he realized the importance of the journey.

My journey from those fearful days to graduation was at times painfully slow and at other times a great blessing. Times of grappling with quantitative courses, managing stress, and forming wonderful friendships all flood my mind. I am grateful for these experiences because they required that I develop new talents by taking risks and trusting that God would send people to help.

Blessed Moreau understood that our response to the love we encounter in prayer is action. Faith-based action requires stepping outside of our comfort zone. Whether intended or not, playing it safe elicits a reliance on ourselves and gives only partial consideration to how God is working. Stepping outside of our routines and responding to God's invitation in a more convicted manner opens us to new possibilities otherwise unimaginable. Living in such a way will be seen by some as outlandish and foolhardy, but to God it will be the proper remedy for a world in need.

Peter McCormick, C.S.C.

July 20

A pilgrimage is no pleasure party; it is essentially a praying movement, an earnest search after divine assistance and protection.

—Fr. Edward Sorin, C.S.C.

WHILE STUDYING ABROAD as an undergraduate in London, I visited some fellow Notre Dame students who were taking classes that year in Rome. We had a wonderful time, sharing delicious pasta, gelato, and vino. Of course, we also visited the important landmarks in the Eternal City.

While at the Roman Colosseum, I saw an elderly woman holding a little prayer book and touching the walls of that ancient edifice. I was stopped dead in my tracks. In the middle of tour groups yelling and cameras clicking, she was praying. How right, I thought. The Colosseum was indeed more than an archaeological treasure or an architectural marvel. It was a holy site. Here, hundreds of Christians were tortured and martyred for their faith in Jesus, and their blood had hallowed the very ground on which we were standing. How right this woman was to treat her visit as a pilgrimage and not merely as sightseeing.

As important as a good vacation can be for our mental and physical health, a pilgrimage changes a mere "pleasure party" into a movement, both physical and interior, toward deeper intimacy with God. When we are on pilgrimage, like that woman at the Colosseum who touched the stone wall and prayed for the intercession of the martyrs, we touch the presence of God in our world and ask our brothers and sisters in Christ, living and dead, to pray with and for us for God's protection. And how much more refreshing that divine assistance is than any vacation or sightseeing.

Stephen Koeth, C.S.C.

July 21

O Jesus, who has said, "Let the little children come unto me," and has inspired me with the desire to bring them to you, deign to bless my vocation, to assist me in my work, and to clothe me with the spirit of strength, charity, and humility, in order that nothing may turn me aside from your service.

—Fr. Jacques Dujarie

DURING BANGLADESH'S LIBERATION War in 1971, my whole family had to flee from our home to a safe place in another village for several months. The people hosting us were cooperative and helpful, but as a young child in an unknown and tense situation, I used to quarrel with the kids there. To get us to stop fighting, my mother would tell us how "Jesus loves all the children and calls them to go to him." It is the same message about Jesus I remembered from my first grade teacher, Sr. Mary Dolorous, S.M.R.A. Amazingly, it worked. While the war waged around us, we were safe and secure as we learned to believe in and rely on Jesus, who protects and saves his children.

These two holy women were the major influences that led me to consecrate myself to Jesus in religious life. They took an active part in my life, leading me closer to Jesus. I believe they are in heaven now. I pray to follow their examples while I teach the kids in our schools in Bangladesh.

In our present day, we speak of a vocation crisis in religious life. If we as the Church are to help raise up the next generation of religious brothers, sisters, and priests to give themselves in service, we as parents, teachers, and mentors must take active roles in the lives of the young. Whatever hardships they may face, we must help them believe by our teaching and example that Jesus loves them and calls them to himself. Then Jesus will raise up new servants inspired by his Spirit.

Bikash Victor D'Rozario, C.S.C.

July 22

To maintain ourselves in the sublime vow of chastity we must, as St. Peter says, make our souls chaste by obedience to charity. This means yielding ourselves more and more generously to the law of supernatural love, which refers all things to God and undertakes and suffers everything for his glory.

—Blessed Basil Moreau

ALL OF OUR souls long for union with God. And this searching, longing, and desiring ultimately can only be fulfilled in God. In grasping at images to try to capture this deepest of human yearnings, mystics from the Old Testament onward have turned to the image of a bride longing for her bridegroom. In using such sensual imagery, the mystics point to the true intensity with which our souls ache for God.

Blessed Moreau knew this intense yearning of the soul for God, and he taught his spiritual sons and daughters the language of making our souls chaste and ever faithful in seeking God. Blessed Moreau did not dwell on the sacrificial nature of the vow of chastity; he invited his religious to experience the vow as a state of being that allowed a person to be more generous in service and to keep God at the forefront of everything in life. And, as history testifies, this vow has allowed Blessed Moreau and his band of men not to be concerned with comfort and personal needs but instead to spread the Gospel for the sake of the kingdom, making God known, loved, and served.

Our coming to know, love, and serve God and then making him known, loved, and served by others is a pathway open for all of us to ever deeper mystical union with him. It is the pathway of charity, that in love for our Lord we might be generous in serving our neighbor. In yielding ourselves in this service, we will be ever more united with the God of love.

Tom Eckert, C.S.C.

July 23

It is at the altar that, in order to console the troubles of our exile, he offers us a manna more appealing than the manna of the desert; it is there that he gives us his flesh to eat and his blood to drink; there that he becomes present in such a way within our soul, his heart speaking to us with all of its affection, and bringing our own hearts to beat with his.

—Blessed Basil Moreau

By God's grace alone, I am a priest of Jesus Christ. "No one takes this honor upon himself but only when called by God, just as Aaron was" (Heb 5:4). The letter to the Hebrews thus describes God's initiative in Jesus, the great eternal High Priest, in the Temple priesthood before him and in all of us ordained priests today.

When I genuflect before the altar, the first gesture of the great Eucharistic celebration, I am reminded to put aside my worries and cares. I let them mingle with everyone's troubles, with those of all the parched and hungry souls who have gathered. For we priests are not untouched by the troubles of our world. We trudge as every person does, stumbling through the confusing chaos of our times.

After reverencing with a kiss the sacred table of Jesus' sacrifice, I face his devoted followers in faith. They seek from Jesus and from me—because I am his priest—wisdom far beyond my reach and a fragment of divine bread. He is traveling with us. From the altar, the words I speak must touch human hearts desiring to love as Jesus loved. The Body and Precious Blood must reach into those same yearning hearts to calm their trials.

Jesus, through me, offers his people what is needed for the pilgrimage: divine wisdom and holy food. When I kiss again his altar at the end of Mass, it cannot be a Judas kiss. With all believers, it must be a holy kiss, the simultaneous, rhythmic beating of his heart and ours. We all go our way, sent to change the world, carrying in our hearts the new manna, the bread from heaven. By God's grace alone and at his initiative, we step to the beat of divine love.

Bob Epping, C.S.C.

July 24

Making ourselves all to all must be learned and practiced at home, in order to gain all to Christ, in whom there is neither Jew nor Greek, all having been equally

redeemed in his precious blood. We know there is no
difference of persons with God.
—Fr. Edward Sorin, C.S.C.

DISCIPLESHIP BEGINS AT Baptism, but our experience of redemption is deepened by our life experiences. Ministering on three continents over the years—trying to be all to all—I have seen the possibilities of true human community. Though people speak different languages and have different religious beliefs, there is a commonality that makes us all brothers and sisters. Muslim and Hindu children living in poverty in India and Bangladesh can still smile with hope. African children love to sing and dance to celebrate their joy of learning. Children around the world are anxious to enter the adult community in spite of society's strange prejudices and preferences that confuse them.

The possibility of true human community, our hope for God's redemption, begins with all children deserving to start out on life's journey in a community of faith, hope, and love: learning to share and not simply compete, learning to accept rather than judge, learning to develop their own minds and hearts and not just absorb the habits of others, learning to pray and work and not just expect all to be given to them. Ultimately, all children need to learn that there is no real difference of persons in God's eyes. There is enough divine love for everyone.

Holy Cross men and women and their legions of lay collaborators and students—parents and children together—are fulfilling this vision of education and community in homes, schools, and parishes around the world. It is a Gospel vision from the

Good News of Jesus Christ. And it summons every person to discipleship, for we all have a part to play in God's kingdom.

David E. Schlaver, C.S.C.

July 25

Let us march with courage under the banner of the Cross.

—Fr. Edward Sorin, C.S.C.

IN THE EARLY hours of July 25, 2000, on the Feast of St. James, three Holy Cross priests and their driver were hit by gunfire directed at their vehicle by insurgents in northeast India. Bullets struck Fr. Victor Crasta, C.S.C., in the heart and head, but he prayed aloud, "Forgive them, Lord, for they do not know what they are doing." As the brave son of Holy Cross breathed his last, he encouraged his fellow priests to move ahead and stay true to their mission.

I was one of those priests in the car. I also was hit by the insurgents' bullets but survived the attack. Holy Cross's profound faith, courage, and hope in the face of the Cross give me the strength to move on in spite of losing an eye in this assault. Lack of sight in one eye reminds me every day that it is the Lord who works through me and through us all. As St. Paul reminds us, God's grace works through each of us, especially when we are weak.

I continue to live my life in Holy Cross, trusting in Divine Providence and in hope. In this life, each of us faces challenges.

Some of them are small, and others are large and difficult to bear. Fr. Sorin reminds us that these daily crosses, if we but bear them with courage, will strengthen us to be effective disciples of Jesus, whom we continually experience and radiate in our lives. The death of a loved one, a car accident that cripples, the diagnosis of an incurable cancer, or the deviant behavior of a son or a daughter are all heavy crosses that some among us may have to bear. The Cross, however, becomes light when we are rooted in the Lord and march under his banner.

Paul Pudussery, C.S.C.

July 26

Let us enter into the Sacred Heart of Jesus forever loving and so prolific in good deeds, especially those of us honored to be priests and charged with bringing others into his heart. Let us celebrate the holy mysteries within the Heart of Jesus; let us recite our office there; let us hear the confessions of our penitents there; and let us proclaim God's Word there. In a word, let us fulfill all our duties there, and he will permeate the work of our ministry with the most abundant blessings.

—Blessed Basil Moreau

I WAS ALREADY in bed when the phone rang. It was an urgent request from a nearby hospital. I was on call at the parish where I live in residence, yet I had already worked a long day at Family

Theater Productions, my full-time assignment. I grudgingly got dressed, grabbed my kit with oils and stole, and drove to the hospital. Even at midnight, parking was hard to find in the West Los Angeles area.

Cranky and grumbling, I found my way to the wing and waited for someone to let me into the ICU unit. As I got close to the dying patient's room, I saw a crowd gathered, spilling out of the door, many crying. The gravity and need of the situation hit me. I needed an attitude adjustment, quick. I ducked into a storage area. I pulled my rosary from pocket. The little medal in the center showed an image of the Sacred Heart of Jesus. Looking at the image, I prayed, "Lord, my heart is tired and stressed. Those people in that room do not need to deal with my petty temper and fatigue. Please use my heart to show your compassion." Immediately, I sensed Jesus replying, "No, you use my heart."

When our own life is weak, we are invited to enter into his. The Sacred Heart of Jesus is self-giving love, mercy, compassion, and hope. From these come gifts of wisdom, healing, and comfort—a flow of grace surpassing our limitations and weakness. "You use my heart."

I prayed a decade of the Rosary, then calmly and confidently went to the room, gathered that grieving family in prayer, and anointed the woman in the presence of her children and loved ones. Amid all the tears came a sense of peace and love and hope.

David Guffey, C.S.C.

In consecrated obedience we join with our brothers in community and with the whole church in the search for God's will.

—Holy Cross *Constitutions*

IN WRITING TO Mother Mary of the Seven Dolors, Blessed Moreau advised, "Let us abandon ourselves to Divine Providence. You can be certain that you are where God wants you to be." I wasn't always sure about this. But over the years, I have discovered that such assurance can only come in living each day in abandonment to Divine Providence. Consecrated obedience is about conversion, conforming one's life to Christ—for it is God's will that I seek, not my own.

It is in the search for his will with my brothers in community that I am guarded against the deceptions of my own self-will. For the community can see and call forth in me gifts and talents I may not have seen in myself. Consecrated obedience is the path inviting me to move beyond self-will and to trust that God is speaking through the very human means of a community, calling me beyond myself even though I may not fully understand it at the time. Obedience invites me to set aside my agenda and to allow God's to take center stage.

Whatever our calling in life, we like to believe that we are capable of thinking for ourselves and deciding what is best. Whether lived as consecrated obedience in religious life or as the obedience of faith, obedience remains a choice made in love in order to liberate ourselves from self-will. It is through our openness to trusted friends, wise mentors, and confidants that we move beyond self-interest and become attentive to the voice of God speaking in our lives. As we respond to this voice and enter ever more fully into the life to which we have been called, we discover that we are capable of more than we ever thought possible.

Ken Molinaro, C.S.C.

July 28

God gives so much more help to the faithful ones, the zealous ones for even the smallest things. Then grace becomes abundant. It gives strength to our courage, and courage strengthened by watchfulness and fervor leads to the greatest virtues.

—Blessed Basil Moreau

DURING MY DEACONATE in Holy Cross, I once stood over-whelmed in the ruins of my father's home. He and his family had been murdered during the Rwandan genocide. My father had been a catechist and was my only family member who encouraged me to become a priest. Now, pouring out my anger and resentment through my tears, I prayed, "Lord, let me bury my father when I become a priest." I was asking for a miracle because most people had been dumped in mass graves.

After my ordination, I returned to Rwanda to celebrate a Mass of thanksgiving. At the end of Mass, a man approached me and led me and the other survivors in my family to a mass grave where he claimed my father was buried. As we began to unearth the grave, the first remains that we uncovered were my father's, his identification card still intact. I could hardly believe it. As the priest my father always hoped I would be, I then celebrated a funeral Mass for him, giving him the send-off in the faith that he deserved. My prayers fulfilled, I exclaimed, "Indeed, with God nothing is impossible!"

In my ministry as a priest, I meet many who have suffered so much that they doubt God's love for them or even his very existence. There are those who remain faithful to the Lord and find strength and courage in him to weather the storm. Like St. Paul, it is when they are weak that they become strong through the abundance of God's grace. Their bravery and perseverance inspire us to do the same.

James Burasa, C.S.C.

July 29

What is true of a palace whose foundation has been laid and which is rising gradually to completion is verified, likewise, in a great work of charity. It is not one person alone who builds; nor is it one stone, or one single beam of wood which forms it. Each worker contributes something from his or her own trade; each stone is cut to fit into its one appointed place; and each piece of wood is arranged and placed so as to enhance the general effect of the entire building.
—Blessed Basil Moreau

FROM OUR FOUNDING, we as Holy Cross have gone forth together—to work together, to found institutions together, to pray together, to bring the message of the Gospel in various corners of the world together. What we in Holy Cross have accomplished, we have accomplished together. This is the essence of our religious life.

As a Holy Cross priest, I have served at both the University of Notre Dame and the University of Portland. Whatever work I have done, whatever things I may have accomplished, I have done so as part of a community, a community of faith-filled, prayerful, talented, and diverse men who have come together as Holy Cross. In that community, I find strength and hope and inspiration. In that community, I have been blessed.

Having served in leadership at these institutions, I have been privileged to witness the fruits of many Holy Cross men and lay colleagues who toil together as educators in the faith. Alone, each one of us probably could have accomplished little, but together we have used the gifts God has given us—including our idiosyncrasies—and we have accomplished much. Most importantly, in accord with the vision of Blessed Moreau, we have worked together to educate both the minds and the hearts of our students. This is the character of any great work of charity: it is the outcome of individual talents brought together for the greater good.

E. William Beauchamp, C.S.C.

July 30

Yes, all who are deeply conscious of the real presence make it visible in a thousand different ways in their external behavior, their movements, their posture, and especially by where they look, keeping their sight devoutly on the sacred host or modestly lowered. In a word, they appear convincing and convinced, edifying the faithful and bringing them to reverence this glorious sacrament.

—Blessed Basil Moreau

WHEN IN THE seminary, I spent a summer in Canto Grande, Peru, teaching at our secondary school. Despite having a substantial background in pedagogy and Spanish, the idea of working in a different culture was very intimidating. I was not sure how well I would do or if I would enjoy it, but I prayed that in all things God would work through me.

I wasted no time getting to know my students and their families. I learned about their interests, customs, favorite sports, and music groups. Before I knew it, the fears that I had arrived with were transformed into moments of grace because I was focusing my energies not on anxieties but on relationships—relationships rooted in Christ. The summer flew by, and soon I was headed back to the United States. My time in Canto Grande remains one of the most rewarding and life-giving experiences I have ever had.

It was very difficult to leave Peru. I had given all I could. I had invested so much in those children. I wondered what they would do after graduation. I wondered if they would ever break free of poverty. I wondered when—or if—I would see them again. Yet on that flight back, I realized that we would be forever connected. In Christ, all are drawn together. It is the Eucharist that gives us a real, daily encounter with the risen Lord and with all those we care for (and don't care for!)—those near and far, alive and deceased. In the power of this sacrament, time meets eternity, heaven unites with earth, grace is poured into our hearts, and we are transformed into one body, becoming more like him whom we receive, bound together in love.

Dennis Strach II, C.S.C.

July 31

A soldier of the Cross expects to rest only when under the sod. Indeed, a very serious task stands before us to meet the views of Divine Providence.

—Fr. Edward Sorin, C.S.C.

WE IN HOLY CROSS have never been particularly good at waiting around for God to get something done. This is not to say that what we have accomplished and what we continue to endeavor has not been, from beginning to end, from inspiration to completion, primarily God's work. It's just that, seemingly, we like to try to quicken God's hand from time to time.

We have taken our cue from Abraham, who through love of his people and faith in God's goodness bargained regularly with God. Memorably, as God prepared to destroy Sodom, it was Abraham who got the Lord to hold off in the name of forty, then thirty, then twenty, then ten just people. Moses later would follow suit, changing Yahweh's intent to destroy the stiff-necked Israelites with a last-minute plea bargain. We spend our days and nights like Jacob, wrestling with God's angel, demanding that God bless our work, then limping off—but often with blessings in hand. Perhaps one of our patronesses should be the woman in Luke's gospel who refuses Jesus' refusal to heal her daughter. Instead, she stands before Jesus and, as Notre Dame professor Frank O'Malley once said about the task of any great teacher, "demands to be engaged."

The life in Holy Cross into which we seek to invite those entrusted to us is one of holy impatience, of restlessness. Passivity—not to say contemplation or gentleness—is not an option for all soldiers of the Cross. We are restless in our pursuit to make God known, loved, and served. All the while, we recall that "unless the Lord build the house, they labor in vain who build" (Ps 127:1).

Timothy Scully, C.S.C.

August 1

Go on, my brave little band, with your noble work of gratitude; be just and honest; make good returns; give in proportion to what you receive.

—Fr. Edward Sorin, C.S.C.

WHILE IN THE desert of Arizona, near the place where many immigrants die attempting to cross into the United States, I met a woman named Maria who had crossed the border without papers. She had come north from Guatemala, looking for work so she could provide food and medicine for her family. After stowing away on a freight train for a week, she tried to cross the border three times. The first time, her *coyote*-guide attempted to rape her. The second time, gangs mugged her and took everything she had. The third time, she walked across the treacherous desert in 120-degree heat, ran out of food and water, suffered heat exhaustion, and began to vomit. Ultimately, border-patrol agents detained her and sent her back over the border.

After listening to her story, I asked her what she would say if she had fifteen minutes to talk with God. She said, "First of all, I do not have fifteen minutes to talk with God. In my journey, I have felt that God is always with me, and I am always talking with him. But if I could see him face-to-face, the first thing I would do is thank him for having given me so much and for having been so good to me." In Maria's eyes, her difficult life, from leaving home in Guatemala to attempting repeatedly to find work in the United States, was all an act of gratitude. To praise God amid such adversity is a source of continual inspiration to give in proportion to what we have received.

Daniel G. Groody, C.S.C.

We want to live our vows in such a way that our lives will call into question the fascinations of our world: pleasure, wealth and power. Prophets stand before the world as signs of that which has enduring value, and prophets speak and act in the world as companions of the Lord in the service of his kingdom. We pray to live our vows well enough to offer such witness and service.

—Holy Cross *Constitutions*

I REMEMBER WELL the day of my profession of first vows in Holy Cross. The twelve of us young men had filed into the church and were very excited for what we were about to do. The priest giving the homily—a wise Holy Cross religious who had lived with us at the novitiate during the entire year—started his homily with the words, "Gentlemen, this is not about you." I remember thinking, "Did I hear him right? I mean, this is our vow ceremony, isn't it?" He went on to say that today was about what God has done and is doing in our lives. Indeed, our whole life as vowed religious was to be an attempt to imitate the love that God has for each one of us. Through our vows we allow God to work in and through us: let it be done unto me according to your will.

Professing the vows of poverty, chastity, and obedience takes only a moment; living them out is the work of a lifetime. In order to do that well, I must humble myself and let go of my wants, my desires, and my plans. And while this may seem to be a strange and radical thing to do, I know that after living the vowed life in Holy Cross for nearly twenty-five years that I could not imagine being more at peace or content with my life. If I live my vocation well as a religious and priest, I know that I will be helping others to be faithful to their commitments and vows. And other people's faithful living of their commitments and vows inspires me as a religious and priest. In this way, each of us can pray that our very lives become sacraments, signs of God's presence and love.

Bill Wack, C.S.C.

August 3

His Eucharistic presence is the pledge of the God who chose to dwell in the midst of his people. It is especially appropriate then for us to pray in the presence of the reserved Eucharist. Each of us needs the nourishment of at least one half-hour of quiet prayer daily.
—Holy Cross *Constitutions*

IN OUR MAJOR houses, the chapel is the central room; in our rectories, it is sometimes more modest and tucked away. Yet in both, there in the tabernacle the living Lord Jesus is at home with us, and we seek to become more and more at home with him. What a tremendous blessing it is to have a special room where we can welcome Jesus and invite him to stay with us.

When we are faithful to gathering in the chapel with Jesus at dawn and dusk, we have the graced opportunity to remain focused on him, the center of our lives. Alone, in that profound quiet, time is not measured, and intimacy steadfastly grows into oneness—the unity Jesus wished for when he gave us himself in the Eucharist. That is the rhythm of religious at prayer, a rhythm in which time and presence nurture our relationship with the Lord.

Not every home will be privileged to have a chapel in it, nor will every person have the keys to a neighboring church. Nonetheless, Jesus dwells in every Christian home and makes each a domestic church, where he, indeed, is at home with us, and we can grow to be more at home with him. Through time spent in prayer and love shared as family where we live, we can come to discover his presence ever more in every heart and in every home. Then, intimacy and union with Jesus will grow in us each day.

Bob Epping, C.S.C.

August 4

After a good confession we feel interiorly recollected, filled with heavenly internal joy. Sometimes we are even so moved with devotion that our hearts are filled with happy sighs and our eyes with tears. Our spiritual pace is quickened by new ardor.

—Blessed Basil Moreau

CONFESSION IS INTIMIDATING. I have heard people say, "Father, it must be easy for you to go to confession!" I never know if they think that priests don't have as many or as serious sins—a charitable, if naïve assumption—or that since we are around the sacrament so much, it must not worry us as much. I still get nervous before confession, and I imagine that I always will, to some extent.

When we have been away from the sacrament of Reconciliation for too long, however long that may be, our sins slowly pile up like stones on our chests. We may be able to breathe in the Spirit, but it becomes ever more labored. Even if we, by God's grace, avoid the most serious sins, there can still be a kind of spiritual and emotional "shortness of breath." We can be entirely too tolerant of that shallow breathing and let fear or justifications keep us away from the confessional. We lower our gaze, grit our teeth, and pretend that we aren't wheezing.

After receiving absolution, I have felt, at various times, as if a burden had been lifted from my shoulders, chains had been unshackled from my wrists, a malignant tumor had been removed, or R2-D2 had just disabled the garbage compactor. Sometimes, it's not that dramatic. Sometimes, it's just a feeling as if I have been to the dentist for a routine cleaning. Whether dramatic or not, we are sent forth from the sacrament in peace, knowing that we are much more prepared to face the challenges of life as we again breathe in deeply the Holy Spirit.

Jarrod Waugh, C.S.C.

August 5

Through Mary salvation came to this world—such was, and forever will be, the channel through which the divine grace is to flow to us.

—Fr. Edward Sorin, C.S.C.

I REMEMBER THE first time, as a wide-eyed freshman, that I saw the Grotto at the University of Notre Dame as well as Mary's statue atop the Golden Dome. Those images of her made me feel right at home because I had grown up valuing devotion to the Mother of God. Yet it was only in the Congregation of Holy Cross that I encountered Mary as Our Lady of Sorrows.

At first I failed to resonate with this image of Mary. But through my ministry in Holy Cross, I have developed a growing appreciation for her under this title. The more I have worked among those who suffer—whether with recent immigrants, people with AIDS, and struggling families in suburbia or with those in soup kitchens, hospices, nursing homes, and homeless shelters—the more kinship I have felt with Jesus, who suffered and died for us, and with his mother, Mary, who stood with her Son at his Cross.

In God's wisdom and goodness, Mary bore much sadness that she could not understand—she heard the prophecy of Simeon, escaped from Herod's jealous rage, lost her Son for three days and found him in the Temple, met him on the way to Calvary, watched him die on the Cross, held his lifeless body, and ultimately witnessed his burial. And so, in her, our Lord's first and truest believer, we can find a channel of faith and hope in the midst of the crosses of our lives. For through Mary, Our Lady of Sorrows, Christ continually offers his saving grace to all God's children.

Michael Belinsky, C.S.C.

August 6

God has breathed his very breath into us. We speak to God with the yearning and the words of sons to a Father because the Spirit has made us adopted children in Christ. The same Spirit who provides us with the energy and impetus to follow after the Lord and to accept his mission also gives us the desire and the utterance for prayer.

—Holy Cross *Constitutions*

IT WAS THE Feast of the Transfiguration, and I was celebrating Mass at a three-quarters empty church in a village in the west of Ireland. With my voice still echoing, "The peace of the Lord be with you," in the vast emptiness of the cavernous church, I greeted the young girl who was serving for me and invited her to come with me to greet the reader and the Eucharistic minister in the front pew. Everyone else was so far away, firmly embedded in the back pews where they have been forever.

When I returned to my proper place at the altar, I noticed that my young assistant had not returned to the altar with me. She kept going, and going, and going—all the way to the back. Over there to the group on the side. There by the other door.

She went to everyone in the church while the eyes of everyone else followed every step she took and every greeting she made. The look on the face of every person in that church, with the possible exception of her mother, was truly one of transfiguration. When she finally came back to her place at the altar and stood ready to serve, the whole church erupted in applause. She had brought more joy and meaning to the celebration than any of the homiletic thoughts that I had shared trying to explain the unexplainable.

The Spirit that provides us with the energy and impetus to follow after the Lord often uses the very people we serve to provide us with those gifts. We all hope and pray to continue to allow the Spirit to enter into our lives and inspire us through the lives of others.

Steve Gibson, C.S.C.

August 7

Triumphant and glorious, victor over death and hell, the Divine Redeemer mounted up to heaven. He rose up to his Father; he sat down at his Father's right hand. Yet he does not cease to live and dwell in our midst. He makes this the joy of his heart.

—Blessed Basil Moreau

I REMEMBER WHEN my nephew, Steve—a brilliant, gentle, and thoughtful young man—was diagnosed with Lou Gehrig's disease. This incurable illness gradually undermines muscle function and is ultimately fatal. It was painful to watch Steve's struggle as he was unable to speak, unable to eat except through a feeding tube, and unable to walk without labored steps. It seemed so cruel and unfair. His courage, however, was remarkable, and his death, peaceful. He died in the arms of his loving and attentive wife. His son was with him as well and bid him a gentle goodbye.

During his illness, we as a family began to realize ever more profoundly that Jesus was in our midst. For no matter our position or status, no matter how important we think we are or how insignificant we portray ourselves to be, the work of caring for others brings us ever closer to the right hand of God. It was the Lord and Blessed Moreau who comforted Steve and the rest of us. Steve kept a relic of the founder of Holy Cross with him throughout his illness. Through Steve's grave disease, our family became holier and far more prayerful. We prayed for healing, we prayed for comfort, and finally we prayed for peace—all the while knowing that the Lord was in our midst comforting us and letting us know that he was at our right hand. I always marveled at Steve's courage and strength. Each day now, I pray to him, trusting that he is enjoying God's good graces. I ask him to be with me, joined in courage, to face whatever challenges come my way.

Jerome Donnelly, C.S.C.

August 8

Let us listen to the Good Shepherd, and pray that he will speak to our soul. Then, by means of us, he will speak to those we have been charged to teach and sanctify.

—Blessed Basil Moreau

GOD'S WORD IS a life-giving word. Genesis tells us that God spoke and all created life came into being. To take in God's word, to have God's Word enter our being, is to allow God to change us, to reform us, and to make us into something new. In a very real sense, the Word becomes alive in us, and so people begin to see God's Word incarnate through us.

This is certainly an important part of what preachers are called to be and do. As proclaimers of God's Word, they must let it into their very being. By praying the scripture, studying the scripture, and letting the scripture speak to their souls, preachers allow the Word to change them so that by grace they might become the very word that they are preaching. In this way, it is the Good Shepherd who speaks through the preacher. This is one of the great gifts and wonders of the ministry of preaching. As a preacher, I never cease to be amazed at how the Lord has used me to speak his Word of healing, or forgiveness, or challenge, or direction through the vehicle of my preaching. It is an amazing grace and privilege.

Inner transformation by God's Word is essential for preachers, but it is a grace and gift to all who are willing to let his word seep deeply into their being. Through our own personal prayer and study of scripture, we learn to heed the words of Blessed Moreau and listen deeply to the Good Shepherd in order that his words might change us into living witnesses for all the world to see.

Tom Gaughan, C.S.C.

August 9

It is surprising, people often ask me for healings, but rarely for humility, the spirit of faith.
—St. André Bessette

IF I ENCOUNTERED Br. André Bessette, C.S.C., in his youth, I imagine that my impression of what he needed would have focused on his "presenting" needs. Beholding an orphaned, uneducated, and sickly youth, I would have concluded that he needed a foster home, an education, and medical attention. However, the movement of St. André's life suggests that he was aware of a deeper need. His attentiveness to the frailty of his life and to the longing of his own heart enabled him to know that God alone could fulfill his deepest needs. In humility, he knew that his deepest need was for the gift of faith.

In a pastoral counseling course, the instructor advised us not to presume that we understood the needs of the people seeking our assistance or that the people themselves were always aware of their real needs. She suggested that, like Jesus, we remain deeply aware of our dependence upon the Father, and we ask those who come to us to speak from their hearts about their deepest longings. She taught that we would have compassion for those who come to us only if we truly listened to their hearts and remained aware of our own frailty and need for God.

Orphaned, uneducated, and sickly, St. André nurtured the gift of faith that the Lord offered him. He realized that faith was the deepest need of the human heart and the greatest gift that God bestows. Deeply attuned to his own frailty and need for faith, he was surprised and saddened when others did not share the same awareness. In prayer, St. André turned to the Lord, asking that those who came to him would ask for—pray for—the deepest healing of the human heart: the gift of faith.

Thomas P. Looney, C.S.C.

August 10

Afflictions, reverses, loss of friends, privations of every kind, sickness, even death itself, "the evil of each day," and the sufferings of each hour—all these are but so many relics of the sacred wood of the true Cross which we must love and venerate. We must enclose these precious souvenirs in a reliquary made of charity which is patient, resigned, and generous and which, in union with the Divine Master, suffers all things and supports all things.

—Blessed Basil Moreau

As I LAY on my hospital bed in Uganda after my third attack of malaria, I often looked at the crucifix hanging on the wall.

I was suffering, and I really wanted to die. My patience had just about run out; my generosity was almost spent; indeed, my resignation was complete: "Take me, Lord." Then one day as I received the Eucharist from the hands of our bishop, I felt renewed as he said, "Body of Christ." It was as if God had said, "Not yet." The crucifix on the wall gave me hope just as the Eucharist within my body nourished me. I felt, for a moment, at one with Christ on the Cross. I believe my real recovery began at that very moment in union with Christ who suffered for me and supported me.

Our daily crosses in life are so many splinters from the Cross of Christ. Blessed Moreau teaches all who would follow Christ to see these crosses as gifts from God to assist us on our journeys. Our lives are reliquaries made up of many sorrows—loss of relatives and friends, sickness and privations, sufferings and afflictions. All of these sorrows are splinters, or relics, from the true Cross that we must hold on to and encase in our very lives. Our love, our charity becomes the gold to make our reliquaries. Our patience, resignation, and generosity become the gems that adorn it. Then our crosses are made beautiful in our God, who suffers all things and supports all things.

Robert Nebus, C.S.C.

August 11

Prayer and devotedness to duty are universally accepted as essential to community life.
—Fr. Edward Sorin, C.S.C.

IT WAS A hot August afternoon in 1962. I had just arrived at St. Joseph's Novitiate, located on a farm in Rolling Prairie, Indiana, to begin my life in Holy Cross. My first work assignment was to clean up after the pigs. I was a city boy who had never seen a live pig before. I still think of this day when I reflect on a phrase from our *Constitutions*: "to stand by duty when it has become all burden and no delight."

During meditation the next morning, I asked Jesus if this was the way things were going to be from here on out. As I looked up at the crucifix, Jesus seemed to reply that there would be more days like this and that there would be better ones, too—but that was not important. What mattered was that I do whatever I had to do, as he done what he had to do. I had to take that path if I wanted to share in the life and work of Holy Cross.

Our *Constitutions* link prayer and duty: "The more we come through prayer to relish what is right, the better we shall work in our mission for the realization of the kingdom." This linkage is critical in any life. Duty not only requires that we do things right but that we do the right things. It is all too easy to focus on our personal preferences, to do well what is easiest for us, and to let other responsibilities slide. We fight these tendencies by bringing everything before the Lord in prayer. "To serve him honestly, we must pray always and not give up."

Patrick Sopher, C.S.C.

If, as St. Paul says, "Knowledge without reverence makes one proud," and thus becomes dangerous, it is likewise true that reverence without knowledge makes a teacher useless and compromises the honor of the mission of the teacher. That is why Daniel, speaking of the reward prepared for those who teach others, does not assume that they are merely "just" and hence reverent, but also "learned and knowledgeable."
—Blessed Basil Moreau

KNOWLEDGE IS ONE of the necessary gifts of our ministry in Holy Cross as educators in the faith. This is not just true for those in the classroom. We spend our lives trying to attain it. We struggle for it. We spend so much effort trying to attain it. Then we look for new and effective ways to pass it on to each other and to our students. But it is always so partial, so maddeningly incomplete, so changing and quickly obsolete.

Blessed Moreau spent his life pursuing knowledge and teaching it to others. But knowledge for him was never isolated from faith. He championed the full use of reason rigorously to pursue knowledge in all disciplines, including the sciences. Yet he always filtered whatever knowledge he gained through his humble life of prayer. We are privileged to have his life of learning and prayer as an example to guide and inspire all who seek knowledge in this way.

Each one of us is unique, with his or her original insights. And from time to time we need to be reminded that we have something distinct and original to say. If, however, what we say is to be knowledge that we would communicate to others, it cannot go unexamined by the convictions of our faith. Likewise, our faith must be informed by the knowledge we discover. Blessed Moreau knew that the two were not opposed to each other. In his example, we can simultaneously and humbly live the quest for both the purest faith and the deepest knowledge.

Claude Pomerleau, C.S.C.

August 13

"Learn from Christ to put aside the old self and to put on the new self." But I am addressing you in a particular way, since that is the purpose of your receiving the habit and the grace to ask for as you begin your novitiate. This is not merely a question of changing worldly fashions for clothes of a different quality, style, and color; that would not need to be blessed by the Word of God. It is, rather, a question of effecting in your life, in the eyes of faith, the transformation symbolized by the changing of attire, which will take place before this assembly.

—Blessed Basil Moreau

IN MY YEARS as a high school principal, our school had a pretty strict dress code. But it always amazed me seeing the students after school hours, as they experimented with the latest fashions of the day. Each new fashion statement was simply part of the adolescent search for identity and a sense of belonging. Unfortunately for some, this process continues into adulthood as they try to claim an identity outside of themselves instead of looking within. It is a fruitless search, however, because our true identity as God's beloved sons and daughters lies within—in the very image of God in which we were made.

The novice habit we present to the young men as they are officially received into the Holy Cross Novitiate may appear simply to be another piece of clothing to be added to their closets. Yet the novice habit is not meant as an exterior answer to the novices' interior search and identity. Rather, the habit is to be a reminder, an outward manifestation of an interior transformation taking place. It is to be a visible symbol of the interior garment of the heart—a heart clothed ever more in Christ—as they seek to conform their lives to his. The habit does not create an identity, as much as it reveals, reminds, and draws out the identity deep within, indelibly marked from their Baptisms, growing and bearing fruit.

In this regard, the habit is like the white garments we all received at our Baptism, garments blessed by the Word of God. That new garment did not create our new identity as God's adopted children; instead, it made it visible to help us claim and live out that inner transformation, our call to holiness, that began with our Baptism. It is that interior transformation of the heart that matters. The exterior simply draws out and reveals the interior. For while our habits and white garments will eventually wear out, the conformity of our hearts to Christ will carry us to eventual union of mind and heart with God.

Ken Molinaro, C.S.C.

I have a full list of all the religious of Holy Cross. I carry it with me everywhere; and whenever I enter a celebrated church or chapel, I take the dear roll in my hands, and as soon as I make sure that I am listened to, I begin my litany and go through.
—Fr. Edward Sorin, C.S.C.

TO CALL INDIVIDUALS by their name is to recognize them in their uniqueness. God calls each of us by name when he brings us into existence. He affirms us in our being with each breath that we draw. Each of us is unique in the eyes of God—a child of God, cherished and loved, affirmed in dignity.

We can imagine that as Fr. Sorin took the list of the religious of Holy Cross in his hands and read through the names, the faces of so many brothers and priests of Holy Cross would have come before his mind's eye. He would cherish each one in his uniqueness, for who he was and for what he contributed to the mission of Holy Cross. Then Fr. Sorin would lift each of them up in his prayer.

There is a "communion of the saints" at the deepest of levels that comes from faith. It binds us one to another with the bonds of love. It is a sharing in the love of God, the love of Christ. In our own prayer, each of us has a dear roll of those for whom we pray. As we recite their names, their faces come before us. We affirm them in their uniqueness, as objects of God's love and of our love. We lift them up through our prayer so that God will bless them with the gifts and the graces that they need. It is one powerful way that we share in the love of God, the love of Christ.

Arthur J. Colgan, C.S.C.

August 15

After the humanity of the eternal Word, the heart of Mary is the most beautiful masterpiece of the hands of the Creator.

—Blessed Basil Moreau

ONE DAY, WHILE entering my doctor's office, I held the door for a mother whose daughter was in a specialized medical chair. It was evident that she had cared for her special-needs child for several years. I was meeting a sorrowful mother. While sitting in the waiting room, I prayed my Rosary for them.

I have been praying to the Blessed Mother daily since I was a child in French Canada. At my home parish, Our Lady of Lourdes, we had a grotto, and I would often visit to pray and drink from the spring. Every evening, my family would kneel by the radio to recite the Rosary. My mother and grandmother each had a small statue of Mary on the windowsill above their kitchen sinks. They would pray their *Aves* while doing the dishes.

I've lived at the University of Notre Dame for more than forty years and have always loved praying and lighting candles at the Grotto. I live now at Holy Cross House because as a senior priest I have special health care needs. Yet from the far side of St. Joseph's Lake, I can still see our Blessed Mother on the Golden

Dome, and I continue to pray. In fact, I have more time to pray now and say my Rosary a couple of times a day.

Mary was always there for Jesus, and she will always be there for us. That is the beautiful part of cultivating a devotion to Mary. This devotion is often the last one to remain in our advanced years and even at the hour of our death. I have often witnessed this in my ministry to the elderly. As we pray to Mary today, our hope is to have her at the hour of our deaths, leading us to her Son for all eternity.

André Léveillé, C.S.C.

August 16

Happy those who understand this spirit of denial; happier still those who have tasted its sweetness and opened their hearts to it. For them, obedience becomes easy, and subjection to rules and superiors, sweet and light. Each subject does the will of God and not his own.

—Blessed Basil Moreau

WHEN WE ARE asked to accept assignments we would rather not take or to leave a place we have come to love, obedience can be the toughest vow. As effective ministers, we often give our hearts to the people we serve. When asked to go elsewhere, the letting go can be difficult. And yet it is in the surrender, in obedience to the will of the community as expressed through our superior, that we grow in freedom and give life to others. It is a lesson taught to us by those who loved us first and who in their own obedience to God's will let us go so we could be free to become the people God was calling us to be.

I still remember the early morning when I said goodbye to my mother and left for the seminary. As I drove off, I could see her silhouette framed by the light of the open garage door. My father had died when I was just sixteen, and as the youngest, my departure meant my mother would now live alone. I did not fully appreciate it then, but her encouragement of my journey to Holy Cross and subsequent letting me go was an example of her surrender—of her obedience, really—to God's work in my life. It would have been far easier for her to keep me close, to ask that I not venture so far away and into a new family, but she let me go as a gift to God and to Holy Cross. Her surrender reminds me of the Widow's Mite. In obedience to God, the widow gives from her want what little she has, trusting that God will use it. That is the surrender that is freeing and life-giving for us all.

Peter Jarret, C.S.C.

August 17

You will need to fill and nourish your heart with Jesus' teachings, to meditate on these mysteries in silent recollection as well as on the abundance of his mercies. You will also need to ask God to enlighten your mind and heart so that you may understand and savor them in such a way that you may come to that kind of knowledge of Jesus Christ which is life-giving, profound, luminous, and practical and which makes his virtues almost palpable, so to speak, his lessons familiar, and remembrance of him as habitual as it is enjoyable.

—Blessed Basil Moreau

BEFORE I JOINED Holy Cross, I worked for a trucking company. I tried to convince manufacturers to ship their products in our trucks instead of someone else's. Lancaster County, Pennsylvania, was part of my sales territory, including the neighboring towns of Blue Ball and Intercourse. You might think that to live in towns with such suggestive names would be embarrassing, but none of my mostly Amish and Mennonite customers ever gave any indication that they found the names of their towns remotely awkward or funny. I admired them for their obliviousness.

Some of us are old enough to remember when every family seemed to have a "maiden aunt" who, all unawares, would say things with humorous sexual connotations. Then, while everyone else dissolved into giggles, she would look around with a bemused smile wondering what was so funny. Alas, those ladies are long gone. Nowadays we all get the joke. No sexual reference, no matter how obscure, can be slipped past any of us. I wonder if we're the better for it. What, after all, does our knowingness say about us except that we are part of our hypersexualized culture?

It seems to me that, as Christians, the incidents of our daily lives should evoke a different set of associations for us. We ought to be so steeped in the gospels that a chance encounter, an odd coincidence, or a friend's slip of the tongue will trigger a scriptural allusion. We might smile and say, "Ha, that reminds me of the loaves and fishes." If our minds, hearts, and imaginations belong to Christ, we will find intimations of him time and again. The Good News will never slip past us!

Charles B. Gordon, C.S.C.

August 18

Our rules certainly ensure the necessary training for the mind, but their first and foremost concern is with the formation of the heart through the development of those religious dispositions which alone can make a good person and a Christian.

—Blessed Basil Moreau

As a young child, I remember the excitement I had getting ready for my first day of school. How thrilled I was with new clothes, books, and school supplies. I had new pencils and pens, notebooks, and even a ruler. As the years progressed, life became more complicated. Braces on my teeth made me afraid to smile. Eyeglasses for reading made me look silly but saved me from headaches. All sorts of new, unwritten rules of conduct had to be learned, like how to get along with the "in-crowd" or how to act around members of the opposite sex. Sometimes I thought I was the only clueless one.

When Blessed Moreau offered the first rules, or *Constitutions*, for his young Congregation, he was offering a pattern for living, loving, and growing as Christians, as children of God formed into a holy community. At the heart of the definition of "rule" is "pattern." For all Christians, Jesus Christ is our pattern for discovering the way to the Father and communion with all people. Just as the Word was made flesh, the rule is a pattern enfleshed in us through a relationship with Jesus, whose heart burns with love for all of his children. He is unyielding until our hearts are set on fire, too. Blessed Moreau gave to both his community and the Church the transforming pattern of the Cross as our only hope. To embrace this pattern forms our hearts to receive the One who is the way, the truth, and the life. For indeed, God loves truth in the heart. And in the secret of each heart he will teach us wisdom.

John Donato, C.S.C.

August 19

The spirit of the Congregation is a spirit of peace and charity; the brothers shall live together in the most perfect union, loving each other and helping one another equally. If any dissension arises, however small, they should come to reconciliation before evening prayer.
—Fr. Jacques Dujarie

WHENEVER I ATTEND a community function—a profession of vows, a celebration of a feast day, or, most notably, a funeral—I look at the members of the community and reflect. I will be here to bury most of these men, and some will bury me. For me, this is not a morbid thought but a life-defining experience. We are part of a brotherhood that's larger than each one of us.

Besides being colleagues in ministry, we are partners in discipleship, sharing a particular response to the Lord's summons. It is clearly a call to do something, but it is perhaps more importantly a command to be somebody, along with others called to do likewise.

More than forty years of community life have yielded many ups and downs for me. There have been disagreements with and even estrangements from some members. But that does not change the fundamental dynamic of life in community—brothers living in perfect union.

Community life is primarily this sharing of individual lives lived in imitation of the Lord. In that regard, the dynamics of a Christian family, business, or parish are no different from those of the religious life. All of these require the same give and take that aims for perfect union, including the realization of our solidarity with each other and the will to reconcile with those we have hurt. Perhaps that's why I look upon Holy Cross as I do when we are together. Just like any of us, I am not who I am without my community. Nor are my fellow community members who they are without me. We are brothers.

Joseph H. Esparza, C.S.C.

August 20

We must lay down deep in our hearts the foundation of a new spiritual structure; in other words, we must humble ourselves before God, for "he gives his grace only to the humble."

—Fr. Edward Sorin, C.S.C.

I STILL REMEMBER vividly the ordination Mass of a new priest in Uganda, where I lived and worked. Hundreds were present. At the time of the offertory, everyone came forward with their donation clasped between their two hands, as is the custom in that culture. As they reached the large woven basket set on a table, each in turn placed his or her two hands over the basket and released an offering. Typically, most of the offerings were a fifty shilling coin, the smallest minted currency, not because of the poverty of the people so much but because, as in so many cultures of the world, the Church often gets the smallest coin of the realm. As the line was ending, an old woman of perhaps eighty years came shuffling barefooted with her donation in her clasped hand. When she reached the offertory table, she carefully left her offering, a fresh egg, on the table. The market value of an egg at that time was one hundred shillings.

Immediately, the gospel passage of the widow giving her last coin came to me. I realized again that what matters in our offering is not the amount that we give to the collection but rather the sincerity of our motivation at the time of our giving. Ultimately, it is a reflection of the sincerity and generosity with which we live out our daily lives. Simply put, being poor will not guarantee the graces of God. Instead, living humbly, no matter what our economic situation may be, is what will be blessed.

James Nichols, C.S.C.

The bark of Peter has been assailed before, but has never sunk. Jesus may seem to sleep in it and not to mind the fierce tempest that rages around it; but let us remember St. Matthew: "Jesus said to the disciples: 'Why are you fearful, you of little faith?' Then rising up, he commanded the winds and the sea, and there came a great calm."

—Fr. Edward Sorin, C.S.C.

HOPE IS AN essential Christian virtue, and we in Holy Cross strive to nurture hope in our lives as a central part of our charism and spirituality. And yet, I must confess, I can sometimes become a bit anxious about the future of our community, of our apostolates, and even of our Church.

All of these things we hold so dear exist in the midst of a broader culture that seems constantly to assail our gospel values and to dismiss our faith. Despite our best efforts, it is sometimes easy to think that one day soon it simply will be too much, and finally we will sink under the weight.

At times like that, I like to read the stories of our Holy Cross forefathers, including Fr. Sorin, who more than one hundred fifty years ago brought our community's charism and mission to the wilds of northern Indiana and the swamps of New Orleans. The stories of these intrepid missionaries and the amazing odds they overcame inspire me to have faith and hope as they did. It is a faith and hope not so much in our own abilities to overcome tremendous adversity or to keep the ship afloat and on course but in Christ's promise that he will be with us until the end of the age and in his assurance that we have nothing to fear. Whatever tempests may rage, however the boat may be swayed or swamped, the One whom even the wind and the seas obey is present in our midst. He will sustain us and, at the last, bring us to safe harbor.

Stephen Koeth, C.S.C.

August 22

Whether it be unfair treatment, fatigue or frustration at work, a lapse of health, tasks beyond talents, seasons of loneliness, bleakness in prayer, the aloofness of friends; or whether it be the sadness of our having inflicted any of this on others . . . there will be dying to do on the way to the Father.

—Holy Cross *Constitutions*

IN THE HOLY CROSS Chapel in the Stinson-Remick Hall of Engineering at the University of Notre Dame, a stained-glass window depicts the Blessed Mother with seven stars in the golden nimbus surrounding her head. They shine as the seven transfigured sorrows of Mary, the seven dolors of the Blessed Mother, her dying to do on her way to the Father.

Seven trials are listed in today's reflection from the eighth and final of our *Constitutions*: The Cross, Our Hope. There could be more; there could be less. Life itself crucifies everyone sooner or later, one way or the other. We all must die. We are not in control, yet we in Holy Cross profess to be men with hope to bring. No one asks to be born, in this particular body, at this particular time and place. Like Jesus in Nazareth, we find ourselves dependent, limited, blessed yet burdened with our own crosses in life. Jesus spent thirty years of his short life in a village where his abilities were hidden from the world. There was dying to do on the way to the Father.

As a child, I was shy and very lonely. I was not happy much of the time. Even then, there was dying to do on the way to the Father.

If today I am blessed with an interior life of prayer, it was born out of the sorrows of long ago. God in his mercy will take our sorrows and our wounds on the road to Calvary and transfigure our pain and our dying into the "glorious wounds" of our Christ-life. Each and every one of our personal lives embodies that mystery of the Cross.

Nicholas Ayo, C.S.C.

August 23

Ours should be a perfect chastity that purifies all our thoughts and affections, words and actions, in a word, our bodies and our souls.

—Blessed Basil Moreau

DUE TO IT coming as the result of some well-intentioned trickery, our only photograph of Blessed Moreau—and every subsequent portrait—depicts him with a stern and dour expression.

Yet I wonder if this expression does not reveal a truth about our founder's rigorous discipline in the spiritual life. Whatever the case may be, it is clear that Blessed Moreau worked very hard to develop a "perfect chastity" that allowed him to focus all of his energy and attention on the mission of Holy Cross and on the kingdom of God.

When I first explored a vocation in Holy Cross, the one thing that most impressed me was the fun-loving joy that seemed to radiate from the religious I met. We spent our first days as seminarians each new academic year at our summer camp in Deep Creek, Maryland. There we would discuss the upcoming year, get to know one another, and learn to play and relax as brothers. I can remember pondering at camp how proud the founder would be to see his children relating to one another with such uncomplicated joy.

I believe that both Blessed Moreau's legacy of self-discipline and the community's fun-loving joy are two sides of the chastity not only that we seek in Holy Cross but that the Christian tradition teaches all Christians are called to live. On the one hand, our vow of celibacy commits us to the sort of purification which makes room for God alone. Our entire person, body and soul, is called to surrender to the project of growing into the likeness of Jesus. And yet, such perfect chastity cannot be lived without an openness to love that makes our joy apparent and our commitment true.

Steve Wilbricht, C.S.C.

We should find our greatest consolation and even our delight in spending ourselves in the glorious task of training up young and childlike souls for heaven. Let, then, God's holy remembrance permeate all our efforts and their efforts.

—Fr. Edward Sorin, C.S.C.

WHEN I WAS rector of a residence hall, I received students at my door daily for tape, recommendation letters, screwdrivers, confession, even needle and thread. I gave ironing lessons and knotted bow ties. I cooked a five-gallon pot of chili every week. I learned to tune out stereos that could be heard halfway to Ohio. I told them not to wear brown shoes with blue suits to job interviews—then suggested a haircut. I was asked, "Do you know how to boil water?" I told freshmen's parents, "I'm just a stay-at-home priest!"

Our more humdrum tasks test our patience while cumulatively nurturing our devotion to our students. If they emerge from our universities as mature, thoughtful, and prayerful adults, it is because their personal and spiritual growth outside the classroom outpaces even the expansion of their intellects. The constant friction of aspirations butting up against failure and frustration teaches them patience, wisdom, self-discipline, and perseverance.

So it is, too, for all who spend themselves in service of youth. We are predictably pleased when they return transformed from a summer experience in Africa, receive their diplomas as seniors, or later join hands with their life's love at the altar, but it also is our delight simply to journey with them as their lives and ours intersect. We mark the milestone moments joyfully, but we know that our embrace of unsought knocks and mundane routines is what grounds our service in Christ and demonstrates the depth of our obedience to God's call.

James B. King, C.S.C.

August 25

It was a call that came to us from without, but also one that arose up within us, as from his Spirit.
—Holy Cross *Constitutions*

MY CALL TO religious life as a brother in Holy Cross came through the back door, so to speak. During my junior year of high school, my best senior buddy told me that he was joining the brothers. I was stunned but, at the same time, intrigued. I had no idea that he had been thinking about such a radical move. Certainly, I had not been entertaining such a commitment myself. But the Spirit began to percolate in me, and I joined Holy Cross at the end of my senior year. Now, looking back upon more than fifty years as a religious brother, I am aware that the Spirit has been moving me in directions that I never consciously would have chosen.

Perhaps the greater mystery is that I have responded at the very moments when I was unaware that anything positive might occur. The Spirit's gift to me, indeed to all of us, is the courage to move out into the unknown—to step out of the boat onto the waters of uncertainty because the Lord Jesus beckons.

I know in my own life, if I have been effective in ministry, it is because the Spirit has led me to step out of one comfort zone after another. I am who I am right now because of my responsiveness to the Spirit—because I have been able to say, even timidly, yes. True power to be for others, in each of our lives, arises from the Spirit breathing power upon our powerlessness and transforming that into action for the Church and the world.

Philip Smith, C.S.C.

August 26

Above all, let us work with that strength, unity, and clear understanding which come from mutual cooperation and the possession of all things in common. We must never lose sight of the fact that strength of numbers, joined with unity of aim and action, is the greatest of all strengths and is limited only by the bounds of the possible.

—Blessed Basil Moreau

AS A NOVICE, I was taught about the three branches of Holy Cross—priests, brothers, sisters—but this was a theoretical vision at best. In the novitiate, we were all brothers from the same province, with a priest chaplain. In the scholasticate at Notre Dame, however, I lived with student brothers from all over the United States and elsewhere. There were many Holy

Cross priests, brothers, sisters, and seminarians at Notre Dame, too. Living in this milieu sparked in me an intuitive appreciation for the uniqueness of our Holy Cross religious family in practice, although those of us in formation were pretty limited in our "external relations" in those days.

That situation began to change in 1973 with regional gatherings to celebrate the centenary of Fr. Moreau's death. I was serving in ministry in New England, and we discovered that all the branches of Holy Cross had been serving in our region for many years. From that time forward, I have had the opportunity to serve and live with Holy Cross priests, brothers, and sisters literally around the world. I now find myself at Holy Cross College at Notre Dame. In this "tri-campus" location with the University of Notre Dame and Saint Mary's College as our neighbors, we have great opportunities to collaborate proactively as Blessed Moreau asked.

The vision of Blessed Moreau for Holy Cross and the Church remains prophetic in our day, as it was in his. Our task, whatever our calling or state of life, is to take the risk to work with that strength, unity, and clear understanding that come from mutual cooperation. We must find concrete ways to live that unity of aim and action that is our greatest strength and extends the bounds of the possible for the Church and world.

John Paige, C.S.C.

There are many ways of carrying out this imitation which can be summed up as the study of Jesus Christ. When we study him, we get to know him; as we get to know him, we love him; in loving him, we are led to imitate him.

—Blessed Basil Moreau

BLESSED MOREAU WAS an intensely passionate man when it came to the task of teaching Christians to discover and live their calling in life. For many in Holy Cross, the calling as educators in the faith is carried out in institutions of higher learning. For these members, to study a particular field is a lifelong endeavor. They are always immersed in the debates and research of their fields whether they are theology, the sciences, or the fine arts.

The knowledge mined from a life marked by study is vast, but for it to remain mere knowledge, while humanly impressive, would be spiritually sad. True fruit arises when that knowledge bursts into a love for the topic of study and consequently for the God by whom the arts and sciences were created and receive their continued inspiration.

So, too, is it with Christ Jesus who, far from being a mere topic for study, is the very subject of our lives. It is, therefore, as Blessed Moreau tells us, the duty of all Christians to study Christ so as to know, love, and follow him. Just as the scholar daily takes up the book, so too do we daily place in our hands the Word of God in sacred scripture and our breviary, the daily prayer of the Church. We also place ourselves among other believers in the Church's public prayer, the liturgy. How can those unfamiliar with the discoveries of science dare name themselves scientists? Or by what claim can those who fail to view and be knowledgeable of works of art enjoy the title of artist? Likewise, we who hold the title "Christian" must have knowledge of, love for, and discipleship in Christ Jesus.

Michael Wurtz, C.S.C.

August 28

The Lord's Supper is the Church's foremost gathering for prayer. It is our duty and need to break that bread and share that cup every day unless prevented by serious cause. We are fortified for the journey on which he has sent us. We find ourselves especially close as a brotherhood when we share this greatest of all table fellowships.

—Holy Cross *Constitutions*

WHEN I FIRST came to know Holy Cross as an undergraduate at the University of Portland, two things struck me: these are men who work hard, and they are men who pray. It wasn't until later, as a member of the community, that I learned the vital connection between the two: work only becomes ministry when it is nourished by prayer. In every Holy Cross house I have lived in or visited, the Eucharist is the center of our daily life. Sure, it's nice to have a thirty-minute retreat every day when we come together for some peace and inspiration at Mass, but the

Eucharist is so much more for us. It reminds us who we are as Christians and as religious, and it strengthens us to serve our Lord well.

Every time I come to the altar, I remember the words of St. Augustine, who taught that we actually mean two things when we hold up the consecrated host and say, "The Body of Christ." We are saying both that this host in my hand is the Body of Christ and that those who receive it are the Body of Christ. Thus, when we gather as the Church, and partake of the Eucharist together, we become ever more who Christ created us to be—his Body here on earth. If we are to continue Jesus' mission, we must fortify ourselves by receiving his body and blood. It is only then, nourished and bound together at this greatest of all table fellowships, that we become bread broken and wine poured out for the life of the world.

Dan Parrish, C.S.C.

✠

August 29

Resist the evil one stoutly, having frequent recourse to prayer, constantly imploring the aid of our dear Lord and his Holy Mother.

—Fr. Jacques Dujarie

ON A VISIT to the University of Portland, Anglican Archbishop Desmond Tutu regaled the students with a personal, heartfelt exhortation on living a life of faith. "To believe against all sense and reason and logic, that is grace," he encouraged. "The world will say you are silly! Be proud of that!"

How much more does the world call us foolish, downright ignorant, and even stupid to believe in Satan! We have no choice but to be humbled in that belief, which is based on Jesus' own teachings, for we are sinners. All too often, it seems, our sin can get the upper hand. As St. Paul confesses to the Romans, "What I do, I do not understand. For I do not do what I want, but I do what I hate" (7:15).

In those early centuries of Christianity, when some believers went to the desert to test and confirm their faith, they wrestled mercilessly with their desires and seemingly innate contradictions. In doing so, however, they encountered more than their empirical selves; they encountered the grace of God and the temptations of demons. They became so engrossed in the profound mysteries of the natural and the supernatural realms that they could not *not* believe in something beyond themselves.

Without the grace of silence and solitude in our lives, we may abandon faith to keep from appearing silly and foolish. We may eagerly embrace our illusions and those of the world. But in the prayer of the desert, with the aid of our dear Lord and our Holy Mother, there's no denying the truth that evil exists—and even more profoundly, that the power of grace is engaged in a great battle for the purity of our hearts. And it is in this battle that we are set free truly to live.

Hugh Cleary, C.S.C.

August 30

I am a priest to be father to the orphan, the consolation of the widow, the support of the poor, and the friend of the suffering.

—Fr. Jacques Dujarie

OF ALL THE people who have had an impact on my life as a Holy Cross priest, I am convinced that teachers hold the first place. I remember on one occasion asking Frank O'Malley, my English professor at Notre Dame, what he thought was the most significant mark of a good teacher. Without hesitation he replied, "Knowing how to ask questions and tell stories; that was Plato's way and Jesus', too." I have never forgotten that answer. It has given my life direction and focus whether as a teacher at the high school and collegiate levels or in the pastoral work that I enjoyed for many years, flying to small villages in rural Alaska as a sacramental minister.

Without a doubt, the natural human desire to find life's meaning amid the issues and circumstances of our age continues to consume our deepest efforts and longings. There are moments in all our lives when our restless hearts incite us to ask such questions as, Why am I here? What is my call and destiny? Does it make any difference?

Fr. Dujarie clearly had discovered the answer to these questions in his own life. It was to live for others, especially those with the greatest need—the orphan, the widow, the poor, and the suffering. As we ask these same questions about life's meaning today, we can look to the answer that Fr. Dujarie found for guidance and inspiration. The answers we discern matter greatly because they necessarily affect how we reach out to those most in need around us.

LeRoy E. Clementich, C.S.C.

August 31

My great and ever-growing ambition is now to finish the work I have commenced or continued, that, when I disappear, it may remain and go on increasing and developing for the glory of God and the salvation of souls.

—Fr. Edward Sorin, C.S.C.

As ONE WHO has never lived or ministered at the University of Notre Dame, I always stand in awe when I arrive on campus. I visit the Log Chapel, pray at the Grotto, and imagine Fr. Sorin and the first Holy Cross religious arriving in 1842 and deciding that this place would be the site of their mission. I then wander around campus and take in the sights and sounds of students and faculty engaging one another in the wisdom of the ages and the search for new knowledge. I also visit the retired religious who live at Holy Cross House, the community medical facility, and share in their stories and memories.

Fr. Sorin came to America as a young priest to found a place where the young could learn. In his wildest dreams, he never could have imagined the university that stands today. Yet he believed in a dream and allowed it to sustain him through many trials and tribulations. That dream was taken up by successive generations of Holy Cross religious and their lay collaborators who have helped to build a place where literally hundreds of thousands of young people receive an outstanding education and become the next generation of Catholic leaders in our society.

We, too, must dream and imagine a world different from our own. Our efforts must look toward a reality beyond ourselves and our own time. And we must do so recognizing that it is God who is both the source and the goal of our service. When we do this, we truly participate in the story of salvation, a story that continues with each generation and has as its end the proclamation of the kingdom.

Mark Cregan, C.S.C.

September 1

Our vows not only bind us in community; they are to mark our life as community. Open and generous and hospitable love is to characterize our houses and our service. As a congregation and in each of our local communities we are committed to the use of few belongings and to simple living.

—Holy Cross *Constitutions*

WHEN I WAS at Moreau Seminary, we had many family members and friends join us as guests, especially during football season at Notre Dame. I was always struck by how profoundly grateful our guests were for our hospitality because what we offered was not much: a spartan room, an adequate bed, and, for most, neither a private shower nor air conditioning. Yet despite our less than luxurious accommodations, our guests always expressed their immense gratitude for our hospitality and welcome.

It is easy for us to think of hospitality as something that is dependent on material things—that to be hospitable is to serve dinner on the finest china or to offer the best liquor or to have the most grandiose accommodations. The characteristic warmth and simplicity of each of our Holy Cross communities, however, is a reminder that true hospitality is found not in the lavishness of the accommodation but in the love and attention afforded the guest. What our guests appreciate the most is the care demonstrated to them by the residents at the house—through sharing conversations around the dinner table, directing them to the bookstore, or sitting next to them and guiding them through the breviary at prayer.

Hospitality is not something that can be purchased. It is found in the core of our hearts. It is in our care, concern, and love that true welcome is found. Simplicity of life can be such a grace because it aids us in finding that core. It allows us to remove some of the distractions in our life and to key in upon that which is most important: our ability to share the love that God has for us with those around us.

Brian Ching, C.S.C.

September 2

We accept the Lord's call to pledge ourselves publicly and perpetually as members of the Congregation of Holy Cross by the vows of consecrated celibacy, poverty and obedience. Great is the mystery and meaning of these vows. And their point is simple. They are an act of love for the God who first loved us.

—Holy Cross *Constitutions*

ALL VOWS ARE sacred. Religious cannot love without them, but how do we speak about them? We profess them publicly and often wear them outwardly, but their living is internal. Indeed, the vows are more the quiet expression of the confessional than the bold proclamation of the pulpit. This is not because of any offense committed, but because poverty, chastity, and obedience are about God and the individual's experience of contrition and conversion in the depths of being. Who wants to make public such an inward vulnerability?

At twenty-seven, I made to God forever vows of celibacy, poverty, and obedience. I sought to make absolute the identity I had been working toward since college. As St. Columba once said, I felt "wounded by God's love" and believed that I was called. At twenty-seven, this identity, especially as called by God, was what mattered. I would soon be taught by God that the vows were less about strength and security in my religious identity and more about friendship with God.

Why any of us make a commitment and why we continue in it are two different things. Something hopefully changes in us in the living. It strikes me, after almost three decades as a vowed Holy Cross religious, that more than anything else the pursuit of fidelity repositions us to see and love in ourselves what God sees and loves in us—that is, Christ Jesus. The soul wounded by God's love is one that enters Christ's wounds and discovers a wide compassion and care for the stranger.

Daniel J. Issing, C.S.C.

September 3

The Sacred Heart of Jesus is the chief source of the affections of Our Lord, and the center of the most perfect virtues which ever existed: a veritable treasure-house of sincerity, innocence, purity, meekness, patience, and humility. In a word, the Heart of Jesus is a living mirror of the most admirable human perfections, and of the choicest gifts of grace.

—Blessed Basil Moreau

As the story goes, Fr. Patrick Peyton, C.S.C., was giving an address in Uganda, speaking in his Irish brogue about the foundational experience of praying the Rosary with his family as a child. The crowd was immense and hushed as he spoke and urgently begged them to take up the practice of the family Rosary to strengthen and save their families.

Among the thousands of rapt listeners was a man from a tribe that did not speak English. One of the many reporters spotted him and studied his countenance. The man could not have been more riveted upon the glowing face of Fr. Peyton. He was hanging on every word that came from the Holy Cross priest. Bemused and curious, the reporter spoke to the man in his native dialect.

"Do you agree with that fellow?"

"I certainly do," came the immediate reply.

"But you do not speak English, do you? No members of your tribe do. How can you agree or disagree?"

"You are right," admitted the tribesman. "I cannot speak or understand a word of the English language. But I know I agree with this man."

"How can that be?" the reporter questioned.

"I can read his face. This man is sincere, innocent, meek, and humble. I don't understand the exact words, but I know they come from someone close to God, so I agree with them. When I stand before the judgment seat, I would be privileged to stand next to such a holy man. Why, he has the Heart of Christ!"

This, too, is our call—to put on the Sacred Heart of Jesus.

John Phalen, C.S.C.

September 4

To struggle for justice and meet only stubbornness, to try to rally those who have despaired, to stand by the side of misery we cannot relieve, to preach the Lord to those who have little faith or do not wish to

hear of him . . . our ministry will hint to us of Jesus'
suffering for us.

—Holy Cross *Constitutions*

WE ARE KNOWN for crossing borders of every sort, and many of those I cross are related to migrants and refugees. If there is ever a time when I stand by the side of misery that I cannot relieve, it is when I go to a place where people have just been displaced from their homeland because of war, violence, or a natural disaster.

When I was doing research along the Syrian-Lebanon border a few years ago, I came upon three sisters-in-law who had just lost their husbands in their country's civil war. They and their children were living under a plastic tarp, exposed to a vulnerability I had never seen before. At one point their mother-in-law rushed in, weeping and sobbing uncontrollably, holding in her hands the heart-breaking news added to an already burdensome plight: her fourth grandson was just killed, and her last son had just been put in prison. Although she was speaking a different language, her grief pierced right to the heart. Up until that time I had only seen the Pietà carved out of stone. Here I saw it carved out of the suffering of Syrian refugees. The more I heard, the more powerless I felt and the more speechless I became, recognizing that no thought or words could relieve their pain. By the end I was weeping. Then I began to realize that God not only suffered for us, but he also suffers with us.

As we accompany those in pain, we begin to learn to surrender all we cannot control. As we do, we open ourselves even more to discovering the crucified and risen Christ present among us—even when it means just standing with those being crucified today.

Daniel G. Groody, C.S.C.

September 5

We can scarcely realize how much is at stake for us when we begin to study. But we may be easily convinced that one of the surest means to obtain such an enviable result as an exceptional success in our studies is to place them, as so many wonderfully learned men have done, under the special protection of Mary.
—Fr. Edward Sorin, C.S.C.

WHEN I TEACH, I always begin with a prayer—first, the Our Father, the prayer that Jesus taught us, followed by "Mary, Seat of Wisdom," to which the students dutifully respond, "Pray for us." It is fitting in whatever we study, whether theology or politics or science or business, that we turn to the woman who "kept all these things, reflecting on them in her heart" (Lk 2:19). Reflection is the fruit of learning, and analysis and application can happen only when we have taken the basic ideas to heart. Mary, then, is the model for the scholar, whether student or teacher.

For the student, Mary shows us how learning is related to love. Her openness to new and surprising realities, such as bearing the Word in her womb and her questioning how this could be, reflect a thirst for the truth that is never so much satisfied as eternally whetted. For the teacher, Mary shows us the desire to share the truth with others as she generously displayed her newborn to the shepherds and the Magi. She also shows us the possibilities for knowledge to change a situation as when she approaches Jesus at the wedding feast to tell him, "They have no wine." Her direction to the servants at Cana is, no doubt, what catechists throughout the ages have taught to those who wish to follow Jesus: "Do whatever he tells you" (Jn 2:5).

Mary knows that all knowledge and all wisdom lead to her Son, and it is for this reason that she is our special patroness in learning.

Brent Kruger, C.S.C.

September 6

God's help will not be wanting in our hour of need. Providence never fails to provide for all the necessities of those who, by fidelity to their duties, abandon themselves to its guidance, even if it becomes necessary to send angels to help them.

—Blessed Basil Moreau

BY DIVINE PROVIDENCE, I contemplate the work of God in my life—that is, how we are God's instruments for one another, how through our actions we can make known his presence, the presence of a living God who loves us profoundly as daughters and sons and who continues to speak to us. It is enough that our hearts are open to listen.

I work as a chaplain with students ages eleven to fourteen at St. George's College in Santiago, Chile. Caring for their school supplies, especially by not ripping the sheets from their notebooks, is a difficult task for them. So I told them a story from my pastoral experience in Santa Cruz College in Tacna, Peru.

There, I met a boy named Michael who was thirteen. I noticed how he gathered leaves of different sizes and colors both in the classroom and on the playground. His constant preoccupation was that the leaves were relatively clean. Day after day, I watched as Michael gathered and collected the leaves. Before ending my pastoral experience, I decided to congratulate him for his concern for cleaning and caring for the planet. His answer, however, surprised me: "Thank you for your congratulations, but those are not my concerns. I gather all these leaves, and when I have collected enough, I glue them together. That's how I make my notebooks, as my mother is so poor that she cannot afford to buy them for me."

More than big speeches, the witness of Michael was the way the angel of God taught me—and perhaps can teach all of us, my students included—how to care for and value what we have and yet do not always appreciate.

Rodrigo Valenzuela, C.S.C.

September 7

Distance only increases affection, if it is real and sincere. Should I go to the end of the world, my imagination would bring my friends likewise, as daily companions of my every step.

—Fr. Edward Sorin, C.S.C.

ONE OF THE greatest joys of my life is my large family. When I was younger there was always someone around with whom I could talk or play games. Even now when we are all adults, I know that I can still call them night or day and they will always be available to talk with me. Holy Cross has been a natural extension of that experience, bringing me into an even larger family that reaches across many time zones and borders. There is great comfort in knowing that, wherever I go, I will always have my brothers in community with me.

Every time we move to another assignment, we take the experiences and friendships that we have made, and we continue to remember the people that we have left behind with phone calls, letters, and especially prayers. Because of this, we never lose them as companions on our journeys, and if we cross paths again, we have a joyful family reunion that picks up right where we left off, celebrating our brotherhood around the table of the Lord.

We strive to do the same with all of our brothers and sisters in the Body of Christ, to keep in our hearts all who have traveled on our journeys with us. That way, even if we do travel to the opposite side of the world, we will never lose them because they are part of who we are—and who we hope to be—as companions on the road to God in heaven.

Neil F. Wack, C.S.C.

September 8

We pray with the Church, we pray in community and we pray in solitude. Prayer is our faith attending to the Lord, and in that faith we meet him individually, yet we also stand in the company of others who know God as their Father.

—Holy Cross *Constitutions*

I LOVE PRAYING the Liturgy of the Hours, the daily prayer of the universal Church that marks the time—morning, midday, evening, and night. As a vowed religious, I am committed to praying it daily, and my faithfulness to this obligation has become an important part of my life. The hours force me to stop what I'm doing at different parts of my day and to pray, acknowledging that all of those things that have been keeping me so busy don't mean much unless I am offering them to God for his greater glory. This rhythm of prayer is a hallmark of religious life. We may be tired or distracted, we might be experiencing dryness in our prayer, but we pray anyway. We may be busy or even overwhelmed by the demands of our day, but we pray anyway. Prayer is nonnegotiable.

But our prayer lives, whether as priests, religious, or lay men and women in the Church, aren't just about ourselves. We offer our prayers together as a Church, the People of God trying to lead each other closer to heaven. Our prayer will never be perfect, and often it will even be frustrating. But we trust that God will speak to us in the liturgy, in our common prayers, and even in the silence. So we're called to make that extra effort to spend time with the Lord each day, however imperfect it may be. Because whatever imperfect prayer we can offer—as individuals, as a community, and as a Church—God can use it to transform our hearts and our world.

Steve Lacroix, C.S.C.

September 9

If idleness leads to boredom and to the grossest of vices, study on the contrary is a course of pure delights. Let us then be men of study, but let us study the things we should know and in their proper order.
—Blessed Basil Moreau

OFTEN IN HIS instructions, Blessed Moreau leaves us with as many questions as answers. Let us study the things we should know, he tells us. But what should we study and know? I have been thinking about this especially in my role as Vice President for Student Affairs at the University of Portland. It is essential that all of us in university ministries help develop our students' intellects. Those of us who work in student affairs, however, also have a special responsibility to help students in their personal formation.

Part of our challenge in student affairs is to know how to share what we have learned with our students. We can do this through the interactions we have with them and by the example of the lives we lead. It is sometimes in the difficult moments of life, when our students have made a mistake and have to face the consequences of their actions, that their greatest personal growth and formation occurs. Often that happens in the context of a pastoral conversation or a conduct meeting when there is an amazing opportunity to teach about the importance of being intentional with their decisions and actions. We strive to show how their character is not something that is static, but rather is formed by choices made over time in both the big and the small matters in life.

I think what we teach our students is what Blessed Moreau instructs all of us to do for ourselves: learn about and be intentional about our own lives and choices so that we can develop most fully into the people whom God calls us to be.

Gerard Olinger, C.S.C.

September 10

Let us not forget that it is not money or talents which do great things for God, but faith, prayer, and fidelity to the rule.

—Blessed Basil Moreau

WHEN BR. ANDRÉ MOTTAIS, C.S.C., set foot on Algerian soil in 1840, he knew little about the country to which he was sent, but he accepted that Blessed Moreau wanted him to use his administrative and teaching talents in this new mission territory. Br. André had been the most important of the Brothers of St. Joseph, founded by Fr. Dujarie, who later became the brothers of Holy Cross. He had served as novice master and spiritual director in the community for fifteen years. Yet when Br. André's new superior, Fr. Moreau, sent him to Africa, he did not hesitate even when it seemed that the place had less use for his talents than he and his superior had hoped. Debilitated by disease and wracked by spiritual darkness, he nonetheless continued on, realizing that talents alone are not the most important things in life. Fidelity to God's will—that is what is most important.

We sometimes think that our greatest obligation to God is to hone our talents for mathematics, or preaching, or counseling. When we find ourselves in situations where our talents are underutilized, however, we must make the greatest act of faith we can and accept with childlike grace what God sends our way.

Like Br. André Mottais, we wait in silence and peaceful reflection for God to manifest his expectations. Then we swallow hard and move forward, trusting in prayer that God knows what is best for us. Faith is a greater gift than any accomplishment of our own doing. Acceptance of Divine Providence makes greater sense than the greatest of talents developed in the absence of God's guidance.

George Klawitter, C.S.C.

September 11

The God of justice and mercy may, and often does, afflict his faithful servants here below in order to reward them hereafter with an eternal happiness.
—Fr. Edward Sorin, C.S.C.

EACH ONE OF us is caught up in the ageless fight between good and evil. It is a struggle for which we are ill prepared because we cannot predict the afflictions that will come our way. Moreover, we live in a world well beyond our immediate control. And so it seems that the only match for evil is our omnipotent God, who is just and merciful.

And yet, we must face our imperfect human situation, filled with weakness, illness, accidents, and tragedy. The ravages of nature—tsunamis, tornados, earthquakes, fires, and floods—also burst suddenly upon us, disrupting our lives. And we honestly wonder why these things happen to us. Then there is sin, our own personally chosen affliction. So much of our interpersonal turmoil and sadness stems from ill-chosen words and acts of unkindness. Their consequences can heap bitterness and resentment onto our already trying lives. In our suffering, caused both by the course of nature and by our own free choices, we cry out to God asking where he is. Has he really conquered evil?

When we face afflictions and are tempted to give up, we are peering directly into God's inscrutable ways. Even Jesus prayed in anguish to the Father, seeking to understand his ways before he endured his passion and death. Yet Jesus' faithfulness was ultimately rewarded in the glory of the Resurrection. All God asks of us, too, is faithfulness. And so even when we fail to understand God's ways, we can "boast of our afflictions, knowing that affliction produces endurance; and endurance, proven character; and proven character, hope; and hope does not disappoint" (Rom 5:4–5).

Bob Epping, C.S.C.

September 12

The tree of the Cross has been planted where our worthy religious dwell. But these religious have learned to savor its life-giving fruits, and if God in his goodness preserves them in the admirable dispositions which they have chosen thus far, they will never taste death, for the fruits of the Cross are the same as those of the tree of life which was planted in the Garden of Paradise.

—Blessed Basil Moreau

SORROWS ALWAYS COME unexpectedly, suddenly, without warning. Conversely, to feel joy for life normally takes time and is the fruit of great sacrifices. This reality has been a part of my life, but it makes more sense when I think of my first years as a Holy Cross religious in Chile.

We had suffered the breakdown of democracy and a painful military coup. Several of my classmates from high school as well as from university were detained; others, like myself, suffered exile. I remember painfully my friends who were killed. We were young people who simply aspired to a more just society with less poverty. We wanted to bring down these immense social and economic inequalities. We who believed in Christ could not be indifferent, and these words of Jesus resonated in us: "Unless a grain of wheat falls to the ground and dies, it remains just a grain of wheat; but if it dies, it produces much fruit" (Jn 12:24).

Today, I see that the sufferings of these years were not useless. It is not that I have seen the promised paradise, but I feel that in such a difficult moment for my country, God took care of us, and we could be his witnesses. The reality of having surrendered myself to what faith in Christ asked of me fills me with joy today. Moreover, I now understand that the most painful and difficult thing in life is not to change others or society, but to change oneself. None of the pain and suffering was in vain, and above all, it has made me grateful for life.

Whatever our circumstances, God gives us each day the possibility of a new life. He is the tree that sustains us and gives much fruit. He is our only hope.

José E. Ahumada, C.S.C.

September 13

Wherever through its superiors the congregation sends us we go as educators in the faith to those whose lot we share, supporting men and women of grace and goodwill everywhere in their efforts to form communities of the coming kingdom.

—Holy Cross *Constitutions*

BEING EDUCATORS IN the faith might sound pretentious to some, yet the gospels call all Christians to take on this role. In my more than three decades serving as a priest and professor at the University of Notre Dame, I have learned that this task is the work of a community.

Since coming to campus, I have been a member of Corby Hall, the Holy Cross community at Notre Dame. Upon arriving,

I was welcomed by many of my brothers in Holy Cross who have been models of faithfulness and holiness for me. Over the years, they have quietly lived Christ's call to educate students and colleagues in the faith. They are both generous and engaging, patient and giving. They challenge respectfully and multitask with grace. They educate best by their very example. Young religious bring vigor, energy, and hope to the apostolate. The elderly religious, who are most faithful to prayer and to the common life of the community, provide an important grounding to sustain the mission. Together we mold one community of educators, and we join with the rest of our colleagues at Notre Dame to form the university into a community of the coming kingdom.

Now I have been assigned by Holy Cross to serve as the religious superior of Corby Hall. As we continue to strive to build this community, we know that we are all human. Along with professing faith in Jesus Christ, we also admit that we are sinful. As much as we have the ability to do good, we also have an equal or greater ability to do evil. And so reconciliation becomes an essential part of the work of education if we are truly to form communities that will educate the next generation in the faith. Shaped by community and renewed by reconciliation, we go as educators in the faith to those whose lot we share.

Austin I. Collins, C.S.C.

There is no failure the Lord's love cannot reverse, no humiliation he cannot exchange for blessing, no anger he cannot dissolve, no routine he cannot transfigure. All is swallowed up in victory. He has nothing but gifts to offer. It remains only for us to find how even the Cross can be borne as a gift.

—Holy Cross *Constitutions*

OUR FUNDAMENTAL SACRAMENT, the Eucharist, is named for Jesus' acts of thanksgiving at the Last Supper. On one level, Jesus simply did what observant Jews always do before they eat: he thanked God for bread from the earth and fruit of the vine. But the Passover was no ordinary meal, and the Last Supper was no ordinary Passover, for the bread and wine Jesus blessed and shared anticipated his sacrifice on the Cross. Since we offer thanks precisely for gifts, in this meal Jesus first revealed how even the Cross can be borne as a gift.

Just hours later, however, Jesus prayed, asking the Father that this cup might pass from him. Christ himself seemed to want to return the very gifts he had instituted at that first Eucharist. And yet these two different attitudes—thankfulness and reluctance—reveal the paradoxical truth about suffering. For if we cannot give thanks we do not bear the Cross as *gift*. But if we do not acknowledge the reality of our suffering, we do not bear *the Cross* as gift. Only in reluctance, only in the plea to God for deliverance, do we really bear the Cross. To bear a cross without fear is an act of extreme denial or inhuman stoicism. If God's gift to us is a real cross, then our gift back to God is the acceptance of this cross with our real, unglorified humanity, the very humanity assumed by his Son. For only in light of the eternal Easter will we understand the gift's true reality; only then can we proclaim with the risen Christ that it was necessary to suffer these things to enter into glory (Lk 24:26).

Charles McCoy, C.S.C.

September 15—Solemnity of Our Lady of Sorrows

When Jesus Christ wished to express the great love of his Father for us, he said that God the Father loved us so much that he had delivered his only Son up to death. This is what Saint Paul referred to as the excess of divine love for human beings. Now, the heart of Mary was capable of this same excess because she gave her only son, the adorable child of her womb, for the redemption of the world. The suffering of Jesus caused deep and bitter suffering to the Virgin, such that we will never be able to find suitable expression to give an accurate idea of the martyrdom she suffered. This martyrdom did not begin on Calvary, but at the very moment when she was visited by the archangel. That we may better understand this, let us remember that Mary's heart was the most tender and most loving heart imaginable, after the heart of the Savior himself.

—Blessed Basil Moreau

IN A LAND where, by and large, crucifixes show as much as possible the marks of the cruel torture and agony Jesus suffered on the way to his death on the Cross, it is no surprise that among the most popular images in Peru of Mary are those that show the great sorrow she bore in her heart on the long journey with Jesus from the presentation to his burial in the tomb.

In our parish of *El Señor de la Esperanza* or "The Lord of Hope," there is a very large processional statue of Mary, robed in untraditional green, whose crystalline tears flow from her eyes and drip down her cheeks but without disturbing the contemplative and serene countenance of her face. This particular statue is called Our Lady of Hope rather than Our Lady of Sorrows, and except for the color of her dress, it would be difficult to tell the difference between the two Ladies. But the difference says something about how the woman whom we in Holy Cross celebrate as our principal patroness moves us from sorrow to hope and shows us the way to being bearers of that hope for others.

Among its many ministries, our sprawling parish on the edge of Lima has a health-care apostolate whose members look after shut-ins, transport sick people to medical appointments, pray with the bedridden, visit hospitals, comfort the dying, and lead families in prayer in their homes at wakes for their beloved deceased. Most of these ministers are women. I like to refer to them as *las santas mujeres* after the acclaimed "holy women" of the scriptures, including those who walked with Jesus to Calvary and to his empty tomb. What these women share in common is not just that they have chosen to participate in the same ministry in their parish but, more importantly, that they themselves have suffered: life-threatening health issues, great personal losses, long-lived family crises, separation from family, and so on. They know all too well those tears they contemplate on the face of the Lady in green. If we were to meet any one of them on the street, in church, or on a visit to our own homes, however, we probably wouldn't have a clue as to the extent of their personal suffering. What we would find is a smile, a hug, a cup of tea, and a reason to hope.

These holy women, like Mary, carry a lot in their hearts—things they hope someday to understand—but they don't let the pain, sadness, grief, or anguish that they bear overwhelm them, stop them, or define them. Rather, what pours from their hearts is like that overflowing love that Blessed Moreau saw in Mary's heart. They are credible and effective ministers! Somehow the people to whom they minister know that these women understand and embrace their sorrow because it's their sorrow, too. But they also feel their warm invitation to move from that sorrow to a better place where their sorrow can be turned into strength.

We in Holy Cross know that, if we accept suffering in our discipleship, we will move without awkwardness among those who suffer and will have hope to bring. The Lady of Sorrows is for us, in fact, Our Lady of Hope.

Donald Fetters, C.S.C.

September 16

Since, however, our sad experience with the inconstancy of our hearts prevents us from trusting in even our better resolutions, let us go to him who holds in his hands the will of humanity. Let us ask him to establish

*and confirm us in well-doing, to proportion his grace
to our needs and weaknesses.*

—Blessed Basil Moreau

As **young religious** and priests, my brothers and I accepted the call of Jesus to follow him, professing our vows to live publicly and perpetually as members of the Congregation of Holy Cross. We were filled with an idealistic desire to search for God's will and to be prophetic signs of his great love and mercy. We saw all of the wonderful things we could do in the name of Jesus by following in his footsteps right to the Cross.

We zealously set out to fulfill our ministries of teaching the young, assisting and preaching in parishes, and working as missionaries abroad. But then reality struck. We quickly discovered that we had not truly understood or appreciated the rigors of discipleship. We had overestimated our own resources to remain constant to our calling to live and work among God's chosen faithful. Our resolve to follow Jesus even to the Cross was constantly stymied by our own needs and weaknesses.

As all of us Christians come to realize in our own lives that our work is not ours but God's, we must turn to the Lord, asking for the help we need to do his work. Our constant challenge is to be linked to Jesus in such a powerful way that he fills us with the grace that we require to overcome our own needs and weaknesses. For then, and only then, can we fulfill God's will for us and for those we serve each day.

Charlie Kohlerman, C.S.C.

September 17

Look not to the number, but to the quality. Twelve men
sufficed, in God's own mind, to convert the world.
—Fr. Edward Sorin, C.S.C.

NEAR THE CREST of the hill that rises above Saint Mary's Lake at Notre Dame there is a small monument of stones resembling a cairn. Rather than a burial marker, this cairn marks the birth of the mission of Holy Cross in the United States. At this spot, a small group of seven Holy Cross religious first beheld the abandoned Potawatomi mission that would become their home and the site of their life's work.

Often on a football weekend, visitors to campus, clad in sweatshirts and green plaid slacks, stand at the monument and read off the names. Next, they follow the path to Old College, where they read the plaque for the "cradle of the university" in a loud, inspired voice. Over the years, countless undergraduate seminarians in Old College have had their Saturday mornings—the one morning they are allowed to be college students and sleep late—interrupted by the repetition of these names and by some variation on the refrain, "Imagine, Mildred—so much grew out of so little!"

I can think of no better introduction into the mystery of the kingdom, as preached by Christ, which rises from the tiniest seed. Like the Twelve sent out by the risen Christ, like the small band of immigrant missionaries by a snow-covered lake, like these countercultural few in Old College who choose religious life in our own day, we can feel overwhelmed by the wideness of the work before us when compared with the scarcity of our numbers. When venturing out, we can be too cold in our assessment of our own qualities, not to mention those of others. This is why the very quality about which Fr. Sorin speaks is zeal, the zeal that arises in us when we believe that what we find lacking, God to his end provides.

Peter J. Walsh, C.S.C.

September 18

The more we come through prayer to relish what is right, the better we shall work in our mission for the realization of the kingdom.
—Holy Cross *Constitutions*

IN OUR DAILY lives, we need to care for so many things that it is not always clear that we are directly working for the realization of the kingdom of God. Doing research, teaching, going to meetings, living in community, joining in household chores, and raising children might not at first seem to be clear images of serving the mission of Christ and ushering in the kingdom. The core of our mission, however, both as baptized Christians and as Holy Cross religious does not reside so much in what we do but how it is that we do it. Since we are called to carry out Christ's mission, we first of all are called to have the same sentiments as Christ Jesus, no matter what the task or labor at hand.

Yet we all know the difficulty of being of one mind and heart with Christ. It is impossible without prayer, for our thoughts are not easily God's thoughts nor our will his will. Our union with God through prayer brings us deeper into the mystery of his presence within us where we can discover his will for us. For to know his will is to hear the call, as Blessed Moreau describes it, to lead with our Lord a life hidden in God. Then, grasping more clearly the will of God for our lives, we come to relish more and more what is right. That is, we seek to live our every action with the same sentiments as Jesus Christ. Then we, too, shall contribute to the realization of his kingdom.

Gérard Dionne, C.S.C.

September 19

In our common life we give an immediate and tangible expression to what we profess through our vows: in the local community we share the companionship of goods and the united efforts of our celibacy, poverty and obedience.

—Holy Cross *Constitutions*

FOR ALMOST FIFTY years, couples have used *Together for Life* from Ave Maria Press to prepare for their marriages. The book's scripture readings and reflections portray the beauties and ideals of marriage. But one day, not long after the ceremony, dishes sit in the sink or leaves cover the yard and ideals meet day-to-day realities. So, too, in religious life. Our *Constitutions* describe ideals, but like the ideals of marriage, they must be grounded in the daily life of a community.

One can attend to dishes, yard work, common prayer, or meetings simply because they need to be done if the marriage or religious community is not to fall apart. But is there more to it than that?

This quotation on our common life, which comes from the constitution on Brotherhood, echoes the earlier constitution on Mission. The constitution on Mission clearly states that brotherhood in mission and prayer lived out locally incarnates the Congregation as a sign of hope in the world. It is to be a virtuous circle. A community or a marriage cannot run as a well-oiled machine as if that alone were the ideal of common life or marriage. Nor can one claim to be living any ideal if the demands of everyday life remain unattended. No matter how beautifully an ideal is worded, it must be lived out in deeds. No matter how perfectly a common life is lived, it must be grounded in an ideal. For a marriage to show the sacramental splendor of Christ's love in the world or for a religious congregation also to be a sign of that love, word and deed must be read and done together.

Thomas P. Gariepy, C.S.C.

September 20

Whether he afflicts or consoles, whether he leads to the gates of death or brings back therefrom, let us praise the Lord.

—Fr. Edward Sorin, C.S.C.

EVERY DAY THAT I served at Portland's Downtown Chapel, I was reminded that I could not control people's lives. I could not fix the heroin addict to make him love himself. I could not change the decisions of the mentally ill who clung to patterns from childhood abuse. I could not influence our guests to search for housing and to seek employment. I could suggest nothing to motivate my friend to move out of his depression, his anxiety about never feeling loved. These could be days when the inconsolable suffering of people turned me toward fear.

On days like those, even now, God alone points me in a new direction. Faith allows me to trust God and not the gifts I think God should be bestowing on those who suffer. This awareness brings me great humility and profound patience. It teaches me to learn from other believers. I now understand the leper who waited for Jesus on the margins of his village. I see the mother who begged Jesus to cure her daughter. I empathize with the man whose withered hand was cured on the Sabbath.

The profound treasure that the Holy Cross tradition passes on to all believers is an unwavering trust in God's presence, regardless of life's circumstances. We grow in faith through life's adversities and seek God's love even in despair. We demonstrate perseverance when uncertainty brings us low. We worship with full hearts when we let go of the illusion that we are in control. And we grow in gratitude when we move beyond ourselves and finally seek God.

Ronald Patrick Raab, C.S.C.

September 21

*Jesus went to heaven to prepare a place for us, and
what a place! There, as he does now, we will one day
have no more pains to suffer, no good thing to wish
for, no change to fear. God himself will wipe away
the tears from our eyes. The source of tears will be
forever dried up. All capacities of our body and soul
will be satisfied.*

—Blessed Basil Moreau

THREE YOUNG ADULT children sat on one side of the table,
their parents on the other. Again, I was meeting with a family
to prepare the funeral of a loved one. What was unusual was
that the loved one was present, not just in spirit but very much
in the flesh.

This wife and mother was fully engaged in parish life; her
greatest joy was choir. Sheri loved to sing, and she sang like an
angel. She battled the scourge of cancer. Now she was preparing
to sing with the angels. Sheri wanted to "make her arrange-
ments" to ease the burden on her family when that time came.

Previously she asked about funeral preparation. "I meet with
the family," I said, "to choose the scriptures, music, and let them
share memories." She had selected the scriptures and music. "I
want to gather the family," she replied, "and share memories!"

The prospect was awkward, but the bond of family and faith
was strong. The tension was palpable as we assembled. I asked,
"What qualities of your mother will you treasure most?" The
eldest son spoke. His younger brother continued. Their sister

chimed in. The heaviness was obliterated; joy and laughter prevailed as memories flowed. Her husband, always stoic, held his wife's hand. They glowed with pride over the fruit of their love, three times revealed.

I thanked them for this privileged exchange. Sheri was radiant. The reality of why we had gathered returned. Silent tears flowed from her children's eyes. "How can you not cry?" her daughter protested. "This makes me so happy," replied her mother, gesturing toward her family. It was, for her, a glimpse of heaven on earth when pain is vanquished. Here the hope of Resurrection dawned, for God himself will wipe away the tears from our eyes.

Ed Kaminski, C.S.C.

September 22

As religious, we spend daily considerable time before the tabernacle; these precious visits alone should amply suffice to keep the fire of faith burning in our hearts day and night.

—Fr. Edward Sorin, C.S.C.

Cardinal John F. O'Hara, C.S.C., referred to Notre Dame as the "City of the Blessed Sacrament." Today, with sanctuary lamps burning before tabernacles in more than fifty chapels, it is easy to see why this name is appropriate. And yet Notre Dame has been a city of the Blessed Sacrament from its earliest days. One of the most touching letters Fr. Sorin wrote to Fr. Moreau tells of how encouraging it was for the young Holy Cross community to see the flickering of the sanctuary lamp through the window of their simple residence as they returned from hard work clearing the fields each day.

In view of the many trials and hardships that Fr. Sorin and the other priests and brothers endured—and among many graces and consolations they enjoyed—the presence of the consecrated host in their simple tabernacle must have been special. While they always would have the grace to celebrate Eucharist together, the last measure of oil to keep their sanctuary lamp burning would mark the temporary end of their ability to visit Jesus Christ present in the reserved sacrament. I suspect it is not too far-fetched to imagine that the first item on their shopping list even when funds were scarce would have been oil in order to keep lit the lamp that beckoned them so warmly, inviting them to visit their Lord and Savior and be renewed.

So, too, must all of us seek this same spiritual nourishment by making time to be in the Lord's presence before the reserved sacrament. In return, he will keep the fire of faith burning in our hearts day and night.

Richard V. Warner, C.S.C.

September 23

Let us join to truly religious conduct a love of work and especially study.

—Blessed Basil Moreau

ONE AFTERNOON AT the end of a rather long lecture, a seminary professor engaged the class in a discussion about our future ministry in the Church. I remember sharing that I very much wanted to become a college professor. A fellow student rather abruptly injected, "That is not ministry!" Taken aback, I remained silent. However, my professor, a renowned scholar and Jesuit priest, interjected gently but firmly by recalling, among other things, the numerous figures from Church history who dedicated their lives to God by also dedicating their lives to study.

Needless to say, in whatever career we pursue in life, all of us engage in some type of preparation for it. Whether such training be technical or theoretical, we spend time, perhaps even years, enlightening our minds through practical exercises, critical reading, and analytical writing in order to be ready to undertake the work of our chosen profession. Blessed Moreau always emphasized the importance of the pursuit of learning for religious of Holy Cross. In turn, he exhorted his religious, in whatever ministry we undertake, to share the knowledge we learn with those whom we serve. For Blessed Moreau, however, learning was incomplete if it only increased an individual's academic knowledge. Rather, it has to be transformative and affect both the mind and the heart of an individual so that she or he will be able to see the world anew, ultimately through the prism of Christ.

In our busy lives, we are all invited to follow this wisdom and allow ourselves to continue to learn and grow. Our God has created a magnificent and wonderful world with layers upon layers of mystery and meaning, so may we continue to explore

and learn from it with an open mind and heart as we encounter
and attempt to decipher the depths of God's creation.

Kevin P. Spicer, C.S.C.

☦

September 24

*Come into solitude to re-enkindle your faith, your fer-
vor, and your zeal. Imagine you hear our Divine Lord
inviting you as his apostles of old: "Come apart with
me to rest for a while." It is a rest which your soul
needs, a period of quiet during which it can become
more attentive to the inspirations of grace.*

—Blessed Basil Moreau

BLESSED MOREAU WAS a man committed to ministry while
grounded in prayer and solitude. His practice of solitude was
born from his intimate love of God. By reminding us of Jesus'
invitation to "come apart with me to rest for a while," Blessed
Moreau reinforces our own desires for intimacy with God,
which are purified only in the solitude of our own hearts.

Solitude is resting in God. Even when my prayer often gets
tangled up in myself and my preoccupations, time alone with
the Lord continually teaches me to let go and simply to rest in
God. Yet I never have as much quiet time with God as I need. I
struggle to make time for solitude. This is especially true when
I am caught up in my deepest fears and the seductions of doubt.
I need actively to pursue moments of quiet where I rest in God
and set aside everything else. As a result, I seek solitude in a

number of ways. There are spectacular places, such as the top of the Rockies, where my awareness of God is so acute I could burst. There are special times, such as during a long run, where I find myself one with the God of all creation. There are ordinary spaces, such as my prayer space, where I can rest in my hunger for God and God's hunger for me.

Union of heart with God is essential for Christian discipleship. Ultimately, our universal call to holiness is grounded and renewed in this union that can only be cultivated by prayer and solitude.

Richard S. Wilkinson, C.S.C.

September 25

Let us bear with everything as Christ did, and unite, if possible, our blood with his blood, our death even with his death, that we may share in his Resurrection—a favor to be granted only to those who shall have been associated with him in the pains and torments of his Passion.

—Fr. Edward Sorin, C.S.C.

IN MY EXPERIENCE, the familiar expression "misery loves company" can convey two separate messages, neither of which is very encouraging. If the phrase suggests that miserable people relish the companionship of those who are similarly pitiful, it offers little comfort, except perhaps for businesses that promote the marketing of antidepressants. If it means that miserable people make the most appealing dinner guests, then the idea of "loving company" needs a new definition, since the problem then arises as to how, by stark contrast, to describe guests who are cheerful, sociable, and gracious.

When Fr. Sorin urges us to identify our blood and our death with that of Christ, we might understandably be tempted to leap ahead quickly to his Resurrection because of a reluctance to accept suffering as truly belonging in a healthy community that strives to be happy and caring. But this impulse to try to skip over the pains and torments actually prevents us from coming to know in the flesh that it is love and not misery that brings our company together. We are not called to share misery as if it were, like virtue, its own reward. Rather, in bearing with everything as he did and in spreading the Good News wherever we find ourselves, whether sowing or reaping, we partake in that courageous movement of grace that frees us and all people from the very source of misery.

Patrick D. Gaffney, C.S.C.

September 26

We must not be attached to earthly things, otherwise we cannot be attached to God.

—St. André Bessette

WATCHING A BABY reach out and try to grab things reminds us that we are not that old before we start spending our days claiming things for ourselves. Growing up as the firstborn in a family of five kids, I enjoyed first claim on earthly things before my younger brothers. I had my own bed, and they had to share a double-decker. If my clothes no longer fit, they were passed on to my brothers.

All this changed when I joined Holy Cross. From my earliest days in the community, I was taught that religious life was a life of sharing all I have and all I am, a vowed life lived for God and others. It was also a life detached from earthly things so that we could be attached to God.

Fortunately for me, God called me long ago to be a missionary. In the remote parish in northern Tanzania where I serve now, the parishioners are farmers and herders. Their lives have not changed greatly during the past centuries; they plow their fields using oxen and use their ox carts to fetch water. Life is simple and lived very close to the land, and that is probably why I have discovered here real faith and lives attuned to God and his providential ways.

Even after being a Holy Cross religious for more than fifty years, I still cannot claim such detachment yet from earthly things. But I do know the wisdom of Jesus' teaching about trying to serve two masters (see Lk 16:13). And with St. Paul I admit that when I was a child I behaved liked a child and tried to claim the world for myself (see 1 Cor 13:11); but now I have the Lord, and through his grace and the witness of my poor sisters and brothers, I continue to discover ever more that he is all we really need.

George Lucas, C.S.C.

September 27

Since we form with Christ but one Body and draw life from the same Spirit, he urges us to remain united with him, like the vine and the branches, borne by the same root and nourished by the same sap and forming together but one plant. Just as the branch cannot bear fruit of itself unless it be united to the vine, so neither can we unless we are united in Christ Jesus, the vine of which we are the branches.

—Blessed Basil Moreau

THE TREE OF the Cross is planted in the soil of Canto Grande in Lima, Peru. The *barrio* is located in a valley surrounded by the Andes where dirt fills the air and covers everything. Small houses—some with three walls, half walls, or no roofs—cover the sides of the mountains in no apparent pattern. Holy Cross is in the middle of it all, staffing a large parish of 250,000 souls, a large school with two thousand children, and a formation house for young Holy Cross.

As I look out, the houses that meander up the mountains look like the twisted branches and tendrils of a vine. They seem to branch out from the house Holy Cross has built. Holy Cross is far from numerous here, less than twenty men united in Christ Jesus, working together to be the love of Jesus to the Peruvian people.

This vine is planted in other places around the world, some exotic, some ordinary, some beautiful, some plain, but all with the same strong branches and tendrils. This is the Body of Christ made visible. United in Christ and giving glory to him, all of his members across the world work together to make this body alive in the Spirit. Wherever we are, each of us is called to help draw others into his body, by extending the love and knowledge of Jesus to them. For with that love and knowledge, we root them in Christ, the precious gift of hope.

Thomas A. Dziekan, C.S.C.

September 28

If we drink the cup each of us is poured and given, we servants will fare no better than our master. But if we shirk the cross, gone too will be our hope. It is in fidelity to what we once pledged that we will find the dying and the rising equally assured.
—Holy Cross *Constitutions*

I'VE LOST TRACK of the number of weddings and final professions of religious vows in which I've participated. Each is unique, yet there are common elements—joy, hope, excitement, the support of community and family, and a sense that everything is indeed possible with God's grace. Yet we veterans of life know something that the young often do not. Fidelity to one's commitment, which in the moment seems so forever easy, will eventually reach a point where what we once pledged has to be confirmed again and again, and yet again.

Life is not static. We change—or resist change—and must honor and obey our growth and experience. Our spouses or communities change—or refuse to change—and we must remember our promises, for better or worse. Neighbors and coworkers change, as do parents and children, and we must somehow remain faithful to them. The Church changes, as does the world in which we live. Even God seems to change, in the sense that the One whom we thought so close and so supportive now seems absent and unheeding.

There is no doubt that fidelity will sometimes tear us apart, as it did Jesus on the Cross. Hard choices may be necessary as we seek to balance the demands of being faithful to God, self, and others, whether in family or religious community. All we know for sure is that God will be with us, every step of the way. Somehow, someway, that which is torn apart will form the fertile ground for yet one more renewal of our fidelity.

Herbert C. Yost, C.S.C.

September 29

Before the Lord we learn what is his will to be done, we ask that no one lack daily bread, we dare to match forgiveness for forgiveness and we plead to survive the test. We desire that his name be praised, that his kingdom come and that we be his faithful servants in the planting of it.

—Holy Cross *Constitutions*

LET GOD BE God. This is the heart of the first half of the Lord's Prayer. We are not in control; it is God's world, and religion is about what God is doing more than about what we are doing. "Hallowed be thy name; thy Kingdom come; thy will be done." I believe God wants what we want, just as good parents want their children to lead their own lives. God, however, wants what we want at the deepest and truest depths of our beings. Alas, we are often bewildered and confused about what we want because we try to mimic what our culture tells us we ought to want. But at heart, we all do want to give our lives to God and for God.

The second half of the Lord's Prayer says, in effect, let human beings be human beings. I look at a small child, and it reminds me of my human needs. I need to be fed: "Give us this day our daily bread"—which includes both emotional and spiritual food. I need to be cleaned up when I make a mess: "Forgive as we are forgiven." I need to be secure and protected: "Do not put us to the test or lead us into temptation"—be it divorce, cancer, death of a child, loss of a job, or any other trauma. We thus pray not to be given a cross heavier than we can carry, and we know that this prayer, prayed by the Lord himself, will always be heard.

Nicholas Ayo, C.S.C.

September 30

We are sojourners in this world, longing for the coming of the new creation as we seek to be stewards on this earth. The world is well provisioned with gifts from

God's hand, but the gifts are often worshiped and the Giver is ignored.

—Holy Cross *Constitutions*

ON A FINE, sunny day during my novitiate year in Bangalore, India, a beggar came asking for food. Since I was the guest master, I asked the cook to give him some food. An hour later, the cook informed me that the man had disappeared with a silver cup. Immediately, we went after the man and brought him back to the novitiate. I could see the cup hidden on his person, so I became angry and scolded him.

Our novice master, Fr. Reginald McQuaid, C.S.C., seemed to have watched the fracas. When I realized he was there, I froze, but he went into the house. The beggar feared that he had gone to inform the police, so he pleaded with me to restrain the novice master. To my surprise, our novice master returned with a few more silver cups and gave them to the man. The man was spellbound, moved to tears. He fell at the novice master's feet and asked forgiveness. Since the novice master had treated him with dignity, the beggar went away a changed man, resolved to steal no more.

Our novice master's response helped me change my perspective on people, things, and the world. He had a choice either to react or to respond to that beggar. He had an option either to punish him or to restore his dignity and let him go as a human person with his honor intact. He chose the latter and thereby turned the beggar's heart from the silver cup to God, the Giver.

How do we act when confronted by such situations in life? Hopefully, we want to be stewards of God's creation and not masters. By reacting, we can demean the other, but by responding generously, we can restore the person's rightful relationship to our Creator. As our novice master taught us, we can awaken to the Divine, igniting it in both ourselves and others.

P. A. Devadoss, C.S.C.

October 1

Fidelity to our vows is the basis and the whole foundation of the whole structure of Holy Cross, in which each one of us has become both a living stone and the builder.

—Blessed Basil Moreau

WHEN I WAS on staff at Moreau Seminary, we had a table in the refectory known as "Table #1." It was the table where some of the older brothers regularly sat. The ones I knew best were Br. James Edwin, C.S.C., Br. James Lakofka, C.S.C., and Br. Chet Ziemba, C.S.C. They taught me as much about fidelity as anyone.

They were men of work. I can still see Br. Chet in his overalls, caring for the grounds at Fatima Retreat Center and feeding the squirrels peanuts. I remember Br. James Edwin huddled in his old brown coat, walking to work in the winter at Ave Maria Press. I recall Br. James Lakofka's visits to his little office at the seminary, shipping vials of Lourdes water across the country.

They were men of prayer. Every day began with 6:40 a.m. Mass. Br. James Lakofka read, and Br. James Edwin was sacristan and server. His challenge each day was to light the two altar candles with one match.

They were men of simplicity. Br. Chet spent his stipend on birdseed and peanuts. Br. James Lakofka would treat the seminarians to ice cream. Br. James Edwin turned his stipend back in to the superior each month. They wanted for nothing.

They were men of community, always at Table #1. There was never a compelling reason not to be. They loved it when we joined them there, and they were always interested in what we were doing.

They taught me that fidelity in life, whether to the vows or any other commitment, is really about faithfulness to the little things. These gentle and kind men became saints, I believe. They were truly living stones and builders of Holy Cross.

Patrick Neary, C.S.C.

October 2

For the sake of both charity and humility, all should look on others as superior to themselves, should give others the respect and honor due their station, should see in the neighbor the image of God and honor the guardian angel attending him.

—Blessed Basil Moreau

BLESSED MOREAU'S WORDS here seem to echo St. Paul's directive to "humbly regard others as more important than yourselves" (Phil 2:4). I've never liked that verse. It seems to urge me to be disingenuous, to attempt to will myself into a sense of inferiority, or a false humility.

Perhaps that is why a good friend advised me to "start with the guardian angel." At first, I simply smiled; I had already decided to ignore that part of the quotation, thinking it superfluous. Then, I recalled some other quotations from Blessed Moreau. While I am not familiar with any specific discourse on angels by Blessed Moreau, I noticed that references in his writings to angels were not infrequent and were usually associated with his powerful belief in Divine Providence. He often expressed astonishment at how the founding and growth of Holy Cross had come about, believing he was simply an instrument in carrying out what God had already willed. What he couldn't accomplish, he remarked, angels would come and complete. Angels, then, were an expression of God's closeness and God's gifts to him in mission.

This is the key. True humility is a profoundly honest self-knowledge. I am created from the earth (*humus*). As a creature, I have no claim on the Creator. I am completely dependent at all times on the One who brought me into being and sustains me in being at every moment. Yet I, who can claim nothing, have been given everything, including a share in God's very life in Christ! All is gift. This awareness is the essence of true humility. As this awareness grows, along with an awareness of how I have abused what I have received, I can truly honor all other human creatures and love them—and let them love me.

Don Dilg, C.S.C.

As in every work of our mission, we find that we our-selves stand to learn much from those whom we are called to teach.

—Holy Cross *Constitutions*

ALL TEACHERS HOPE that their students will remember what they have learned. Christ the teacher sent the Holy Spirit for this very purpose: "The Advocate, the holy Spirit that the Father will send in my name—he will teach you everything and remind you of all that I told you" (Jn 14:26). According to our Savior, then, true and lasting teaching and learning are fundamentally spiritual activities. And some of my students have taught me lessons I'll never forget.

I teach a subject—college mathematics—that unfortunately seems to bore or terrify more than it inspires. Many find math to be a challenge or even a cross. Yet every so often, students accept that challenge or embrace that cross with remarkable zeal, determination, or cheerfulness. They don't all achieve the same results. Some scrape by with a barely passing mark; others overcome early setbacks and excel. But in their willingness to strive, all of them remind me of my vocation as an academic and as a Holy Cross religious. They call me to renew my own research, for how can I expect them to work on new and difficult problems if I'm not willing to do the same? They call me back to our motto—Hail the Cross, Our Only Hope—for in their willingness to struggle through confusion, they prove their hope for the joy of understanding.

Warning against intellectual and social pretensions, our Lord told his disciples, "As for you, do not be called 'Rabbi.' You have but one teacher" (Mt 23:8)—namely, Christ himself. Perhaps these words are not only an admonition but also a divine call. As all of us form Christ's mystical Body, so all of us must teach one another.

Charles McCoy, C.S.C.

October 4

Jesus was not content simply to become one of us in the Incarnation. To become one with us, he chose a life of poverty. His was the life of the most humble people. His life was obscure. He worked with his hands. He knew what it was to be poor and disowned by society.

—Blessed Basil Moreau

"I WANT TO thank God for all I have." One of our guests shared this as we gathered in prayer before we opened our hospitality center at our Holy Cross parish in downtown Portland, Oregon. I know him. He carries all his possessions in a backpack and prays in thanks for God's generous gifts. He lives outside and prays in thanks for God's protective care. He knows the loneliness of days and nights and prays in thanks for God's loving presence. The grittiness of his poverty contrasts with the richness of his faith. His prayer of gratitude reveals his intimacy with God—simple and honest, face-to-face.

My years as pastor of that downtown parish taught me that the poor cannot hide who they are. Poverty strips away money, possessions, intellect, and power and exposes the real person behind the pretense and false appearance. The poor cannot hide who they are from God. Nor can any of us. Jesus understood this. He wanted nothing so he could have what he most desired—loving, prayerful intimacy with the Father. He embraced a life of poverty, knowing that living anything more than that would raise walls that hide what is genuinely human, including fear, uncertainty, and suffering. Only in his poverty could he see the Father and know the fullness of intimacy with him.

For many of us, the spiritual work we need to do is to strip away the false self. We need to acknowledge our poverty, to stop hiding, to confess our need for God. We seek to live faith from a place of grateful honesty, just like the guest at the parish.

Bob Loughery, C.S.C.

October 5

O Lord, come to my aid, make haste to help me; Lord, give me a burning desire to seek you, to find you, to follow you, at whatever price.

—Fr. Jacques Dujarie

TWICE EVERY DAY, in our morning and evening prayer, we begin with the pleas, "Come to my aid," and, "Lord, make haste to help me." The goal of every baptized Christian is this union with God. But what does this mean for our everyday lives?

As a young brother, I went to work in Africa on fire with the desire to save, if not all of Africa, at least the country to which I was sent for Christ. I worked side by side with many other Holy Cross religious driven by the same desire. Sickness, however, brought me back to the United States, and I tried to understand why this had happened, begging, "Come to my aid; Lord, make haste to help me." The answer came to me from an unexpected source—a child with multiple disabilities. He lived in a state medical facility when I started working with him. His needs were enormous. God, in a sense, took Africa from me and gave me a young man to love, saying, "Deal with it."

The great lesson that I have learned is that, when we love others at whatever the price, we need look no further—we have encountered God. By striving to love in this way, we are participating in God's gratuitous and all-encompassing love for others and ourselves, thus becoming one with him. This can happen in Africa, at a state medical facility, in a classroom, or at a family table. God is always at our side, always helping us, both enkindling in us the desire to seek, find, and follow him, and guiding us to its fulfillment.

Raymond Papenfuss, C.S.C.

October 6

The sacraments are as the last effort of Jesus Christ's tenderness toward those he came to save, for they serve as the channels through which he communicates his grace and gives us his own life and spirit. They are the sacred fountains of which the prophet spoke from which we joyfully drink the waters that purify our souls from all stains of sin and give them sweet peace, divine strength, and new ardor to go forward in the ways of salvation.

—Blessed Basil Moreau

I WAS THINKING the other day about the first time I could not remember what my father's voice sounded like. He died when I was young, and some years later, when I was in my late teens, I was trying to recall something he'd told me, and I realized I could not remember his voice. It both frightened and saddened me. I think that is what is hard about goodbyes in general: we fear losing touch with someone important; we fear that what once was about a particular relationship will never be again.

The disciples were afraid like that before Jesus' Ascension. How would they survive without his presence? How would they ever feel the power of his love? The all-encompassing embrace of his forgiveness? His gentle and healing touch? The wisdom of his counsel? What they did not realize at that time was that Jesus was not going to leave without giving them—and us—an incredible gift: the gift of the sacraments, the gift of his very self, given with love beyond all telling. It would be through the sacraments that they and we would be able to experience all that Jesus was and is—his presence, his mercy, his healing, his Spirit. There would be no goodbye.

The sacraments allow us to be one with Jesus in a real, profound, and transformative way. They are the fulfillment of the Lord's promise that he will be "with you always, until the end of the age" (Mt 28:20). Through the sacraments, we remain in the heart of God, and we are never left alone. The sacraments allow us to live into the words spoken to Jesus by his Father and which the Father speaks to us in every encounter: "You are my beloved son. You are my beloved daughter." It is a voice we never have to worry about forgetting.

Peter Jarret, C.S.C.

October 7

For those who live by faith the Cross is a treasure more valuable than gold and precious stones. If we were truly worthy of our vocation, far from dreading these crosses, we would be more eager to accept them than to receive a relic of the very wood which our Savior sanctified by his blood.

—Blessed Basil Moreau

WHEN A BIT of debris becomes wedged in the flesh of an oyster, the irritated mollusk responds by coating the offending fragment with countless layers of a substance called nacre. In time, a pearl is produced. What began as a source of pain to the shellfish ends as an iridescent jewel. Of course, if the oyster had kept its shell firmly closed, the debris could never have gotten inside in the first place. But an oyster needs to open its shell in order to breathe and feed. So if the oyster hadn't taken the risk of opening its shell, it would have suffocated and starved, and there would have been one less pearl in the world.

Blessed Moreau's reflection on the Cross suggests that something analogous is true of us. If we respond to the sufferings of each hour by enfolding them within a life of patient, generous love, we will in the course of time become jewel-like adornments of the kingdom of God. But if fear of suffering causes us to withdraw from others and the world, we will be spiritually stifled. And someone beautiful, with whom God intended to adorn creation, will never come to be.

In at least one respect, though, the analogy fails. While a pearl is precious, the fragment of debris at its center, considered on its own merits, is valueless, whereas the suffering that occasions a Christian life well-lived is itself a priceless reminder of the saving Cross of our Lord Jesus Christ.

Charles B. Gordon, C.S.C.

October 8

Jesus wants to be our father, not our judge. He is our friend, our brother who has for us only words of mercy and bounty, provided always we bring him a contrite and humble heart.

—Blessed Basil Moreau

LEARNING TO DO marriage preparation was invigorating, exciting, and somewhat terrifying. I quickly learned patience for the couples, who must have been equally nervous coming into those sessions. Eventually, we would reach some intimate, private, personal point of conversation as we discussed their life together.

I could see them tense up. Maybe they asked themselves if I would judge them, if they would get in trouble for giving a wrong answer. If only they understood beforehand that I was not there to pass judgment on them but to minister to them, to walk this Christian journey with them.

I wanted to meet them right where they were, and I did not care if it were the ideal place, as long as it was the truth. I would stress over and over again that there were no right and wrong answers about their lives; there were only true and untrue answers. How could I or any priest serving in this way judge them? Not only would it be a tremendously ineffective way to minister but it also would be entirely against how Christ himself ministers to us.

It may be true that sometimes we do not live up to the expectations of Christ, others, or from time to time even ourselves. But Christ does not approach us with contempt or judgment, and nor should we, then, approach others in that way. Perhaps we, too, must realize ever more that Christ is inviting all of us to deeper communion with himself, especially in those areas that we are hesitant to share with him. He is our friend and has only love to offer us.

Matthew Hovde, C.S.C.

October 9

At the altar, the word of the priest through the power of the Holy Spirit transforms the gifts that are presented there into the body of Jesus Christ, and in the pulpit, the same word ought to transform us in a hidden manner, making us become the mystical Body and members of the Lord.

—Blessed Basil Moreau

DURING MY YEARS as a priest, I have presided and preached at countless Masses. A danger of celebrating Mass daily is that it can become routine and perfunctory, a mere ritual that the priest performs over and over again.

Our holy founder reminded his fellow priests of Holy Cross how blessed they were to celebrate Mass *in persona Christi*. To stand in the person of Christ, to pronounce his word of blessing over the bread and wine, transforming them by the power of the Holy Spirit into his very body and blood, is such an awesome mystery of grace. Each time I celebrate the Eucharist and speak those words of Christ, I try to do so reverently and prayerfully, mindful of how unworthy I am to do so.

Christ also becomes present to the gathered community through the proclamation of his Word. Each time I announce the Good News from the ambo, the assembly acclaims, "Glory to you, O Lord!" "Praise to you, Lord Jesus Christ!" As those present acknowledge the grace of hearing Jesus speak to them, so, too, it must be for the homilist who heard this admonition at his ordination as a deacon: "Express by your actions the Word of God which your lips proclaim."

By its very nature, ritual behavior is repetitive and predictable. Therefore there is the danger of even the Mass, the source and summit of grace, becoming routine and boring for any of us. If, however, we are attentive to what we hear and do, entering as intentionally as possible into the pulse and rhythm of the liturgy, the Mass will shape and transform us more and more into the person of Jesus, whose Word is ever new and challenging and whose body and blood refreshes and strengthens us.

Peter Rocca, C.S.C.

October 10

Let us then renew our generosity in his service, and if our work seems hard and difficult, let us remember that, after all, it will last only a short time, whereas its reward will remain forever.

—Blessed Basil Moreau

"LIFE IS NOT a dress rehearsal." A priest once gave me a T-shirt with this slogan on it when I told him I was considering the seminary. It was inspiring to me because, like similar mottos—"*Carpe Diem*," "No pain, no gain," or "Just do it"—it reminded me that I have to face the present challenges of my life with strength and courage. Holding back, giving less than our best effort, is never the better option.

Some challenges in life—often the most important ones—are both difficult to do and slow to show any results. But we are called to do them anyway, even when they're difficult. A life dedicated to teaching, preaching, or working among the needy means using our abilities and talents for others, not because we're going to get instant gratification but because it's our vocation. We feel called by God; we feel compelled to reach out and do what we can with the gifts that we've been given.

Blessed Moreau felt compelled to found the Congregation of Holy Cross, and some of us have felt called to follow him. Yet each Christian has his or her own unique calling in life as well, filled with its own challenges, the fruits of which might not always be very obvious. The truth is that God may never show us the real impact we've had on others in our lifetime. But holding back is not an option. Our lives are not just rehearsals for the next life; we are called to action right here, right now, so that we may be blessed with the rewards of the life to come.

Randy Rentner, C.S.C.

October 11

Our hope and our need are to live blessed by faithful and loving relationships with friends and companions in mission, relationships reflective of the intimacy and openness of God's love for us.

—Holy Cross *Constitutions*

AS TIME PASSES, these words take on different meanings. This passage is the last sentence of our constitution on celibacy. It expresses the confidence that, in forgoing family and a secular career, we Holy Cross religious will be rewarded by life in a community of friends dedicated to serving the Gospel.

For young religious, forgoing and loss are often not the dominant sentiments. Students naturally form friendships based on shared work and mutual aspirations. In my case, studying theology during the four years of Vatican II created intense intellectual and vocational excitement. We seminarians shared a belief that we would work in a renewed Church, that the *aggiornamento* would produce a new Christian age. This excitement diminished in middle age. Many hopes of Vatican II were not fulfilled, and the opportunity costs of this vocation became more obvious. People of all callings face such midlife thoughts. This is when lay people find support in family, and religious look for encouragement from community members.

Now that I am seventy-five and retired, these words have assumed another meaning. I can calmly acknowledge successes and failures over many past years. Neither the excitement of youth nor the uncertainties of middle age mark my life. What remains at this point is the satisfaction that I may have made some contribution and the hope that my failures will be forgiven. And I give thanks for the companionship of my fellow Holy Cross religious who sustained me.

Every person, lay or religious, will have a similar story. The passage from early to late life runs an ineluctable course. On this journey, the greatest blessing and deepest need are friends and family who keep us faithful from youth to old age, for they make real to us the God who remains ever faithful.

Louis Manzo, C.S.C.

October 12

Just as abyss calls to abyss and one sin begets another, so one grace gives rise to another if we are faithful to the first. Let us then go to the foot of the altar to thank

*the God of all goodness for the new proof of his mercy,
which he has bestowed upon us.*

—Blessed Basil Moreau

THE MOST IMPORTANT question I was asked while studying for my MBA was put to me by a close friend while walking across the quad. As I was ranting about the crises in the Archdiocese of Boston and how squandered trust was impacting me and future generations in the Church, Lex interrupted me and asked, "How's your gratitude?" My first response was an incredulous bark, so calmly he asked again, "How's your gratitude, Fr. Tom?"

In physics, momentum is a function of mass and velocity. In human organizations, momentum is a powerful, intangible force that can mysteriously propel or thwart progress. Sin and selfishness have a cunning way of self-perpetuating, but they are rendered impotent when confronted with gratitude. Gratitude, with its source in Christ, is the first and fundamental disposition for a Christian. And when personal gratitude is prayed for, cultivated, and cherished, it proves contagious, spreading rapidly and transforming both those with whom we have contact and ourselves.

The Eucharist itself is the greatest thanksgiving, the greatest act of gratitude, drawing into one and enlivening all who share in Jesus' gift of himself. So it is that when we bring our grateful selves to the altar and hear the line from the Eucharistic Prayer, "Lord, we thank you for counting us worthy to stand in your presence and serve you," we and all the world are transformed, one grace after another.

Tom Doyle, C.S.C.

October 13

The doctrine of the Cross is the most mysterious secret of divine wisdom. The Cross, which should be eminently our own, as religious of the Holy Cross, is the science of the heart more properly than the mind.
—Fr. Edward Sorin, C.S.C.

WE HUMAN BEINGS typically avoid suffering if we can. Yet the great danger is that our lives become all about avoiding everything that might be a little painful for us. This fear can cause us to avoid risks and to play it safe through life. The Cross, however, reminds us, as it did Fr. Sorin, that there are some things worth suffering for and that the greatest danger in life is not suffering itself but never caring for or loving others enough to suffer with them and for them. Fr. Sorin believed that God was calling him to serve others through education. At the request of Blessed Moreau, Fr. Sorin left the familiarity of France to serve God's people in America. He did not play it safe. He was willing to suffer hardships and disappointments in order to found the University of Notre Dame, which he firmly believed God would use to inspire generations to make the sacrifices necessary to learn and to serve.

While our heads may tell us that it is foolish to choose to suffer at all, our hearts and the Spirit of Christ tell us that it makes all the sense in the world to suffer for what is right. For Christians who believe in the death and Resurrection of Christ, suffering for what is right is the only option because they know in their hearts that denying the Cross leads to meaninglessness.

While we would rather avoid suffering, if we love as Christ loved, we will suffer as he did. But in the end, we will rise as he did as well.

Robert A. Dowd, C.S.C.

October 14

The vow of obedience includes the entirety of our life in Holy Cross, and through it we hope to discover and accept the Lord's will more surely.
—Holy Cross *Constitutions*

WHENEVER A MOVIE portrays a priest or religious, it almost inevitably has a scene in which religious obedience is portrayed as obeying unquestionably. This, however, is merely blind obedience. While Jesus tells us that he has come to do the Father's will, his is not blind but loving obedience. As we see most clearly in Gethsemane, Jesus dialogues with his Father even as he ultimately follows in love.

We religious profess the vow of obedience, yet ours is to be the loving obedience of Jesus to the Father. Over my years in ministry, I have served as a math and science teacher, missionary, religious formator, financial officer, archivist, and mentor. The community had a need in each area and asked if I would serve. Many were not my choice; some I questioned. But as I followed in love, each has turned out to be a blessing, an opportunity to know myself better, to discover my gifts, and, most importantly, to walk closer with Jesus, the model of obedience.

While those who are not religious sisters, brothers, and priests do not have a superior calling them to obedience, all disciples are called to love as Jesus did: with a loving obedience to the Father. Through listening with a loving heart to spouses and family, to friends and coworkers, to the Church and the cry of the poor, we ultimately seek to listen to God and discover what God wants us to do. At times, we might question; we might not be fully sure. Yet, unlike Frank Sinatra, we seek to sing not "I did it my way," but "I did it the Lord's way." We seek in love to say our yes with Jesus, for together with Jesus, yes we can.

James Nichols, C.S.C.

October 15

Who do you suppose are the most valuable members of our little religious family? Undoubtedly those who pray best. Then each one may say, "Why not I?"
—Fr. Edward Sorin, C.S.C.

WHEN I WAS in the seminary, someone introduced me to *The Practice of the Presence of God*, a holy little book written by Br. Lawrence, a seventeenth-century Carmelite monk. The preface describes him as an ordinary kitchen worker who "learned to live in God's presence so consistently that whether amidst the clanging of the pots and pans, or at the Lord's table, he sensed God just the same."

When I read of Br. Lawrence, I was reminded of Br. James Edwin, C.S.C. Br. James was a shy, quiet, and gentle soul who always seemed to be praying, though not always in a conventional way. He had a smoking niche in our seminary garage where he had a couple of boxes stacked up in a corner. Every time he smoked a cigarette there, he prayed the names of each seminarian written on a note card. While he smoked over the years, he managed to fill two notebooks with paraphrased scripture passages, which we later discovered in an old metal cabinet. Just as Br. Lawrence came to a continual awareness of God, whether in the chapel or in the kitchen, I believe Br. James came to the same continual awareness of God, whether serving at 6:40 a.m. Mass or shipping books at Ave Maria Press, where he worked for more than thirty years. Even smoking, his only visible vice, became an act of prayer.

The most valuable members of our Holy Cross family are those who pray best. Without realizing it, Br. James Edwin became a simple but genuine mystic through his daily faithfulness to prayer. His life is an invitation for all of us to find our own way toward a continual conversation with God throughout the day—no matter what we find ourselves doing.

Patrick Neary, C.S.C.

October 16

Nothing is more opposed to the maxims of the gospel and the spirit of your vocation than fear; nothing is more capable of paralyzing the good which has been so auspiciously begun.

—Blessed Basil Moreau

"BE NOT AFRAID." St. John Paul II opened his pontificate with these words of Jesus Christ, and he repeated them over and over again, in and out of season, as a reminder to the Church and to the world that God's love overcomes all our fears, freeing us to live our callings.

I know the deep truth of Christ's invitation to abandon all fear. God has richly blessed my life and ministry as a priest in Holy Cross. I have even been shocked at what God has done through me when I simply have trusted in Divine Providence. I often wonder how else God seeks to use my life. I don't know. What I do know is that if I let fear govern my life, I will limit the possibilities of what God can do through me because fear restricts us. It inhibits the transformative power of God's love in our lives. But if I trust and take God at his word, there is no limit to the good that he can accomplish in and through even sinners like myself.

When each of us allows God's perfect love to cast out fear from our hearts, we open ourselves to live fully our vocations in Christ. St. John Paul II was not afraid; members of Holy Cross shed their fears in order to serve the Church throughout the world. We, too, must remember that God is never found wanting in our need. There is nothing to fear. "Be not afraid."

Joe Corpora, C.S.C.

You must submit yourself to God's will; it is the teacher of everything.

—St. André Bessette

AN OLD MAN once told me a story about St. André Bessette. When this man was a boy growing up in Canada, he had a hip problem so severe that he had to use crutches. One day, he learned that Br. André would be visiting his school. The boy's mother insisted that he ask Br. André to heal him.

On the playground that afternoon, embarrassed and intimidated, the boy nervously tugged on Br. André's sleeve and asked for his help. Br. André smiled. They said a prayer together asking for St. Joseph's intercession and God's healing. Then Br. André asked, If the boy got better, could he keep the crutches? The boy wasn't sure and said he needed to ask his mother. He got permission to walk the short distance home. Seeing him from afar, his mother was anxious and asked why he wasn't at school. The boy explained, and his mother said, "Of course, just go back to school!"

When the boy returned, he gave Br. André the crutches. Only then did he realize that he hadn't used them the whole walk back to school. He never needed them again. With that experience as a foundation, the boy decided to become a Holy Cross brother.

No matter what our vocation, God most often calls us through the words of parents, friends, and other wise people in our lives. When we follow their challenging advice, we respond generously to God's call, which requires great trust that God will heal us and give us what is best. In this way, submitting ourselves to God's will, we will learn all we need in life. For not only did God's will—manifest in the voices of a mother and a humble, holy man—bring physical healing to a little boy; it taught him the greatest lesson of all: God's call for our lives.

Matt Kuczora, C.S.C.

October 18

It is God who up until the present has directed all those events which appeared most contrary to the execution of his holy will. If we seek only God's glory and are ready to make every sacrifice for the love of so good a Master, then the more trials we will have to face, the better everything will succeed.

—Blessed Basil Moreau

SINCE THE FOUNDING of our universities, we Holy Cross religious have lived among our students in the residence halls. As rectors, chaplains, and religious in residence, we are role models, teachers, and pastors for them. As time unfolds after graduation, our students often become role models to us, their peers, and our world.

I immediately think of a young married couple I know. They were students together at a Holy Cross university. They fell in love and married. I celebrated their marriage. The Lord blessed them with one child and then another. I baptized both children with joy and delight. Then the oldest child sickened, suffered terribly, and died. He was the happiest boy. How easy and natural and normal and understandable it would have been, then, for the parents to be bitter, to rage against the Lord who allowed such pain and sorrow. But they did not rage and roar. They taught me a great lesson. They poured themselves into being deeper in love as husband and wife. They poured themselves into being even better parents to their daughter. They did not question but only worked harder at the vocations they had chosen. They faced their terrible trials with grace and courage and patience and humility. I was awed. I remain awed. A year later a child was granted unto them by the Lord. I baptized the new baby.

I think of them often—this couple, their three children, their love, their humility. I hope and pray that we can be as accepting of terrible trials, as firm in our faith, and as true to our chosen vocations as they are in theirs.

Edwin H. Obermiller, C.S.C.

October 19

"He alone searches the heart," and from his scrutiny nothing is hidden. What a source of consolation and encouragement for the exemplary religious! And what a cause of fear for the lukewarm and "wicked servant," as the evangelist terms him!

—Fr. Edward Sorin, C.S.C.

IN TROUBLING TIMES, we long for a god who vindicates the righteous and inflicts justice on the wicked. When the innocent suffer and their tormentors prosper, we find it comforting to turn to a god who makes all things right in the end. Such a god, however, may not exist, if the Father of Jesus is, indeed, God of all the earth. For Jesus teaches that his Father causes the sun to rise upon good and bad alike, and sends rain for the unjust as well as the just.

The searcher of hearts, it seems, is not gathering up evidence to use against us in a court of law, to ensure that each receives as his or her conduct deserves. A parent does not keep score of the failings of a beloved child. If we who are evil know how to express tender care for those we have loved into existence, would our Eternal Father do less?

A sure comfort is to be found less in the conviction that the upright will ultimately be rewarded and evildoers punished, than in the awareness that nothing can separate us from the eternal love of God. Such awareness is consoling, however, only for those who know themselves as deeply flawed. The righteous do not need a physician or forgiveness. More genuinely to be feared, by contrast, is the possibility of dwelling everlastingly in the presence of such love, even as we know ourselves to be frauds, in the certainty that the Eternal sees right and utterly through us.

Russ McDougall, C.S.C.

October 20

When my mind attempts to measure the great responsibility which weighs on me, I can find no peace save in blind trust in the God of mercies, from whom I expect the help which will compensate my weakness.
—Blessed Basil Moreau

OREGON IS LOCATED on the Pacific Flyway, and at certain times of the year migrating Canada geese can be seen passing overhead in their familiar *V* formation. There's a reason they fly that way and honk loudly as they do. Their formation gives aerodynamic lift to their leader, and their honking is the sound of encouragement. You never see geese traveling alone.

Leaders of universities don't travel alone either. There is no question that there is a lot of responsibility that comes with being president of a university. About 4,100 students attend the University of Portland, and more than five hundred faculty and staff have made the university their life's work. There's a budget that has to be met. But I never have felt all of that to be a burden; it doesn't weigh on me and keep me awake at night because I never feel it is something I am doing by myself. That's because I know that I can rely on the God of mercies from whom I expect the help that will compensate my weakness. But it's also because dozens of talented and caring people share the work with me.

In the more challenging moments of founding Holy Cross, Blessed Basil Moreau didn't have that luxury, and sometimes he had to carry the load by himself. But I am blessed to have brilliant people dealing with finances and enrollment and academics and the sundry other work of running a university. I am surrounded by an entire community of women and men of talent and good will who share the work and make it a joy to come to my office every day. They lift me up, just as I hope I lift them. The lesson I take from all of it is this: our life and our mission is better when we live it and do it together.

Mark Poorman, C.S.C.

October 21

If the imitation of Christ is our duty, it is also our glory.
—Blessed Basil Moreau

As a new kind of apostle, struggling to lead a fledgling Congregation in making Christ known and the Gospel lived across the globe, Blessed Moreau understood the need to put on Christ. Like the apostle St. Paul, whose putting on Christ required a new way of seeing himself and the world around him, Blessed Moreau had to suspend fears and judgments in order to devote himself, and lead his followers, to see as Christ saw. If the need presented itself in India or America, there the Congregation would go; it was the path the Lord had selected.

In my work in a college setting, God asks—often prods—me to put on Christ, to suspend my human and intellectual judgments about what knowledge I might impart in favor of seeing with the heart. Rather than judging how well prepared I think a student is, should I not be more concerned with how I will reach that questioning or indifferent student in the third row? I need constantly to identify and to refuse to surrender to the self that impedes compassionate action, which is motivated by the other's need rather than my own.

Blessed Moreau taught that our goal as Christians is to understand others as God sees and accepts each one of us. It is not really a "duty," except in the sense that we must work at it each day. Rather than being a loss of self, the rooting of our will and ability in the heart of Christ's saving mission enables our fulfillment. When we put on Christ and let God lead our hearts and minds, our lives and our service become a transforming—indeed a glorious—experience of his grace-filled presence.

Anthony Grasso, C.S.C.

October 22

With how marvelous the Lord has been to allow me to be consumed and made whole at the same time, I say to each and all: be consumed, be eaten up by the Lord's call.

—Fr. Jacques Dujarie

CONSUMED IN THE service of the Lord! To be eaten up, so to speak, by my ministry so that I may live in Christ. The paradox is that as I have been consumed and eaten up over the last forty-five years teaching high school English and music, more times than not the spirit has been simultaneously nurtured and made abundant with life. Are there days when I'd rather stay in bed? You bet your life! Yet as the body has gradually been taken over with arthritis and occasional angst, the spirit through God's grace has strengthened its response: "Here I am, Lord."

Sometime in the late 1990s, I heard for first time Richard Gillard's "The Servant Song." For years now, its first verse has become my daily mantra: "Will you let me be your servant, / let me be as Christ to you? / Pray that I may have the grace / to let you be my servant too." Subsequent verses speak of journeying together as pilgrims, mutually holding on to the Christ-light, and weeping and laughing together until "we've seen the journey through." My ministry in Holy Cross has been liberally peppered with teaching ninth graders to place commas in sentences or to play a flam on a snare drum, with assisting the very capable AP seniors to see deeply into a Hopkins sonnet or to write college essays that really demonstrate their ability. The Lord has been marvelous to allow me to be consumed and made whole at the same time. I say to each and all, "Be consumed, be eaten up by the Lord's call in service of others."

Philip Smith, C.S.C.

October 23

Christ was anointed to bring good news to the poor, release for prisoners, sight for the blind, restoration for every broken victim. Our efforts, which are his, reach out to the afflicted and in a preferential way to the

*poor and the oppressed. We come not just as servants
but as their neighbors, to be with them and of them.*
—Holy Cross *Constitutions*

AS PEOPLE BROUGHT near to God through Christ, our primary preoccupation must be to stand with the poor and the afflicted as neighbors. This is a countercultural and difficult charge, but it is only from this position that our message of life will have enough appeal to convert and deliver the world. "Solidarity," in a local language in Ghana, translates into "being a part of the life of another." It goes beyond empathy. It means that we identify with the poor and share their lot. It means we come not just as servants but as their neighbors, to be with them and of them.

To do this, we have to make Christ our model. He identified with the poor in his birth, ministry, and death. He was born in poor circumstances, and the first message of his birth went to shepherds, people considered poor and simple. In his ministry, Christ began by announcing, "The Spirit of the Lord is upon me because he has anointed me to bring glad tidings to the poor. He has sent me to proclaim liberty to captives and recovery of sight to the blind, to let the oppressed go free, and to proclaim a year acceptable to the Lord" (Lk 4:18–19). Even in his death, Christ hung on a cross as a common criminal between two thieves. Thus, as far as solidarity with the poor and the afflicted is concerned, Jesus clearly remains unsurpassed. As we follow his model, Christ is able, through our lives, to bring conversion and deliverance to many.

Michael Amakyi, C.S.C.

October 24

Peter became the Lord's true and reliable disciple not during the days he followed in Galilee but after he disowned his Lord and wept and was given the opportunity not to become as he once was but to serve as he never had served.

—Holy Cross *Constitutions*

PETER DESERVED TO hear the words, "You're fired." Stubborn, self-righteous, and cocky, Peter made his share of mistakes during his three-year apprenticeship with Jesus. But they had become friends, and Jesus was always able to cast a net deep into Peter's heart and draw out the love and goodness that was in there. It was because of this love and friendship, however, that Peter's betrayal of Jesus was all the more shocking and devastating, and no one felt it more than Peter himself. We can only imagine the guilt and shame this rock of the Church must have felt at what he'd done to his beloved friend.

But as we know, there is always more to the story when dealing with Jesus. What Peter was to discover on the shores of the Sea of Galilee, what we hopefully all discover in our lives, is that love is stronger than all the wrong we might do, that it is stronger even than death. On the beach after his Resurrection, Jesus asked Peter the only question that mattered: "Do you love me?" In their exchange, echoed three times, all was forgiven and set right, all was healed and made new. Jesus gave Peter back to himself.

So it is with us. We know what it is like to fail, to disappoint ourselves and others, to bear the weight of sin and guilt. In each of these moments, over and over throughout our lives, Jesus whispers into our hearts his question: "Do you love me?" When we murmur back our yes, however tentative, Jesus heals us and sends us, like Peter, on our way to serve others.

Peter Jarret, C.S.C.

October 25

Education is the art of helping young people to completeness; for the Christian, this means education is helping a young person to be more like Christ, the model of all Christians.

—Blessed Basil Moreau

IN MY LIFE journey as a teacher and administrator in Catholic education, I have discovered, after many years of trying to bring about great success in the classroom and in leadership, that getting to know Jesus is the only achievement necessary. For Jesus himself questions his disciples, "What profit is there for one to gain the world and forfeit his life?" (Mk 8:36). And what profit would there be for us to educate young people without inviting them into a personal relationship with Christ Jesus?

I know from my own education that I profited the most from those teachers who passionately provided me the necessary support and nourishment to model my life on Christ. I recall in particular one scripture teacher who awakened in me a yearning to know God's universe, a yearning that has remained with me throughout life and inspires me still today. Then, in my own teaching, the most graced moments have been those in which I have witnessed this transformation of students as their cloud of unknowing becomes the brightness of understanding, filling their hearts with hope, and preparing fertile ground for the seed of Christ's love to grow.

Yet the work of transforming young minds and hearts is shared by all. For as we witness and give witness to Christ's love in the world around us, we are teaching young people by our very lives how they, too, might model their lives on Christ. It is through our quest to follow Jesus and our teaching of his example that God will open our hearts and minds, educating each of us in the grandeur of his love.

William C. Nick, C.S.C.

October 26

If the teaching body in the Church exhorts, so powerfully and unanimously, all Christians to seek salvation in the Sacred Heart, we, consecrated as we are by our own Constitutions *to this adorable heart, should be foremost in this solemn act by the fervor of our souls and the entire offering of our whole being to the loving heart of our Divine Savior.*

—Fr. Edward Sorin, C.S.C.

TO SPEAK ABOUT the heart is to speak about the very core of who we are, the very center of our being. Traditionally, the heart is also the symbol of the emotions, most particularly the symbol of love. In a rich and powerful way these two ideas come together in the Sacred Heart. For devotion to the Sacred Heart draws us into the core of who Christ is, which is ultimately divine love.

Blessed Moreau chose the Sacred Heart as the patron for the priests of Holy Cross because it drives at the heart of who we are called to be—men who are drawn to the Lord and his divine love and men who offer our lives to him in service of the Church.

Throughout most of my formation and early priesthood, I wondered if I had what it took to be a Holy Cross priest. This question was probably the strongest in my mind as I lay on the floor at my ordination while the litany of the saints was sung. What was I doing? What did I have to offer? As I listened to the words and the beating of my own heart, it slowly came to me: right there on the floor was what I had to offer—only me and my beating heart. And, in the end that is all any of us has to offer to God—our very self and our own heart beating in time with Christ's.

Jeffrey Allison, C.S.C.

October 27

There was no action, no matter how painful, that Jesus'
love for us would not make him do, no position so

*low or so wretched that his love would not make him
undertake to attract our own love. And, after so many
proofs of his love, he asks in grateful response only
that we go to him with confidence like children to
their father. He invites us, calls us, and urges us to
come to him to comfort us in our pain and to calm the
bitterness of our hearts in his own heart.*

—Blessed Basil Moreau

IN THIRTY YEARS as a school administrator, I look back at significant accomplishment. But I also remember messing up, usually when I thought I was in control. When I was disciplinarian at the brothers' school in Chicago, I dreaded the days before Christmas break. Most of the time, the school was a haven of peace and scholarship for our mostly poor, inner-city youth. But for some reason in those dark, December days, the students' tempers flared, stubbornness took root, patience was forgotten, and academic focus was a vague hope. I did not like my job those days and often turned to God for help. I reminded myself I was doing God's work, not mine, and if I let him, God would use me to do good. Since it is my natural tendency to be in control, letting go has been a challenge, but one that makes things easier. When I turn to God and remember things are in his hands, I become less important and more open to the grace I need.

Reflecting on the gospels, I realize I am one among many who identify with Peter—willing to respond to God's call to lead but in seemingly endless need of correction and intervention. We are the ones who ask God to forgive us, again and again. We ask God to inspire us when we feel empty or inadequate. We ask God to heal us spiritually, physically, and emotionally.

And we ask God just to love us—to allow us to let go and feel wrapped in the arms of his love, experiencing hopeful comfort and support in the face of life's challenges. Thankfully, our God never tires of forgiving and loving each of us.

Ken Haders, C.S.C.

October 28

The Lord Jesus was crucified. But the Father raised him to glory, and Christ breathed his Spirit into his people, the Church. Dying and rising with him in baptism, his followers are sent to continue his mission, to hasten along the kingdom.

—Holy Cross *Constitutions*

THE LOVE OF God revealed in the Crucifixion, Resurrection, and Pentecost is the source of our hope, the food for our faith, and the catalyst for the zeal with which we pledge our lives to the mission of Holy Cross. How exciting, yet humbling, to be called to this mission, which is very simply the mission of Jesus, our Savior. Our efforts, stemming from our prayer, brotherhood, and life in community, are not rooted in who we are but rather in who he is, since they are really his efforts. Be it in the classroom, parish, homeless shelter, or a land or culture foreign to us, we are all missionaries of his hope who proclaim the kingdom of justice, peace, and love.

The mission of Jesus, shared by all the baptized, is often misunderstood, rejected, or frustrated by conflicting values. Indeed, we are walking with him on the road to Calvary when we are mocked, ignored, or reviled for being preachers and teachers of the mission. Hope can be hard for us to sustain when we feel the kingdom impeded rather than hastened. Weariness can dampen our zeal or even create for us a Gethsemane of the spirit. In these times we are reminded that, just as the mission is that of Jesus, so also is the strength for it. He sustains us. His unending love for us restores our hope and fires our zeal. And since God loved us first, we are capable of sharing, and yearn to share, that love with others. It is a love that hastens us along in our mission.

David T. Tyson, C.S.C.

October 29

Beyond the liturgy that convokes us into church and congregation, there is the prayer we each must offer to the Father quietly and alone. We contemplate the living God, offering ourselves to be drawn into his love and learning to take that same love to heart. We enter thus into the mystery of the God who chose to dwell in the midst of his people.

—Holy Cross *Constitutions*

ST. PAUL CHALLENGES us to pray constantly, yet every day distractions abound. I live on a college campus, so all the opportunities—including sporting events, presentations, theatrical performances, and various social interactions—can consume my entire day if I'm not careful. Our students often say that meaningful personal prayer time is usually the first casualty when it comes to prioritizing their academic and social calendar. And yet, once the rigors of academic studies are completed, they're easily replaced with the pursuits of career goals, work responsibilities, and family obligations. Our challenge is to make prayer always part of our daily routine.

Our days are filled with choices. How often do we find ourselves checking our e-mail even though we just checked it minutes ago? Or find ourselves perusing the Internet but seem unable to find time to spend in prayer with God?

St. John Chrysostom writes, "Prayer stands before God as an honored ambassador. It gives joy to the spirit and peace to the heart. I warn you, though: do not imagine that prayer is mere words. Prayer is the desire for God, an indescribable devotion, not given by man but brought about by God's grace." God is giving all of us this grace; however, we have to choose it, to receive and accept it, and to let our desire for God manifest itself in time.

If our lives are only filled with activity and void of prayerful reflection, we can become vulnerable to unhealthy life choices and unbalanced lives. Prayer allows us to listen better to what God is calling us to do. Jesus chose to go off into the wilderness to pray, and we aren't any different. The challenge isn't finding the time but prioritizing what time we do have.

Christopher Torrijas, C.S.C.

October 30

The disciples followed the Lord Jesus in his ministry of proclaiming the kingdom and healing the afflicted. Jesus also spent long days alone with his disciples, speaking to them of the mysteries of his kingdom and forming them to the point when they too could be sent on his mission. Later they would return for his comment and for a deeper hearing because of what they had experienced. We too are sent to his mission as men formed and in need of lifelong formation for his service.

—Holy Cross *Constitutions*

AT GRADUATION AND at profession of vows, my brothers in Holy Cross and I thought we had come to the end of our personal formation. Blessed to have lived not a few years after both, I came to realize beyond any doubt that our formation continues in everything we do. We hope to continue to learn and to grow spiritually each day of our lives.

Both my library and my prayer life expanded over the years. In my intellectual life, I tried to keep up with new thoughts and theories evolving from professional research. Every day, every class, every counseling session taught me something about myself, about others, and about God. My prayer, too, changed through the years. As I grew inwardly, I began to spend more time alone with Jesus, to listen to him, to learn from the inner silence and darkness. Like the psalmist and the disciples, my flesh pined and my soul thirsted more and more for God.

So it is that my learning grew and my spirituality deepened. Formation in the Christian life, whatever our calling, is a never-ending story taking us from the kingdom of this world into the kingdom of God. It is with anticipation that we can all look forward to the great adventure of stepping through the veil of death and into the open embrace of the compassionate Father of Jesus.

David H. Verhalen, C.S.C.

October 31

The tears that blind my eyes bear witness that I say the truth when I declare that I had never known before what love God has infused into my heart for all he has entrusted to my care.

—Fr. Edward Sorin, C.S.C.

ST. PAUL USES the image of an earthen vessel to describe how he and all disciples of the Lord carry within themselves a treasure that derives its transcendent power from God alone (see 2 Cor 4:7). All of us who are called to Christian service quickly become aware of our own human limitations. Yet despite our self-doubts and our misgivings about our natural abilities, hopefully we answer God's call like Isaiah the prophet, "O Lord, send me."

In this spirit, Fr. Edward Sorin, C.S.C., left his home and native country to help catechize, pastor, and educate in a priest-poor region of northern Indiana. He was a man of vision, deeply spiritual, with a ready confidence in the plan of

Divine Providence. Despite tragic fires, financial exigencies, disputes with neighbors, and insufficient personnel, his dream to establish a great Catholic university named after Our Lady has, through the decades, borne much fruit.

When I became Fr. Sorin's fifteenth successor as president of the University of Notre Dame in 1987, I was both humbled and honored. I was given the privilege, as a Holy Cross religious, of carrying on a work that had been so nobly begun. All the while, I was fully aware that a great institution of higher learning and thousands of people around the world had been entrusted to my care. I was comforted, like St. Paul and Fr. Sorin, with the knowledge that I shared this responsibility with my fellow Holy Cross religious and with a whole host of dedicated women and men. Together, we could give one another greater confidence that God's holy purposes would be fulfilled.

Edward A. Malloy, C.S.C.

☩

November 1

The spirit of faith fills the just in all the details of their conduct, as the soul is the principle of all the movement of the body. Their thoughts and judgments are always according to the gospel. Their conversation is in heaven. They see God always and everywhere. It is the Holy Spirit which enlivens them. Jesus Christ lives in them.

—Blessed Basil Moreau

As CHRISTIANS WE strive to live as Christ did, devoted to the service of God and enlivened by the presence of the Holy Spirit within us. St. Paul spoke of the Christian community as the Body of Christ. In a sense this is not merely metaphorical. It is Christ who is our soul, the life force within, directing the movement of our lives and service. Whether as priests, religious, or lay men and women, we seek to establish Christ as the source of all of our actions and interactions in our families, communities, Church, and world. This is our ideal aim as Christians.

But day-to-day we often are not conscious of this deep grounding of our lives. We are all too human, it seems, to be the living Body of Christ. The grind of daily life can seem quite ordinary, nothing like the high ideals we hope to achieve. The ambiguities of our human society and of the physical universe can make it difficult to see God always and everywhere.

But if we ponder the implications of Christ living in us, we come to understand that the Divine dwells in the ordinary—in flawed humans, in our common life, and in our uncertain world. The infinite God became one of us and embraced our world; in redeeming it, God filled the ordinary world with extraordinary value and beauty and love. To see God always and everywhere despite the ambiguities of life is one of the deepest blessings of the spiritual life.

Thomas E. Hosinski, C.S.C.

The journey begins before our profession and ends only at our Resurrection. We would be created anew to the point when we can say, "It is no longer I who live, but Christ who lives in me." It is the Lord who gives us both the desire and the accomplishment. For our part we must submit to the wisdom and the discipline that will purify us of our selfishness and will make us wholehearted in the service of his people.

—Holy Cross *Constitutions*

YEARS AGO WHEN I was first discerning my vocation, I came to know several elderly Holy Cross religious. They had an intensity about them that I found intriguing, if not occasionally puzzling. One priest had traded his prayer book for the French edition to pick up a new language. Another religious, then living in the seminary, impressed us all with his austerity. He would also, to our delight, ceremoniously eat a bowl of ice cream at the end of every day. And then there was the brother who, upon hearing me cough during my first Midwestern winter, grabbed my arm, walked me to his room, and gave me medicine while asking how a boy from Texas managed to stray so far from home.

These men have all since died. As I walk alongside their graves, I contemplate how my journey and theirs have merged over time. Someday I will be buried next to them, and I hope that further on, in a way I now only ponder, we will gather again at the Resurrection. But in the meantime, in this life of seeking to discipline my will, of trying to serve the Lord with my uneven set of talents, their presence remains. They speak to me within the intensity of my own discipleship. When I question why I was chosen to perform the tasks before me, I see their knowing smile. When I fear the unknown, I sense their love. Whatever good comes from these hesitations, however, is neither mine, nor theirs. It is the Lord's, whose work within us is but an extension of his presence among all disciples: both those before us and those who will someday follow in our steps.

Aaron Michka, C.S.C.

November 3

Before the Lord all of us are sinners and none is an enemy. We stand with the poor and the afflicted because only from there can we appeal as Jesus did for the conversion and deliverance of all.
—Holy Cross *Constitutions*

IN OUR RELIGIOUS houses, parishes, schools, and other apostolates, we pray for the poor in our midst during communal prayers. When we ask God to raise the poor from their situation and to fulfill their needs, we pray not only for those who are materially poor or who we think are poor but also for ourselves. We are all poor. As the Akans of Ghana say, "*Nnipa hia mboa*"— "All human beings need help." Even if our material abundance blinds us to this reality, we are all bound together in and by our need. Beyond our material needs, we share a hunger and thirst for human communion, a hunger and thirst for the Lord.

The deeper meaning of *nnipa hia mboa* is that all human beings deserve to be helped. The Akans of Ghana also say, "All human beings are children of God; no one is a child of the earth." Each of us bears a spark of the Divine. That being the case, at the very least, none of us should be enemies. Rather, we should all be together as partners both in our need for food, clothing, and shelter, and in our need for each other and for the living God. It is impossible for us to fulfill this obligation to one another in our shared humanity as long as we live in isolation—spiritually or culturally. Instead, we must stand side by side as brothers and sisters before the Lord—saints and sinners, men and women, rich and poor. For it is there that we together can appeal, as Jesus did, for the conversion and deliverance of us all.

Michael Amakyi, C.S.C.

November 4

Some of us may not see many another new year; neither age nor vigor will avail; but a holy life will enable us to look steadfastly upon death as a deliverer from temptation and misery, holding out the crown promised to those who shall have persevered to the end.
—Fr. Edward Sorin, C.S.C.

NO ONE KNOWS how long we will be on this earth. Death will come to each person like a thief in the night. But for us children of God, death is not something to be feared, as though it were a defeat or a total loss. No, death truly is our birth into eternal life with God. In faith, each of us can say with St. Paul that, from now on, a "crown of glory awaits me."

I wonder if we spend enough time dreaming or fantasizing about heaven. St. Paul wrote that it hasn't so much as dawned on the human heart what God has waiting for those who love him (see 1 Cor 2:9). To me this sounds like a dare. It's as if he were saying, "Go on, dream big. Imagine the absolute best existence possible, and you won't even come close to the blessedness of heaven." The more we set our eyes on the kingdom of heaven, the better we will be able to live as true daughters and sons of God while here on earth.

Still, Jesus knew that we might become anxious, or even preoccupied, with our death. That is why he said, "Do not let your hearts be troubled" (Jn 14:1). He will come back for each one of us at an undetermined time. For our part, we must live each day well in this joyful hope so that we will be ready for that great and glorious day.

Bill Wack, C.S.C.

November 5

*Our consecration in baptism is a departure on a jour-
ney that requires us, as it does all his people, to be
refashioned by the Lord's creating grace over and over
again. Likewise with our lives in a religious community,
we must have formed in us by God's enablement the
living likeness of Jesus Christ.*

—Holy Cross *Constitutions*

WHILE SPENDING TIME in northern Wisconsin one November, I decided to go on a run. It had just snowed, and the fine coating of slippery snow glazed the pavement and flocked the tall pine trees that surrounded the north-woods road. In order to avoid falling, I had to take short, stutter steps, and I was disappointed at the thought that I wasn't even going to get my heart rate up on this "run." As I passed a small country store, a woman came running out and cupped her hands around her mouth.

"Hey!" she shouted at me. "You're gonna get shot!" I stopped, stunned, and asked the only question I thought relevant: "Why?" She explained, "You're running in dark clothes, and it's hunting season! You're gonna get shot!"

Wide-eyed, I turned around and shuffled back home. As it turns out, this time I had no trouble getting my heart rate up! After that moment, everything looked different—I saw every squirrel, moving branch, and swaying tree dropping snow onto the ground. I arrived safely, but it struck me how my awareness could change so radically in an instant.

Profound moments such as our Baptism or religious profession leave us changed. In Baptism, "them" becomes "us." In marriage or religious profession, "I" changes to "we." These realities invite us to see the world anew as we seek to live the Paschal Mystery over and over again. Being refashioned means living beyond ourselves as we conform our lives and wills to Christ. This is no easy task, to be sure—one that can easily get our heart rate up! Yet when we are faithful to our vows and commitments, our Lord invites and helps us to live in a constantly new awareness of ourselves and of our God.

Nate Wills, C.S.C.

November 6

If God is our only hope, we must try to deserve his protection.

—Fr. Edward Sorin, C.S.C.

"WHAT'S KEEPING YOU from leaving the priesthood?" The question startled me. But in fairness to the young man who asked it, I recognized how troubled he was by what he saw in the Church of the late 1960s—priests and religious leaving, liturgical experimentation running amok, and Church authority flouted or ignored. Those turbulent times were understandably upsetting for someone discerning a vocation to religious life and priesthood. Could he commit himself to a life so many were abandoning?

Upon further reflection, I might have answered differently, but in the moment I responded, "I'm no prophet, and I have no idea what the future holds. But I'm ready to walk into darkness, if only accompanied by one or two of my brothers in Holy Cross." They were brave words indeed. And many dark days did come along in my religious life and priesthood to test my resolve, just as they had tested the resolve of the men who had gone before me and will test those who will come after me. I admire the generations of Holy Cross men and women who have lived and worked in the shadow of the Cross with little more to sustain them than hope itself—hope in God, hope in the Cross. For it was, after all, in this hope that they found their way to the Lord. Their example inspires all of us who are seeking our way to the Lord to let go of everything that clutters our lives and finally put all of our hope where it rightly belongs, in the Cross of Christ our Savior.

Leonard N. Banas, C.S.C.

November 7

When I speak of visitations from Divine Providence, whether they apply to individuals, or families, or nations, we religious readily understand they are always merciful means which our heavenly Father uses for the salvation of his children. However severe they may appear, if properly received and acted upon, they never fail to create amendment and reach their intended, ultimate result.

—Fr. Edward Sorin, C.S.C.

SOME YEARS AGO I was serving as the superior of a house of eight priests engaged in various activities. One evening at the supper table, two of the priests got into a rather heated argument, the point of which escapes me now. We all left the table in silence, and an atmosphere of tension pervaded our residence. As the superior, I thought that it was my pastoral responsibility to mediate between the two men who had had the argument, but I had no idea how to go about it. Both men were at least twenty years older than me, and one of them had been my teacher in the seminary. I went to bed pondering my options and slept fitfully.

The next morning we all gathered for Mass in the chapel. Just before Mass began, one of the two priests stood up and said that he wanted to ask forgiveness for anything offensive that he had said at supper the previous night. He walked across the chapel and extended his hand to the other man with whom he had been arguing. The other man accepted the apology.

It is tempting to think that by our wit and wisdom we shall solve all our problems. In this instance, it was my brother's welcoming of the grace of God that brought reconciliation and healing.

James Connelly, C.S.C.

November 8

Education, in its proper sense, implies the expansion and cultivation of all the faculties, mental and physical—the cultivation of the heart as well as the mind; and of these, the formation and enrichment of the heart is undoubtedly the most important of the two.
—Fr. Edward Sorin, C.S.C.

MY HEART SANK as I read the quotation assigned to me for this reflection. In my experience, the language of not educating the mind at the expense of the heart often has been used within religious life to promote a lack of aspiration for excellence in academic quality and effort. I still remember one of my fellow religious telling me, "You know, what is more important is what your heart teaches you, not teachers." Afterward, I promised never to let the heart and mind dictum pass my lips. And so, my heart sank even further when I learned that not only Blessed Moreau but also Fr. Sorin, the second founder of Holy Cross, said the exact same thing.

So much of education is, in fact, cultivating the intellect, cramming ourselves with knowledge. In my own case, early on, this was the hard work of understanding the structures of foreign languages and, even harder, memorizing vocabulary without having acquired it from the surrounding culture since birth. Simply put, what Fr. Sorin calls "filling up the mind" is much of what education is. Indeed, the very pursuit of knowledge through study is a reflection of what it is to be human because such intellectual curiosity about all things reveals both our incompleteness as humans and our desire to be with God completely.

Yet the importance of the formation and enrichment of the heart comes to us later, after we have had experience. It comes to us within the struggle to know God with our minds. And so it is that any education moves toward completion in God having cultivated both the mind and the heart.

James E. McDonald, C.S.C.

November 9

Just what does a painter do? He studies his subject. He fills himself with it totally in order to reproduce it and, in a manner of speaking, to create it anew on canvas in a very close imitation of the subject's features. Is it thus that you try to make Jesus Christ live again in you, to the point of his being totally remade or formed again in you?

—Blessed Basil Moreau

I RECENTLY PICKED up a paintbrush for the first time in more than thirty years. My new teacher observed my grief from leaving my previous parish assignment. She suggested that I paint an image of a person who had significantly touched my heart in ministry. I slowly dipped my brush into a dab of paint and began to push the color onto a piece of paper.

The face of a man who still lives in a tent in the woods emerged in acrylic. Our parish had received him into the Church some years ago. He still lives with depression, isolation, and unemployment; however, his face reveals the love of Jesus through his poverty and vulnerability.

People living with mental illness, generational poverty, or loneliness and disease show us the face of Jesus. We discover the tender face of Jesus through his mercy, love, and forgiveness, not through our control, selfishness, and false power. People's stories of suffering teach us about the search for faith in honest relationships as we begin to create genuine community.

In order to create genuine art, we need to be emptied of our judgments, cynical attitudes, and inability to see people for who they are. We also learn to see ourselves in the strokes of paint and dabs of color. In my case, all the years without creating art have passed for a reason. I am now vulnerable enough to see the colorful face of Jesus, who is still with us in people and in me, all of us searching for hope and new life.

Ronald Patrick Raab, C.S.C.

November 10

If we wish to avoid failing, we must do nothing except what is in accord with our vocation and the will of God. We must strive to remain not only in the state of grace, but even more in a state of fervor and in close union with God which makes us want to act always out of love of God.

—Blessed Basil Moreau

WHEN I WORKED at Holy Cross College, I regularly attended Mass with our local community of senior and infirm brothers—men who had steadfastly remained faithful to their vocations and the will of God for fifty, sixty, seventy, or more years. One day in particular, the experience was humbling as only a sacrament could be. Not only had I encountered our Lord and brother, Jesus the Christ, in the Eucharist but I also felt his embrace in the midst of men who fervently strive with unflagging zeal for a close union with God.

Afterward, as I walked the short distance to my residence, I continued my thanksgiving and reflection on that encounter with Christ. I think the encounter was so extraordinary for me in that it was so ordinary for my brothers who, living in the love of God, were beacons to others to seek union with God. If their ability to minister actively had diminished, their power to reach out to others in prayer and hospitality continued to blossom into an even more transforming ministry. Through them and my communion with them, my own zeal was renewed.

Perhaps that is what Blessed Moreau meant when he used "we" and not "I" when writing of our wish to avoid failing. Zeal is not a virtue that can be achieved or maintained in isolation. In isolation, it fades to extinction. Zeal, like every other virtue, requires a family of believers to nurture and sustain it. Zeal for the will of God is found in union with God, and union with God is found in union with others who share our journey.

John F. Tryon, C.S.C.

November 11

Prayer is the key of heaven. With it, the just person opens up all the treasures of heaven where the soul may draw its ease.

—Blessed Basil Moreau

I'M OFTEN REMINDED of what C. S. Lewis said to a friend in William Nicholson's play *Shadowlands* when it became apparent that the cancer of Lewis's wife, Joy, had gone into remission. His friend commended Lewis for his persistence in praying for Joy's healing, and now God was answering his prayer. "That's not why I pray," Lewis responded. "I pray because I can't help myself. I pray because I'm helpless. I pray beca . . . I pray because the need flows out of me all the time, waking and sleeping. It doesn't change God. It changes me."

In light of this truth—we pray out of our haunting need and holy desire—perhaps we can see now that the treasures of heaven to which Blessed Basil Moreau refers are open to us today, here on this planet. Prayer draws us out of our limited, creaturely selves long enough for us—even in moments of darkness—to touch, taste, smell, hear, and see the Divine, who is our *Abba*, our Father in heaven, the longing of our souls. And for perhaps a brief moment, we are transformed—renewed, refigured, refined, made whole. For one blessed moment, we are awash in hope and gratitude and become who we always prayed we would be.

At best the universe is indifferent to human pain. Too often too many of us carry quietly and alone the weight of our own failures and fears and feelings of shame and guilt. But those often desperate prayers that rise from moments of loss and darkness bear strong witness to a more compelling story: In faith, we are never alone. God is always with us. In *Abba* we draw our ease. "My soul rests in God alone," sings the psalmist. Prayer reminds us of this consoling, lovely truth.

Patrick Hannon, C.S.C.

☨

November 12

We are the children of our heavenly Father. Consequently, we must behave as such, putting into his hand a future which is not our lot to penetrate.

—Fr. Jacques Dujarie

WE KNOW THE concepts. God's immense love for us is without limit or depth. We are never out of God's hands. These concepts are really quite simple, and yet they challenge us greatly. For being the human creatures that we are, with faults, idiosyncrasies, and failings, we live in the midst of anxiety. Sometimes anxiety can be good as it motivates us to be creative and to get things done. On the other hand, sometimes it can be paralyzing. Fr. Dujarie reminds us, though, that there is no reason ever to feel paralyzed.

But at the heart of our anxiety lies an enduring difficulty in understanding a love that doesn't count the cost or one that isn't doled out as a reward. We struggle to understand the care that God has for us, a care that envelops and protects. Perhaps we feel that, because of who we are, we are really not worthy of such care. The truth is that we like to think that we are in charge and we like to control, or at least attempt to control, our lives. We are content to let ourselves live in that delusion.

God doesn't seem to mind at all. He lets us live in that delusion and perhaps delights at our silliness, always waiting patiently for that moment of recognition of and total surrender to his love. God delights in us because we are his creatures, created in his image. And so we pray for the courage and grace to live as his children, trusting in the abundant love and care he has for us.

Thomas A. Dziekan, C.S.C.

November 13

Our commitment is an invitation for our fellow Chris-tians to fulfill their vocation, and for ourselves it is a concrete way of working with them for the spread of the gospel and with all for the development of a more just and human society.

—Holy Cross *Constitutions*

I COUNT AMONG those whom I consider heroes and role models in my life a number of contemporary Church ministers: Archbishop Oscar Romero, the four American churchwomen of El Salvador (Sr. Maura Clarke, Jean Donovan, Sr. Ita Ford, and Sr. Dorothy Kazel), Cardinal Joseph Bernadin, Sr. Dorothy Stang, Dorothy Day, and Bishop Dom Hélder Cámara. All but three died a martyr's death, and all preached the gospel message of justice, for which I hold them in the highest regard.

There are likewise a number of my Holy Cross brothers and sisters whom I consider role models because of their work to bring about a more just and human society. They have carried on this ministry in various apostolates here in the United States and in Holy Cross missions throughout the world. In some apostolates, they have ministered directly to the poor and marginalized, while in others they have advocated for the poor and for a more just society in a variety of ways.

We Holy Cross religious work with our lay collaborators in numerous ways on behalf of the gospel call to justice. Our *Constitutions* call us to collaborate with all people of good will in building up the kingdom of God. We are blessed to serve alongside so many faith-filled laity in our congregational ministries of education, parish, and mission through which we minister to the poor and educate all on behalf of justice. Together—laity and Holy Cross religious—we seek to live lives of prayer and service that bring the hope of the gospel to those most in need of the Good News of Jesus Christ.

Jim Fenstermaker, C.S.C.

November 14

Jesus wants us to come into his sacramental presence as often as we can. On each happy occasion when we can visit him in the Blessed Sacrament, we should make a spiritual Communion. This invitation to Jesus to come spiritually into our hearts may be given him at any time, however, even when we are not in his sacramental presence.

—Blessed Basil Moreau

As a seminarian, I spent a week with the Missionaries of the Poor in Kingston, Jamaica. The missionaries' ministry was to care for people discarded by their families and communities because of disabilities or disease. The work that I did with them was extremely powerful and moving. One of the pieces I loved the most was the prayer that they maintained in the midst of their ministry. Every day around 5:00 a.m., we gathered for adoration. I am hardly awake by 7:00 a.m., so at 5:00 a.m. my awareness is usually limited at best. But each morning, sitting in the presence of Jesus, I found myself not only awake and aware but also resting in joy. It took me a few days to put my finger on it, but it was simply joy at being with Jesus, at spending that wee hour of the morning with the Lord present in the Eucharist. And having Jesus in my heart then carried me through the rest of the day.

Each one of us has many things that demand our time and energy, be it our work, our family, or whatever other responsibilities. But God doesn't need us to bring anything more than ourselves to him. All he wants is us. He wants us so that he can fill us with his love, his joy, and his peace. In my experience with the Missionaries of the Poor, I was able to let Christ enter my heart through adoration. I was able to see him clearly and let him fill me. But we can find Christ everywhere—in the Eucharist, yes, but also in our neighbor and in the world. We must only open ourselves to that happy encounter with our risen and loving Lord, and then his presence will carry us.

Timothy Mouton, C.S.C.

November 15

A grand, a noble task has been assigned to us as educators of Christian youth; a task, the importance of which none of us can duly appreciate and for which we shall never be able here below to return proper thanks to God.

—Fr. Edward Sorin, C.S.C.

NOT A DAY PASSES DURING WHICH I FAIL TO RECALL AND REFLECT on the thousands of students—from grade school to graduate school—I have been privileged to educate in my more than four decades of teaching. Fr. Sorin's words to our young community more than one hundred years ago are still a sobering reminder, for all who are helping young people to grow, to be conscious of our role as educators of Christian youth. Teaching and indeed parenting, coaching, and mentoring are all tasks of great importance. Ultimately, beyond all of our efforts, only

God knows the totality of our successes as well as our failures. I have prayed daily that what I do to educate those entrusted to our care furthers his plan for these souls, and I have asked that what I fail to do does not harm them.

More important than crediting our own efforts, though, is realizing that what we accomplish is first and foremost the work of God. Whatever we have been able to do to instruct young men and women is certainly important, but we are effective because education in the faith makes the difference in our students' lives, and we willingly share in that wonderful mission.

Fr. Sorin understood well that all of us engaged in forming youth are unable to thank God properly for the graces we have been given to serve as educators. That, however, does not excuse us from thanking him daily for having given us the privilege of forming men and women in the faith.

Donald J. Stabrowski, C.S.C.

�

November 16

It is a happy self-denial that begets the peace and the liberty of the children of God.

—Blessed Basil Moreau

WHILE IN THE seminary, I had many visions, dreams, and expectations of what I would be and do when I became a priest. I saw myself getting a PhD in physics, getting tenure at Notre Dame, and living happily ever after. My perceived journey, however, was derailed from the very beginning. My first assignment was in high school work, something that had never been on my radar. This was abruptly followed by a stint in a treatment center for alcoholism. Next on the journey was preaching retreats and counseling in our retreat center. Then came an assignment as assistant treasurer of our province along with formation work in our seminary. This was followed by two terms as a superior, including at our medical facility, as well as additional work on formation staff. Needless to say, in my fifty-three years in ministry as a religious and priest, I have never done anything that I had envisioned or dreamed about in my early years.

But I can honestly say from the depths of my being that I have never regretted anything that I have been asked to do. Truly the grace and ability to be obedient to the will of God through my superiors has been a happy self-denial that begets the peace and the liberty of the children of God. As Pope Francis said, "Obedience often leads us down a path which isn't the one we think it should be: there is another, the obedience of Jesus who says to the Father in the Mount of Olives: 'Thy will be done.'" We, too, must be ready to "obey, to have the courage to change directions when the Lord asks this of us," since "he who obeys will have eternal life."

Charlie Kohlerman, C.S.C.

November 17

It is in meditation on the great truths of our faith that one learns to detach himself from the swiftly passing shadow of the world, which, like a rushing torrent, carries off in its waves both people and things. It is in such meditation that we train ourselves to see the hand of God in all the events of life.

—Blessed Basil Moreau

THE EXPERIENCE OF regret, disconcerting as it is, can have sublime allure. In a world that is continually passing away, in a life in which friendships and accomplishments are never set on sturdy ground, indeed in our very selves that slip back and forth between the person we strive to be and the person we hate to become, we see continual change and loss. The stability we seek in order to counteract this instability, the revival of those people, things, and attitudes we so desire, is found in our mantras of regret—or so we think. For it is in entertaining our regrets that—in the briefest of moments—we relive the past. But the past can never be restored.

Even our faith does not stop the past from slipping out from under us. But it does give us reason to hope and not be afraid. When the storm threatened to overtake their boat, our Lord Jesus told his disciples not to be afraid. When we meditate on the truth of this statement, that our God is so loving that even in our darkest moments he rests peacefully beside us, we come to expose the falsity of regret. It is simple. Regret tells us that God is removed from our past and present, but the truths of our faith resound with the "is now and ever shall be." Our healing with the past and hope for what is to come, then, can only be a healing found in God, a healing that begins when we trade our regret for a litany of thanksgiving.

Aaron Michka, C.S.C.

November 18

Never did we need, as much as now, to live by faith,
so as to make of our life an incessant prayer.
—Fr. Edward Sorin, C.S.C.

I NEVER CONSIDERED myself pastor material, nor did I envision parochial ministry as the primary focus of my priesthood. My talents, I felt, were better suited to education or Catholic communications, but God's ways are not always our ways. When the request to serve as a pastor came my way, the divine sense of humor was made manifest with a call to minister to not one, but two parishes. Faced with this awesome responsibility, I find that Fr. Sorin's exhortation to live by faith speaks powerfully to me. For God does work in strange ways, and we can find ourselves faced with responsibilities—and the crosses that come with them—that are not always of our choosing.

Success in any ministry is not the success of the individual, but rather it is the grace of God and the work of the Holy Spirit. For me, this is especially true in the shepherding ministry of a parish pastor. I am simply an instrument. If there is success, it is the work of the Spirit; if there is failure or inadequacy, it must be because I asserted myself over the Spirit's movement.

To be a worthy instrument of God's grace requires a life of faith rooted in prayer. I have never prayed as much or as ardently as I do now. Indeed, the first responsibility of the pastor is to pray for the people entrusted to his care. Every decision, whether pertaining to the care of souls or the repair of a leaky church roof, is for me a prayer decision. Good pastoring, good teaching, good parenting, and good living are all fruits of a rich life of prayer and a deep life of faith. Incessant prayer feeds the life of faith and is the driving force of any Christian worth his or her weight in holy water.

Ed Kaminski, C.S.C.

November 19

Only a religious spirit which understands the power of his Cross can sustain our courage in the midst of all these trials. Happy indeed are we if we know how to profit by them and to understand the unspeakable advantage of becoming more and more conformed to the image of the Divine Christ crucified.

—Blessed Basil Moreau

IN AND OF itself, pain is not good. We naturally do what we can to avoid suffering, and we would like to avoid the trials about which Blessed Moreau writes. The great danger is that we make our lives all about the avoidance of such trials. We can drift into spending an inordinate amount of time and energy protecting ourselves from pain, and if so, it will be impossible for us to love as the gospel calls us to love. The gospel calls us to run toward those in pain and to believe that there is no trial that God's love cannot help us to work through.

Working with university students as I do, I am continually inspired by their willingness to run toward rather than avoid the trials of others. They do an amazing job of "suffering with" people in pain. Further, these students inspire me by their commitment to using the skills and knowledge they acquire to serve those who suffer rather than to serve themselves.

Although it may be natural in some way to avoid pain, if we love as the gospel calls us to love, we will do some suffering, and we will experience trials. We will also experience great joy because we will have managed to let God free us from the fear of the trials that are part of life. We will spend less energy avoiding trials and more on living life to the fullest. We will live our lives with courage and take holy risks in service of others, realizing that no trial can separate us from the love of God.

Robert A. Dowd, C.S.C.

November 20

Our churches have two stately and venerable thrones: the altar and the pulpit—the altar where we present our requests to God and the pulpit where we discover God's will; the altar where priests speak to God on our behalf and the pulpit where they speak to us on behalf of God; the altar where Jesus Christ is adored in the truth of his body and the pulpit where he is recognized in the truth of his teachings. From the one as from the other of these two thrones, we are served a celestial food.

—Blessed Basil Moreau

A PARISHIONER ASKED my opinion on something she heard on Catholic radio. A priest was decrying his parishioners' lack of decorum, whether it was their inappropriate clothing or their talking in church. He was grieved that children were running around the sanctuary, that sacred space and time weren't honored.

Like our founder, Blessed Basil Moreau, I believe in the two stately and venerable thrones of the altar and the pulpit. I also believe in the holiness of the children of God. I don't advertise the Mass, but people show up. Yes, we post times for Masses and confessions, but I don't do commercials or hand out fliers. And yet I serve at full Masses and hear confessions for hours every week. If a child runs in the sanctuary, I call the child by name or I introduce myself. If conversations are occurring in the church, I am usually in the middle of them or I know the people who are talking and what they are talking about. I know my flock, and they know me, their pastor. As for the dress, well, we can improve on that, but I serve in a state where formal attire is your good jeans and dress cowboy boots.

As an ordained priest, I serve Christ the King, and his presence is mediated through me. He is a king like no other. He came to serve, not be served. In Christ Jesus, God is not distant or abstract but human and close to us, whom he calls friends. I love and adore the God I can't see; his celestial throne I long to see. I also love and adore his children whom I can see. All of God's people are to become thrones themselves to receive their King in celestial food.

Paul Ybarra, C.S.C.

Jesus entered into the pain and death that sin inflicts. He accepted the torment but gave us joy in return. We whom he has sent to minister amid the same sin and pain must know that we too shall find the cross and the hope it promises.

—Holy Cross *Constitutions*

"YEAH, CHAPLAIN. HAVE you got a cigarette on ya?" That was not the response that I had been expecting when I told the inmate in the maximum security prison what I thought would be the saddest of news—the untimely death of his mother. His face, however, remained unchanged. There was simply no mourning in his heart for the woman who had abandoned her infant child to pursue her drug habit. Even his bitterness toward her had faded. She had fought her own demons and lost. What was that to him now?

The prisoner calmly explained that it was his grandmother who had compassionately stepped in and raised him. Her death would have broken him up as hers was the only mother's love he had ever known. And now, he lived tormented with the dark thought that his own sinful, angry acts had disappointed her in her old age. It hurt to be away from her and from his own children, who were being raised without a dad's encouragement, just as he had been.

The chain of sin and suffering visits every generation. We who are sent by God to minister know this very sin and pain, but we also know the hope and joy that rise from the devastation of the Cross. Only a relationship to the Crucified can help us bear the crosses of sin and suffering so that the new generation might come to know encouragement, joy, compassion, and hope. It is only when we are anchored in the hope of the Cross that we have the strength and the courage to enter into the darkness of life.

John Phalen, C.S.C.

November 22

We could never complain of the sacrifices demanded by our vow of poverty, if we reflected on what the gospel tells us of the sacrifices which Jesus Christ imposed on himself for us, and if we had a true love of him who for love of us became the poorest of people. How edifying would be our language and our conduct on the score of poverty if we kept our eyes always fixed on this Divine Model.

—Blessed Basil Moreau

MY PREVIOUS ASSIGNMENT as pastor of Holy Cross and St. Stanislaus Parish in South Bend, Indiana, was quite a bit different from my childhood home in sunny southern California. When I was growing up, everybody drove shiny new cars. My friends lived in large homes overlooking the Pacific Ocean. Weekends were spent at the malls. Restaurants were a regular part of the weekly routine, and nothing was ever beyond our grasp. Conversely, on the neighborhood streets of the parish th

I pastored, I observed dented and rusted-out cars that squealed and squeaked as they rumbled along. Dilapidated old homes seemed to slouch under the weight of their many years. The local strip mall and liquor store bustled with activity around the clock. Fast-food boxes and bags littered the streets, and people of all ages lingered on porches and sidewalks with apparently nothing better to do.

For some, this dichotomy might seem depressing. But as religious of Holy Cross, as men with hope to bring, the vow of poverty calls us into the neighborhoods of the poor and working class. It challenges selfish displays of wealth and consumerism that characterize many parts of our society. If we want to follow truly the example of Christ, we must embrace the same self-sacrifice and poverty Jesus endured for us. For a life of simplicity and sacrifice is a requirement for all who dare to follow Christ. Whatever vocation we embrace, our poverty must be a response of the heart to the teaching of Jesus. If any want to become my followers, let them deny themselves and take up their cross and follow me.

Michael C. Mathews, C.S.C.

November 23

*This is what you can and must do for your students,
ou truly have zeal for their salvation. Make haste,
fore; take up this work of the Resurrection, never
ng that the particular goal of your institution is,*

above all, to sanctify youth. By this, you will contribute
to preparing the world for better times than our own.
—Blessed Basil Moreau

FROM THE 1980s into the 2000s, Tripura State in northeast India was marked with intense political turmoil due to its ethnic diversity: threats, abductions, cold-blood killings, and house fires were everyday events. The experiences of Holy Cross religious were no different from those of any normal citizen, including the burning of our presbytery at Mariamnagar and the killing of Fr. Victor Crasta, C.S.C.

As a response to this painful situation, Holy Cross created the North Eastern Students National Integration Movement (NESNIM) to empower our students to shape a better world. Annually, NESNIM brought together hundreds of students from all over northeast India. Along with their teachers, these students experienced the joy of living and working together. It did not matter that they spoke different languages and dialects or that they had different customs and traditions or that they practiced various religious traditions. That was the point: despite these differences, they discovered that it was possible to live and work together and thus create a better future together. NESNIM's rippling effects have been experienced not just in the teachers and students' families and schools but also in the wider community. In recent years, Tripura has witnessed a resurrection in a period of unparalleled peace and development.

In every corner of the globe, there are forces of division threatening to pull society apart. Individuals and communities stand in need of education to overcome ignorance, dissension, and fear. New life is possible when we educate people about unity in diversity. Our Savior said, "When I am lifted up from the earth, I will draw everyone to myself" (Jn 12:32). If we, like him, give our lives in service of drawing together the human family, we fill find a share in his Resurrection. We, and our world, will be lifted up.

Roy Thalackan, C.S.C.

November 24

It is God's own hand which has guided everything, and he it is whom we must thank above all. Hence I beg you to unite your thanks with ours in order that we may draw down more abundant blessings from heaven upon our work, and above all, not stop their flow by a want of gratitude.

—Blessed Basil Moreau

WHEN BLESSED MOREAU looked at the humble yet mysterious beginnings of the Congregation he founded, the talented young people who began to join it, and the missions that were soon established, he felt a deep debt of gratitude to Divine Providence. He knew instinctively that gratitude to God was a sure way to receive even more abundant blessings.

In the United States, we put this spiritual principle into practice through the annual celebration of Thanksgiving. On this one day, we slow down and fuss less, enjoy the company of loved ones and friends, and realize during grace before a delicious meal just how blessed we are.

As a Church, the Eucharist is our privileged opportunity to express our gratitude to the Father for all that we have received in Christ Jesus. The word *eucharist* comes from the Greek word meaning "to give thanks," and for our weekly hour of praise and thanksgiving, untold graces are showered upon us.

In our families, grace before meals and bedtime prayers cultivate in parents and children alike an appreciation for the profound blessings of work, a home, food and clothing, friends, and the gift of one another. As awareness increases, so do blessings.

Forgetfulness is the only enemy of our blessings, for we may stop their flow by a want of gratitude. All of us, like Blessed Moreau, can help each other to appreciate our blessings and to realize that a little gratitude goes a long way. We can learn the power of gratitude, which unites us and opens up the floodgates of heavenly blessings for ourselves and those we are called upon to serve.

Patrick Neary, C.S.C.

November 25

The door of heaven is the heart of Jesus, and the key to that door is prayer and love.

—St. André Bessette

THE PHONE RANG early on a cold winter morning. It was our maintenance man. Our church had been broken into. I needed to come. It turned out that our thief had scaled a high wall and climbed through a small window up high to enter our church.

This was the only possible entry since our church's big, wooden front doors were firmly locked at night and impenetrable.

At times in our lives, especially in difficult moments, heaven—and maybe God as well—can seem far from us and almost inaccessible. We forget Jesus' promise to us in the Gospel of Matthew to be with us always until the end of time (see 28:20). Sometimes, we can't see his presence with us. Sometimes, in all honesty, we are not with him. Yet whether we are with Jesus or not, Jesus is with us, and he loves us more than we could ever know.

Jesus' sacrifice for us on the Cross is the most powerful sign of his love for us. The Cross clearly shows us that Jesus wants our joy to be complete with him in heaven. With so great a love, how could Jesus and the gift of eternal life be a door closed and inaccessible to us? No, we do not need to scale a high wall and climb through a small window in order to break into God's presence, whether in heaven or even here on earth. Jesus continually invites us to open our hearts to him in prayer and in love, trusting that he will lead us on the way to himself and to eternal life.

John Herman, C.S.C.

November 26

We are happy. We have the Lord with us. Only tonight we hung our sanctuary lamp where none had hung before. They tell us we won't be able to afford to keep it burning. But we have a little olive oil and will burn

*while it lasts. We can see it through the woods and it
lights the humble home where our Master dwells. We
tell each other that we are not alone, that Jesus Christ
lives among us. It gives us courage.*

—Fr. Edward Sorin, C.S.C.

FR. SORIN WROTE these words to Blessed Moreau upon the arrival of Holy Cross at Notre Dame, and they hang outside the entrance to the chapel in Siegfried Residence Hall as a reminder—what we do is God's work, and we are never alone.

How bewildered, how busy those pioneer religious were in setting about to make their home, their daily work, their mission. We can only imagine the challenges, frustrations, disappointments, and, yes, the successes they encountered. Life today is busy and has its challenges, too. There is always so much to do, so many choices, so many demands. Sometimes it seems as if the work will never get done—or at least be done the way we want it to be. And still there is no shortage of generosity as people give from their abundant blessings of talent and skill to help one another. Nevertheless, we all face moments of frustration, disappointment, and even failure. Sometimes we wonder if we are working alone and unappreciated.

It is then that we need to remind ourselves that it is God's work we do. It is God's will to which we seek to conform our desires, our will, and our plans. That's why we visit our churches often, to be reminded that we abide in the Lord and he with us. The sanctuary lamp reminds us of this reality. It is a light that from the earliest days has burned at Notre Dame, and it burns wherever Christ gathers his Church.

John Conley, C.S.C.

For many of us in Holy Cross, mission expresses itself in the education of youth in schools, colleges and universities. For others, our mission as educators takes place in parishes and other ministries. Wherever we work we assist others not only to recognize and develop their own gifts but also to discover the deepest longing of their lives.

—Holy Cross *Constitutions*

MY ENTIRE EDUCATION was through the good ministry of Holy Cross priests, brothers, sisters, and their dedicated lay colleagues. I attended St. Joseph Grade School, St. Joseph High School, and have three degrees from the University of Notre Dame. I received an excellent education in everything from the ABCs to theology, but I could have learned those topics well in other schools. What made my Holy Cross education unique was that it taught me that education is more than just gaining knowledge. It is coming to know God's love in all things and learning to share that love, which is our deepest longing, with all people.

I definitely have come away from my education knowing that God loves me. It was evident in classroom discussions and in the way the Holy Cross religious cared for us. It was evident in the way that my classmates and I were formed as a community of disciples. It was even evident in the way that I was disciplined on the rare occasion that I misbehaved.

In my ministry as a priest, I strive to keep God's love as the center of my life. I try to keep myself grounded in good friendships, prayer, and the sacraments so that I might experience God's love in my own life and thus be able to share that love in all I say and do. It is God's love, freely given to all of us despite our sinfulness, that can inspire us when things are good and keep us going when times are rough. For in the end, God has promised that we will be saved, and Love doesn't lie.

Anthony Szakaly, C.S.C.

November 28

Those who care for us and for the kingdom will expect our way of life to be modest and simple. However, our local communities should be generous in continuing our tradition of hospitality to confreres, to those who labor with us, to our relatives and neighbors, and to the poor, especially those who have no one to have them in. The measure of our generosity will be the sincerity, the simplicity and the sensitivity of our welcome.

—Holy Cross *Constitutions*

I LIVED FOR a number of years with an excellent cook, a brother who thoroughly enjoyed preparing a meal. The table and ambiance were always carefully set. We laughingly—and accurately— would describe each meal he prepared as "simple but elegant." The meal was simple: it was at our own table with our everyday plates and silverware, and the preparation was seemingly effortless for him. Yet it was all quite elegant. Not surprisingly, the conversation and conviviality would continue long after the meal was finished.

During my years in East Africa, when visiting families, the meals were also "simple but elegant." Although the food was often everyday fare—like matoke (bananas), millet, sweet potatoes, and maize with some sauce and meat—it was carefully prepared and presented. The presence of a guest would also be a reason for some bottled beer. Our hosts were most grateful to be able to share what they had since it brought us together.

For many of us, time is often experienced as a commodity, maybe even our most valuable commodity. We can feel challenged by the sharing of time and portion it out very carefully, if not stingily. We might willingly share our other resources—but then only our excess. Beyond our excess, we often sense struggle and conflict. Whether in our religious houses, family homes, schools, parishes, or neighborhoods, extending hospitality challenges us to share our time, our resources, and our presence. Yet our welcome need not be complicated or complex. When our lives mirror the hospitality modeled by Jesus, we will find that even a simple hospitality can be quite elegant as it draws us closer together in Christ.

Bill Zaydak, C.S.C.

November 29

Union is a powerful lever with which we could move, direct, and sanctify the whole world. We who are disciples of a God who died for the salvation of souls

who are perishing, we do not realize all the good we could do for others through union with Jesus Christ.
—Blessed Basil Moreau

As I watch the television news, I feel a deep connection to places I have never been and to people I have never actually met: typhoon flooding and political unrest in Bangladesh, civil war in northern Uganda, attacks on Christians in India. These seemingly distant places and events are made close and personal by the fact that I have brothers and sisters in Holy Cross living and working there. From its very earliest days, the Congregation of Holy Cross has been an international congregation. From France, Blessed Moreau sent his spiritual sons and daughters to Algeria and America, Canada and Bangladesh. And so, put simply, I have family around the world.

As Catholics we are all members of an international community. Even though we are spread across the globe, in every nation of the world, speaking hundreds of different languages, we are all still united as one in Christ. Indeed, the plant of which we are all branches is, in fact, the Cross of Christ—the tree of life. And so the sap that nourishes us is the blood of Christ poured out for the world. After all, we are disciples of the One who died for our salvation. It is his salvific death that continues to draw us together into himself. We have Christ's assurance that, if we remain rooted in him, and thus deeply connected to each other across distant places and different cultures, we together will draw from his life, grow, and bear abundant fruit in God's kingdom.

Stephen Koeth, C.S.C.

☩

November 30

The aspirations of a Christian soul should lead to the further imitation of him who never turns his eyes from even the forgetful heart.

—Fr. Edward Sorin, C.S.C.

WE LIVE IN forgetful times. It is not so much that we have forgotten God but rather that we have forgotten our longing for God or at least we have misplaced it. Somehow we have separated from God our longing for God. We direct it now toward lesser things, getting by on lesser joys, which prove passing, fading, and finally worthless. We need to redirect our spirit of longing, which sits at the center of our hearts, back toward its source. Longing is remembering, and remembering where our longing ultimately leads us is the way to retrain our forgetful hearts. For our hearts know longing but no longer know what to do with it. They are hardened by fear of that very longing designed to give them abundant life.

Remembering our longings, though, is not about satisfying them. The deeper they run, the less we are able to find any rest or satisfaction in them. The challenge, instead, is to learn to live in longing, in its open-ended nature, facing honestly its stark reminders of our incompleteness. As the mystics and saints of old have taught us, it is this incompleteness that returns us to the embrace of God. We can trust that, if we live in our longing and follow it faithfully, it will direct us back into the heart of God, a heart that never forgets.

Jeffrey Cooper, C.S.C.

✠

December 1

Sustained by grace, we shall be able to work for our neighbor's salvation without endangering our own, and to devote ourselves to works of apostolic zeal without forgetting the task which should be our constant care and without which the others cannot succeed or at least will be of no avail—the work of our spiritual sanctification.

—Blessed Basil Moreau

EACH YEAR THAT I serve as a priest and religious in Holy Cross, it becomes clearer that Jesus called me to this life. It was not a choice made by selecting one of many equal options, but a choice in response to an invitation. Christ called, and I was able to find the courage to answer, to make a commitment.

Even more, I have come to see that this invitation to consecrate my life came out of God's great love for me. There is the universal call to holiness, to pursue and be drawn into sanctification in Christ. Yet into this fundamental call the Lord weaves a personal call that best leads, challenges, encourages, and supports us along the path to holiness. More than meaningful work, a supportive community, and a solid structure of prayer, religious life and ministry in Holy Cross have provided me the perfect environment to soften my heart of stone and ignite it with a burning love of God and neighbor. It is the workshop and home that affords what I particularly need to enter most fully into the man that God created me with the potential to be.

Others will receive a similar invitation because in religious life and ministry they, too, will find that right blend of what they need to grow in holiness. For many more, the invitation is to some other wonderful combination of community, family, service, labor, and prayer. This is beautiful: in the universal call to holiness lies a personal call from Christ that will lead most directly to our hearts resting in him. The key is to know that the invitation comes from the Lord out of his personal knowledge of us and his desire for our good. He provides each of us with more than a mission; he provides the way to true life in him. We hope not only to hear the call, but also to find the trust and courage to respond.

James T. Gallagher, C.S.C.

December 2

Far from complaining of these trials, we must learn to love them, for if we bear them as we should, they are worth their weight in gold. These nails and thorns will be changed later into the many precious stones which will make up the crown of glory reserved for those who have been faithful to the duties of their vocation and have worn lovingly, even to the end, their Savior's crown of thorns.

—Blessed Basil Moreau

WHILE I HAVE never really learned to love suffering, I must admit that what I have truly learned in my life has usually been at difficult moments. The maturity I have gained and the wisdom I have garnered through these situations are as precious to me as gold tested by fire. Even knowing this about myself, I am also aware of my continued resistance and reluctance when confronted with new challenges.

If anything, however, I have learned that our vocation as Christians is fundamentally a call to hope. And yet we often get caught up in hopes for specific things and particular outcomes, only to see those hopes dashed. True hope, real hope, however, is malleable. It is not merely the belief that this or that will occur or even that all will be well. Rather, it is the belief that, no matter what happens, the result will make sense in God. This truth can only be learned through suffering and loss. For it is only when our hopes for things have been dashed that we experience the meaning of our lives that endures come what may. Having experienced that truth, our hope bounces back, finding rest in faith's abiding trust in Divine Providence, a trust that can transform even the sharpest nails and thorns into the most precious of stones. It is then that hope, indeed, springs eternal, flooding our hearts and teaching us even to embrace our sufferings, difficult though that may be.

Stephen Walsh, C.S.C.

December 3

Above all, let our religious, to a man, strive to preserve in our Congregation a feature which has always been characteristic of the children of Holy Cross—I mean the spirit of devotedness.

—Fr. Edward Sorin, C.S.C.

WE'VE ALL HEARD it said that the devil is in the details. This old saying implies that any great idea will have a countless number of details to which we must attend if our idea is to succeed. Indeed, these little details somehow seem to take up the bulk of our days. Despite our best intentions, most plans will fail if we don't do the little things well.

This attention to detail is a huge part of the Christian life. Our average days are filled with routine things that we do for our families, our coworkers, and our Church. And yet these day-to-day activities are the primary ways that we show our love for these people. Occasionally we might be able to express grand gestures of love, but more often than not we have to show our love in the ordinary things of our day.

The holiest people I know are the ones who can transform simple activities—cooking a meal, making a phone call, saying a prayer—into acts of charity by performing them with love. When we make a conscious effort to do this, we don't just show our love for the people we serve—we show our love for God by serving those around us. Infusing the routine actions of our days with love turns simple jobs into encounters with the Lord. And that is exactly where we can expect to find him—in the details.

Steve Lacroix, C.S.C.

Some of my best friends I may never meet again here below, however brief my absence; but thank God, the hope is laid deep in my bosom, I will meet them again and forever in heaven. God grant that we will all meet there where separation is unknown!

—Fr. Edward Sorin, C.S.C.

DURING MY YEARS as superior of Holy Cross House, our community medical and retirement facility, I witnessed thirty-five of our priests and brothers leaving this world for eternal life. Many were comforted in their last moments by close friends with whom they had shared years of life and ministry together in community. They often sat in silence waiting for the Lord to come. The most common last words were, "Thank you, and I'll be seeing you." Sometimes these blessed reunions between classmates and friends were just a matter of weeks or months away.

The longer any of us lives on this earth, the more friends we have waiting for our arrival into eternal life. And as our longing for reunion with them grows, our longing for heaven itself grows as well. It is for this very reason that one of our elderly priests once told me how he had come to love Advent in his later years. He found comfort in the prayers of the liturgical season that voiced both his patient waiting and his growing desire for the Lord's coming to take him home.

Imagining the deepest human desire to return home, to be with loved ones, and to be in the very presence of God is not so difficult. No matter our age or state in life, this is our desire, too.

Together, then, we can all look forward to the dawn of Christ's coming. Although we make the passage from this world into the next alone, we can give thanks, for we will see one another again.

André Léveillé, C.S.C.

December 5

As a teaching body, here is our first duty clearly revealed: we must excel by a special care to place at the head of all sciences that of religion; hence our chief end is to make of our pupils good Christians before they are learned scholars.

—Fr. Edward Sorin, C.S.C.

I HAVE LEARNED recently that perhaps the first duty of a teacher is not solely to place at the head of all sciences that of religion but rather to put before all else the act of teaching God.

The scripture scholar Sandra Schneiders says that in regard to Divine Revelation through scripture, God never primarily gives us information about himself, but God is always giving his very self. We in turn are called to receive that Divine Presence and give it to others by the giving of our own selves. As Schneiders says, God is never giving us "What" as much as "Who."

I recently lost my mother, the last of my two parents since my father had died eight years previously. In the midst of that fundamental loss, I found myself trying to articulate what my mother meant to me. What I landed on was the fact that she was not only my first educator in the faith but she actually taught me

God. My mother never taught me or my siblings "about" God as much as, through her own giving of self, gave us God himself. She never gave us the "What" of God but really the "Who."

Therefore, the first duty of any theologian or teacher of religion is to give one's "self" to his or her students. It is in this very self-gift that God gives God's self as well. Each of us needs to make it our special care to teach God, thereby continuing to make God known, loved, and served.

Jeffrey Cooper, C.S.C.

December 6

Only this Holy Spirit can make us real religious, as he alone has made us Christians.
—Blessed Basil Moreau

THE HOLY SPIRIT has led me step-by-step along my life's journey. That is not to say, however, that there haven't been major surprises along the way. My childhood days were blessed by the constant support of friends and family, Church and community. Everything seemed stable and my future predictable. But the Spirit summoned me, through the wise advice of my pastor, to enroll as a student at the University of Notre Dame. This prodding of the Spirit continued to guide me until I found myself anchored in the safe harbor of my vocation in Holy Cross.

In my religious life and priesthood, God's holy wisdom has continued to walk step-by-step with me along my journey. Through countless men and women, the Spirit has slowly but surely communicated God's loving guidance to me at every twist and turn of my life. Seminarian classmates and saintly pastors, dedicated teachers and inspiring writers, civil leaders and retreat participants, and indeed so many more, have all shared with me the sparks of their own burning love for God, sparks that have, in turn, fed the fire within me.

And so we should not always anticipate surprises from the Spirit, even though they do come. More often than not, the work of Divine Providence is slow and sure, imparted to us through daily encounters with the people around us. Yet it is the Holy Spirit that is always at work in us, ever continuing to fashion us into the Christians God has called us to be.

Robert Pelton, C.S.C.

December 7

Lifelong formation is lifelong growth. As a daily aid for self-knowledge and self-governance, the examination of conscience allows us to find how we succeed or fall short in both our common life and our mission. A grace more powerful still is given in appropriately frequent sacramental confession, whereby each of us opens his conscience to the Lord, to the Lord's minister and to himself and there finds reconciliation with his neighbors and pardon from the Lord, who gave his life lest any of us be lost to him.

—Holy Cross *Constitutions*

I WILL NEVER forget the first time a priest asked me to hear his confession. I said yes, of course, though with some trepidation. Since then I have been blessed to hear the confessions of many priests and religious. Their humility, holiness, and faith in the midst of their struggles have always given me courage and strength. I see that priests and religious dedicated to the sacrament of Reconciliation exude peace and joy in their vocations. Their commitment to lifelong growth inspires me to remain open to God's grace in my own calling.

The example of these priests and religious also calls me to the sacrament. There, as a penitent before the Lord, I confess my own sinfulness and encounter both my human weakness and the wonder of God's infinite love for me. There I find acceptance of myself as I am, and I find peace. There, too, I discern how deeply and constantly I am in need of God's forgiveness.

The sacrament of Reconciliation and the practice of a daily examination of conscience, in which we review our actions and thoughts before the Lord, can help all of us to evaluate our ongoing spiritual growth. We dare not take that growth for granted, because it is the constant renewal of our spirits, indeed of our very lives in Christ, that readies us for eternal life.

Pat Maloney, C.S.C.

☧

December 8

We understand a bit of the emotion called motherly love, this love of a mother for the children she has brought to life. Motherly love leads her always to think about them and work to assure their happiness. This is but a faint picture of what Mary feels for all people, and the love she bears for us, since she became our mother and she adopted us as her children.

—Blessed Basil Moreau

IT IS A simple truth that all of us have had the experience of having a mother. She was the woman who taught—or tried to teach—us to love our brothers and sisters beyond measure and ability. She challenged us to expand our love for her to those who share her circle of motherly love.

Jesus says of St. John the Baptist, "Among those born of women, no one is greater than John" (Lk 7:28). Very interestingly, Jesus is absenting himself from that list. And yet we all know that Jesus himself was born of a woman, our Blessed Mother Mary. But in saying that, he points to the larger role of Mary in the Church. Mary is the Mother of Jesus and also the Mother of his disciples. More than playing a biological role, Mary was the spiritual formator of Jesus as well as his first follower. She taught them the importance of saying yes to God's will and living out—with love and joy—the consequences.

Though we were not born of blood of the Virgin Mary as Jesus was, we, too, are born of her through Baptism and discipleship. We have been adopted into the family of Mary through her love for us and her hope that we live as she did. Just as Mary converted her love for Jesus her son to a love for all of his disciples, we are called to expand our filial love to a radical love for the whole Church—to transform our biological love for those who share our DNA into a love given to strangers, newcomers,

and former enemies. And we can do this because Mary first
spread her love for Jesus to all of us who take on his name.

Peter J. Walsh, C.S.C.

December 9

*I am convinced that Providence, which has in the past
done everything necessary for the development and
perfection of its work, will continue to bestow on us
most abundant blessings. To ensure this, we must be
constantly animated by the spirit of zeal and generosity which so holy an undertaking requires.*

—Blessed Basil Moreau

WHEN WE INTEND to serve our brothers and sisters with a strong
commitment, we can find ourselves facing many obstacles that
prevent us from carrying our mission and service to completion. It is in these moments that we need to trust in Divine
Providence, boldly entrusting ourselves to the grace of God.
The way to this trust is to seek the experience of God in our
lives through prayer before giving ourselves, just as Jesus did
before carrying out the wonders and miracles that he worked.
He would separate himself from others and in silence would
seek the experience of God in prayer before serving the people.

When I am called to visit the sick in the hospital or in their
homes, I experience a fear of not knowing what to say in those
moments. How can I console and encourage those who are sick?
I have come to know that it is absolutely necessary for me first

to take some time before the tabernacle, asking for the light of the Holy Spirit and entrusting—to the point of abandoning—myself to his action. In this way, I find the words are inspired by the Spirit's wisdom and are just what the people need to hear.

And so whenever we engage in any project or mission in service of our brothers and sisters, we must abandon our own desires, letting go so that the Lord can act in us and work through us. And our provident God will provide. It is so uplifting to hear the people's gratitude for our words and actions, but then we can say to them, "They are the words of God; it is his loving presence." For we are only instruments, servants.

Jorge Armando Morales, C.S.C.

December 10

God never permitted me to entertain, for twenty-four hours, a real ill-will towards any member of our dear religious family; and at this moment there is not one in whom I do not recognize some excellent qualities.
—Fr. Edward Sorin, C.S.C.

SOMETIMES PEOPLE OUTSIDE religious life imagine that everything is always smooth and easy in a religious house. Well, it isn't so. We are human beings, and human beings are frequently in conflict over one thing or another. One of my brothers in Holy Cross captures this reality perfectly: "Where two or three are gathered, there is conflict." While his saying is humorous, it states a truth. The challenge is how we deal with conflict.

Our *Constitutions* speak honestly of the reality of conflict in religious life, reminding us that our disagreements and disputes can and occasionally will unravel the peace in our communities. At the same time, they encourage us to seek frank yet discreet ways to reconcile with one another.

In my own experience, it is rare for me to be in conflict, but it does happen. When it does, I have learned to let the energy and emotion settle a bit before speaking with the other person. Frequently, taking this time and space has revealed to me that the fault is really my own. As a result, whenever I find myself in conflict with another, I go to the person with all the humility I can muster and ask to speak. Often I find that what I thought and what the other person meant were very different. I have never been disappointed when I have sought out my brother or sister in this way.

Alan Harrod, C.S.C.

December 11

As we grow in age, we grow in love for prayer. Let us pray more than ever, and spread around us, by example and teaching, by constant and increasing efforts, the wholesome, the saving spirit of prayer.
—Fr. Edward Sorin, C.S.C.

WHEN I WAS in Catholic grammar school, we were taught during Advent to pray, "Divine Infant of Bethlehem, come and take birth in my heart." We were to say that prayer six thousand times because the world since its creation had waited six thousand years for the coming of Jesus. As a young boy, I actually accomplished that challenge, kept careful score, and even outdid the six thousand. Then, as I matured, I came to find the daily Rosary as a way to pray always. In my growing affection for God, I discovered that I could pray day and night. Over the years, my familiarity with and love for the prayers freed me simply to finger the beads in a holy silence—a growing awareness of the presence of God in our world.

Prayer is the attention of the loving soul. We pay attention to the true, the beautiful, the good. Religion is not about what we are doing. Religion is about what God is doing in us and for us and all around us. Even our prayer of petition is a form of thanksgiving because we know in advance that God hears our prayers. Even our prayer of sorrow is a prayer of praise because conversion of heart in the sinner is impossible by the sinner's own initiative. In the Eucharistic Prayer, we proclaim, "It is right and just, our duty and our salvation, always and everywhere to give you thanks, Lord, holy Father, almighty and eternal God." To recognize God's abundant and perennial Providence is to pray always. This love for God and love for prayer is a wisdom of our waning years that we would share.

Nicholas Ayo, C.S.C.

December 12

Mary's praise went up to heaven like incense because her heart was humble and filled with gratitude and

*love. What love in Mary, who became the mediator
of the grace of her divine Son.*

—Blessed Basil Moreau

To GO TO Jesus through Mary—*ad Jesum per Mariam*—is what
so many students at the University of Notre Dame do when they
visit the Grotto. Modeled on the Grotto at Lourdes, this quiet
place for prayer is never without students lighting candles and
asking for Our Lady's intercession. There, in spring blossoms
and autumn leaves, in winter snow and summer heat, during the
day and into the late hours of night, they are asking her to help
them to follow Christ and to be good Christians. I myself have
often prayed at the Grotto. And each night I say the Litany of
the Blessed Virgin before I go to bed. In that prayer we have a
long list of what Mary means to us and how she can help us to
grow more like her and her Son in all those qualities.

Mary is the mediator between her Son and all men and
women. The safest and best way for all of us to approach her
divine Son, to live our lives in imitation of him, is to receive
advice from her. The imitation of Christ is the Christian life.
And who knows Christ better than his mother? Who was more
loyal to Christ than his mother, standing there at the foot of the
Cross and, in a sense, undergoing the tortures he suffered for
our salvation? She is also our Mother, and she leads all of her
beloved children to a deeper understanding of her Son. That
is the role she fulfills in all of our lives. She wants all people to
take her Son as their Lord and Savior, to come close to him.

Ted Hesburgh, C.S.C.

Happy, then, are the Christians who direct their eyes and their longings to the Heart of Jesus Christ. They will find therein a fertile source of love for God and for his neighbor, because in devotion to the Sacred Heart everything breathes and inspires love.

—Blessed Basil Moreau

As A HOLY CROSS brother and a teacher of photography and filmmaking, I spend a lot of time considering sources of inspiration. Great art, especially a masterpiece, requires constant flows of inspiration. It is, in a way, like grace is for being human. When my students ask for advice about inspiration, I always relate first how in my own life I have longed for and sought after the Divine in so many places. I am also honest about struggles to find inspiration. Often, I get lost in the script that I am writing or in the set of a film or a stage production, looking for answers through the aperture of a lens and the perfect shutter speed of the rawest moment of my subject.

A creative endeavor is nothing without inspiration. We all need to be inspired to fuel our passions and clarify our intentions. In architecture, an example is the Taj Mahal in India. The beautiful structure was built because of the love of a man for his wife. Yet inspiration is also the simple key to our vocations because they are creative endeavors as well, meant to give life to us and others. Whether religious or lay person, writer or teacher, we find the inspiration for our vocations in the salvation of humankind brought forth by the man on the Cross—for his love was true and powerful. Blessed Moreau emphasized that there will be fecundity of our life and passions if they are empowered by the love of God and of neighbors. May we seek that inspiration from Jesus—God-for-us—so that the impetus for what we do, in what we seek, and for what we live may be ever rooted in the joy of the love of God. For if our passion is fueled with God's love, our work is already a masterpiece.

Nich L. Perez, C.S.C.

December 14

In the Christian sense, the finding of the Cross is always that of a precious treasure. In the sense of the flesh, however, the sight of the Cross, in any view it may present itself, is ever frightful, painful, and unwelcome.
—Fr. Edward Sorin, C.S.C.

ONE PURCHASE I never thought I would need to make as a priest was a crucifix. I had been surrounded by them for much of my life. I often carried the processional cross as an altar server, I continue to pray before the crucifix hanging on my bedroom wall during my daily prayers, and I marvel at the various crucifixes in our parishes, university chapels, and religious houses throughout the community. Yet I never really stopped to think about the specific details of the cross until I needed to buy one.

The process of looking through more than a few catalogues for a crucifix—which was a bit odd in itself—led me to reflect on both the gruesomeness and the glory of the most recognizable symbol of our Christian faith. I had a difficult time selecting a crucifix that was neither too sentimental nor too bloody. Perhaps this is because trying to tone down a brutal and inhumane way to die is paradoxical. As much as we might try to sanitize the Crucifixion, there is no escaping the reality that Christ's death on the Cross was frightful, painful, and shameful. At the same time, we Christians know that the Cross is our glory, for through the eyes of faith we can see beyond the nails and the blood to the One whom God raised from the dead three days later. Because of this, the Cross is our most precious treasure. And so we cast it in gold and silver, carve it out of wood and marble, and mold it in plaster and plastic ever to remind ourselves of the true hope and salvation born out of that frightful, painful, and unwelcome death.

Brad Metz, C.S.C.

December 15

Time passes like a dream; eternity should fix our attention.

—Fr. Edward Sorin, C.S.C.

PHILOSOPHERS AND THEOLOGIANS have speculated for centuries about the nature of time and have debated the question of how an eternal God might relate to creatures both temporal and mortal. Jesus embodies this paradox of the eternal-in-time, the Incarnate Word that is both now and always. St. John says in his gospel, "The Word became flesh and made his dwelling among us, and we saw his glory" (1:14).

In our own lives, we experience moments when eternity breaks through to us, when we seem to be, though briefly, in the company of our God. At those times, the paradox makes itself present to us; we have the sensation that we, too, are both now and always. As Fr. Sorin puts it, eternity has fixed our attention. In other words, it is the Eternal who acts, and we respond by focusing on its presence. For me, these "God moments" have occurred while sitting on a hill beneath Pike's Peak at the Holy Cross Novitiate in Colorado; while meditating before the tabernacle and Holy Cross priest Fr. Tony Lauck's stunning stained-glass windows at the Moreau Seminary chapel; and while lying prone on the floor of Sacred Heart Basilica at Notre Dame during the litany of the saints, as part of the Mass of perpetual profession of religious vows. In instants like these, eternity fixes our attention, we become aware of a larger frame of reference, and time passes like a dream. It would be truly divine if only we could experience every moment of our lives this way, in the certain knowledge of God's eternal presence.

George Piggford, C.S.C.

December 16

Strive to be ever mindful of your vows and, once you have consecrated yourselves to God, do not look back.

—Blessed Basil Moreau

LOOKING BACK HAS a bad reputation. We're taught when running a race never to look back because in doing so we inevitably slow down. Baseball teams have base coaches to protect the runner from looking back to see where the ball is and thereby losing a critical step. Most tellingly, the Lord Jesus said, "No one who sets a hand to the plow and looks to what was left behind is fit for the Kingdom of God" (Lk 9:62). Farmers know that unless they keep their eye on where they're going, they'll wander off and the furrows will no longer be straight.

Blessed Moreau seems to have a similar idea. As religious, we spend a long time, years actually, preparing for the moment that we promise to live the vows of poverty, chastity, and obedience forever. We study them, we examine them, we parse them, and we practice living them, renewing them each year until we reach the point of maturity to decide that indeed the Lord wants us to allow those vows to shape the rest of our lives. Once we take vows, Blessed Moreau would have us live them, not wondering about life outside them, about all the infamous "what if" and "grass is greener"-type things that attempt to distract us.

Is this really all that different from the lives all Christians are called to live? Don't the vows of Baptism to which we are all bound require us to look forward and plunge into the Christian journey? If we're married, doesn't our marriage have a better chance of success and final happiness if both spouses are single-minded in devoting themselves to making it work? Living the Christian life in any of its forms requires of all of us who go by that name to live passionately and single-heartedly, attentively and determinedly.

John H. Pearson, C.S.C.

December 17

When we pray, God's ear is pressed to our lips.
—St. André Bessette

UPON GRADUATION FROM high school at the age of seventeen, I entered the US Navy. Having grown up in a small, rural village, I was eager to spread my wings, see the world, and develop a skill. In very little time, I was in culture shock. This was not the adventure I had in mind.

As a young sailor, unhappy and adrift at sea, I was searching for something. Questions surfaced: Why am I in this place? Why am I? Who am I? Where am I going? What is it all about anyway? Where is God in all of this? Nearby, a generous, gracious chaplain on board the vessel opened his door and listened. His patience with an impatient youth full of questions that framed an unfocused future, his gentle queries, and his compassionate insight encouraged me, moved me, blessed me, stirring the deepest longing within. He helped me navigate the storm and set a course.

Years later, that course carried me back aboard ship as a Holy Cross priest and Navy chaplain. Grateful for that devoted messenger who had assisted me, I wanted to open myself to others in the same way: encouraging, blessing. He knew—and I have discovered along the way—that the ear is an invaluable tool.

St. André Bessette was attentive as thousands drew near, presenting their need and expressing their hope. Upon hearing it, he allowed their prayer to become his. The Lord needs healing hands here; the Lord needs an encouraging voice here; the

Lord needs a compassionate heart here. And it all begins with the Lord's open, attentive ear here.

William D. Dorwart, C.S.C.

December 18

Imitating Christ is not a matter of knowing Jesus Christ, his teaching, and his life as we pride ourselves on knowing the story of some famous person. More than this, we must study the details of the Savior's life and know the love which inclined him to act. We must be filled with the spirit of his example.

—Blessed Basil Moreau

WE CAN STUDY a lot about Christ and read a lot of books about him and think through our own personal Christology. But Christ is not bound within the covers of books—no matter how learned their contents. Blessed Moreau understood from his own lived experience that Jesus Christ was different from and more significant than "great figures" from the past, whatever their accomplishments. He grasped profoundly that the fulfillment of Jesus' life on earth came when he freely and obediently chose to suffer and to die so that we in turn might live. Jesus lives beyond books, out among us in the Church and in the world. And he eagerly wants to live within each of us.

Christ's followers today are called to know him such that we might share him with others. In order to do this with any authenticity and conviction, we must deepen our own relationship with Christ. He must be alive in us, and we must know him truly as Savior and also as brother and friend, the One who walks with us through life, even amid doubt, challenge, and difficulty. Our relationship is deepened and strengthened when we spend time with him in prayer and when we seek him out amid the poor and the sick and the abandoned. This relationship ultimately is confirmed not only when we read the gospels but also when we live them out as faithful disciples. We cannot sequester Christ into the category of some worthy figure from the past, but we must allow him to enter our lives this very moment and so guide us along his loving way.

Wilson D. Miscamble, C.S.C.

December 19

All of us are involved in the mission: those who go out to work and whose labors sustain the community itself, those in fullness of their strength and those held back by sickness or by age, those who abide in the companionship of a local house and those sent to live and work by themselves, those in their active assignments and those who are still in training. All of us as a single brotherhood are joined in one communal response to the Lord's mission.

—Holy Cross *Constitutions*

WHEN I LIVED at Stonehill College, the past, present, and future of Holy Cross all came together for me in our community—from young men in formation to some of the venerable patriarchs. Not every member was able to be as active in ministry as others, but all, regardless of age or infirmity, contributed what they could to the house, the province, and the local Church. In some cases this was simply helping to clear the table after a meal, sorting mail, or providing spiritual direction to our seminarians. Our senior members provided us with oral history and insight into our past, while our younger brothers brought fresh ideas and youthful zeal. Together, as a single brotherhood, we then faced issues in the present and planned for the future.

In the scriptures, we find that God uses people of all ages in his plan of salvation. In the Old Testament, we see both the young shepherd David as well as the aged Abraham and Sarah invited to share in the formation of God's people. In the New Testament, we find the young Virgin Mary along with her older cousin Elizabeth both participating in the events that would finally bring Christ into the world. There are no limits to whom God will call to bring about the kingdom. Each of us, no matter our age or ability, has something to offer, whether it is through prayer or serving God's people in a more direct way. All that is needed is our yes.

Thomas C. Bertone, C.S.C.

December 20

Just as the limbs of a human being have no other life except the one they receive from the head with which they are but one body, so does the life of a Christian come only from being one with Jesus Christ. This union of the individual with Jesus Christ came about in you through Baptism, which grafted you, so to speak, onto this divine head of the Body. Confirmation then strengthened and sealed, as it were, this union. Eucharistic Communion renders this union more and more intimate and indissoluble, for Jesus Christ says that he dwells in whoever eats his flesh and drinks his blood.

—Blessed Basil Moreau

RIGHT IN THE wake of my ordination to the priesthood, people were constantly asking, "What was your favorite part of the liturgy?" Most of them expected one of the stock answers: the laying on of hands, the anointing with chrism, the vesting. And yes, those were remarkable experiences, but not the ones I would highlight.

The part of the ordination liturgy that struck me most powerfully was, of all things, the gospel procession. I remember the incense flared up, the organ broke out, Fr. Bill Miscamble, C.S.C., elevated the Book of the Gospels, and the thought hit me, "This is what it is all about." During an ordination weekend, a lot of attention falls on the men being ordained, but in that moment, with everyone focused on the Word of God, I realized, "It's still all about Jesus. It never stops being about Jesus, and how Jesus chooses us for himself."

The same holds true for all the sacraments. They're all about Jesus, which is another way of saying that they are perfectly for us. My students at King's College give me quizzical looks when I tell them, "The only sort of life that persists after death is God's own life, the 'eternal' life that God extends to us, even now, in the person of Jesus Christ." But that's the truth of it!

The sacraments are the life of Jesus as it comes to us and offers itself to us and heals us and raises us to ever new heights of love. In the sacraments, Jesus chooses us for himself and trains us to share forever in the happiness of the Father. Jesus unites us to himself and fashions us into words of the Father. Jesus is all about us so that we can be all about him.

Chase Pepper, C.S.C.

December 21

I shall not attempt to describe for you my inmost feelings during these days of glorious and holy memory. Neither pen nor tongue could adequately express for you the thoughts of my mind and the emotions of my heart as I beheld the touching spectacle of the consecration of our Conventual Church.

—Blessed Basil Moreau

ON SUNDAY MORNING, December 21, 1997, thanks to a ride from a Good Samaritan, I arrived in Duchity, a village in the southern mountains of Haiti, after a seven-hour trip on a bad road that no words could describe. It was my first visit to that place. My eyes took in images of both natural beauty and extreme poverty. This was to be my new parish, and I was to be their first pastor. My heart was quickly beating, like that of an athlete on the field at the beginning of the game, anticipating simultaneously the joy of victory and the fear of defeat.

On that Sunday morning, inside the tiny chapel made of clay, the only visible sign of the Catholic community of Duchity was a group of people gathered for prayer. By the grace of God, I arrived just before the lay leader announced the opening song. Five years earlier the bishop had promised them a priest, and, after all the years they had patiently waited, he had finally arrived. The people's hearts were brimming over with joy, as they loudly exclaimed, "God is good! God never abandons his children! Blessed be the Lord!" These exclamations were clear expressions of gladness, hope, and faith. Suddenly, their joy invaded and overwhelmed me, and my fears disappeared. I quickly understood that my mission was, indeed, demanding and challenging, but I was not afraid. We concluded this extraordinarily joyful moment with the celebration of the Eucharist, that greatest of all thanksgivings in which God draws his people together and builds us into his Church—in Duchity, Haiti, and in every corner of the world.

Fritz Louis, C.S.C.

December 22

Yes, it is a generous love. Jesus is God, and he gives us his divinity. He has a body and gives it to us as food, blood and gives it to us as drink. In this food and drink, he hands over to us his virtues, and he applies his merits to us. And, it is a tender love.

—Blessed Basil Moreau

IN A TANGIBLE act of tender love, the God of the universe is made present in the central experience of our Catholic faith. This is why we truly celebrate the Eucharist. I regretfully admit that often I do not value the generous love of Christ as I ought, but I am constantly challenged to awaken to that love as I witness the love, reverence, and joy of our parishioners in the Eucharist.

Margaret, ninety-three, was a charming woman who had travelled the world as the wife of a major general. After her husband passed, she suffered a series of debilitating strokes and was bedridden. After all she had accomplished, this remarkable lady had one regret: she could no longer attend Mass. She was thrilled to receive Communion in her home. Her son had been away from the Church for over thirty years, and it weighed heavily on her. She asked that I speak with him, hear his confession, and give him Communion. All went as hoped since she had prepared her son for it. The joy on her face was indescribable. When Margaret passed, her son said how he cherished sharing in the Eucharistic banquet again and how proud he was of his mom, who handed on her virtues to him.

Each time I re-experience the joy of the Eucharist, I recall the response of St. Thomas Aquinas when he heard the voice of God: "You have written well of me Thomas. What would you have as reward?" His response: "*Nil nisi te Domine.* Nothing but you, Lord." Our prayer is that the Spirit of the Lord stirs in each of us a desire to want him alone and nothing more, for his generous love is repeated endlessly and multiplied inexhaustibly.

John Britto, C.S.C.

December 23

You must be "all things to all people," like St. Paul—little with the little, great with the great, seeing in all only the image of God imprinted within them like a sacred seal which you must preserve at all costs.
—Blessed Basil Moreau

FOR CHILDREN, EVERY moment is an opportunity to play: holding a napkin is an opportunity to play "peek-a-boo," being fed an opportunity to play "airplane," a long hallway an opportunity to play "chase me." Life—every moment of it, every person in it—is a gift to be wondered at, enjoyed, laughed at, mishandled, cried over, discovered, learned from, and indeed transformed by play. When we watch children play, it is just a small leap to imagine their extravagant Creator, the One who came up with giraffes and elephants, the North Pole and the Caribbean, gravity and neutrons, purple and orange and cinnamon red.

And then there are adults. Perhaps in reclaiming the wonder of little children we in fact can become, as St. Paul exhorted, more open to all. Perhaps in becoming like children we can become all things to all people, for we shed the veil of expectations of what the world should be and begin to experience it again with the fresh eyes of Christ.

Our tradition reminds us that Christ played by the Maker's side at creation. Perhaps that is why, when Christ took on human eyes, he had so little difficulty seeing all people for who they were in the sight of God: the Samaritan woman as the town evangelist; Matthew the tax collector as the biographer of the Son of God; lepers, the blind, and those who mourn as inheritors of the kingdom of God. As disciples of Christ, in the footsteps of St. Paul, we are called to see all people, great and small, rich and poor, healthy and sick, as little children see them, as God sees them—images of himself, imprinted with his sacred seal.

Lou DelFra, C.S.C.

December 24

Reign over us, O Divine Child. Establish in each of us your empire of love that, adorned with the virtues of that time of blessings, we may be capable of offering you in the crèche of our poor hearts, the gold of true charity, the incense of fervent prayer, and the myrrh of mortification made holy by obedience.

—Blessed Basil Moreau

CHRISTMAS REALLY CAME home to me one year when I was down in Baja California and celebrated Midnight Mass for the people of the village near where we were staying. Most who came were very poor with little education. While I preached to them, I realized that all of us are, in some sense, poor and abandoned and lonely in this world. All of us struggle to find hope.

Yet with Christmas, into this darkened and abandoned world comes a Savior. That little child brings with him the promise that, beyond whatever hardships or hunger or troubles we experience here on earth, there awaits immortality and the eternal life and joy of heaven. For the poor of that village, isolated and without a priest to serve them, the celebration of Christmas was something in which they found great joy. In the following fifteen Christmases I spent there, I looked forward to our celebration together. It reminded me that Christmas was the great sign of hope I needed as well.

Jesus came to bring us faith—not just faith in the moment but faith in eternal life. It is the hope of eternity and God's kingdom of love that ultimately gives meaning to our lives, no matter who we are or where we are. Through our charity, our prayer, and our good living, we have to bring faith where things are faithless; we have to bring religion into places where it really doesn't exist; most of all, we need to bring to others the hope of eternity. While Christmas is just a little touch of that, this celebration prepares us to live good lives on this earth so that we can come to the eternal Christmas in heaven.

Ted Hesburgh, C.S.C.

☩

December 25

Christmas and Epiphany are, by excellence, the mystery of the humble.

—Fr. Edward Sorin, C.S.C.

THE CHRISTMAS SEASON is typically one of family togetherness and joy. Yet for many it is a time of stress and division. I witnessed that reality firsthand ministering to troubled teenagers in a residential treatment facility. At Boysville, the young men had conflicted feelings about Christmas, since for them it often was a time of loneliness or family conflict.

We made Christmas at Boysville a time to experience God's love through others. Volunteers would bring gifts of NFL/NBA jerseys, sports equipment, and games. More importantly, they would spend time telling the teenagers that they were important and that we cared about them. One year, these volunteers also brought a large cake and gathered the students to sing "Happy Birthday." The boys were trying to figure out who had a birthday. Sensing their confusion, one of the ladies reminded them it was Jesus' birthday and proceeded to lead them in singing "Happy Birthday." From that year on, it became a Christmas tradition at Boysville. With everyone assembled at breakfast and before the presents were distributed, all would sing a loud, heartfelt "Happy Birthday" to Jesus. It drew all there more deeply into the mystery of God's love revealed in Jesus.

The Nativity is a remarkable story: God became human, just like us. The Savior of the world came in humility, born of a poor family in a simple dwelling in a small town. The Son of God allowed himself to be raised and taught, to work and serve. He embraced the outcast and, through his parables and lessons, challenged us to do the same. As we celebrate again Jesus' humble birth, we seek, like him, to humble ourselves in service of others, so that not only they but we, too, know the true peace, joy, and wonder of Christmas.

Chester Freel, C.S.C.

December 26

Imagine, when kneeling enraptured before the crib, to see the Blessed Mother offering you the Divine Child to hold in your arms for awhile, as she did to some favorite saints; the marvel would be as it always was to my mind, how such a favor could be borne and not burst instantly the poor human heart.

—Fr. Edward Sorin, C.S.C.

I CAN TELL that mothers are nervous whenever I hold their children. I'm afraid of dropping them, and they flop around in my arms and on my lap like a loose sack of potatoes. I imagine that's how most of us would accept the Christ Child, awkwardly and hesitantly. It is more responsibility than we desire or merit.

The kid in my arms quickly grows nervous and scowls before beginning to cry, but the Christ Child didn't wail even when he was handled roughly. God entrusted him to us, and we rejected him. Mary continues offering him to us even after we return him limp into her arms. The image rends the heart even more poignantly than our meditations upon the selflessness of the Father's original gift.

We usually pray cognizant of ourselves as God's children. We constantly ask that he watch over and guide us. We would be better off imagining ourselves charged with the responsibility of holding the Christ Child and keeping him safe. If we live instead as if God is in our care, then the fundamental dynamic of our lives ceases to be a constant struggle against a parent's authority and becomes one of yearning to protect the gift we love most by devoting ourselves to its every need. It is awkward to switch roles, but the more we learn to embrace the Christ Child rather than simply hold him, the more he trusts us and our hearts beat together as one.

James B. King, C.S.C.

December 27

Our one ambition must be to bring forth children of Jesus Christ by means of Christian education or the apostolic ministry.

—Blessed Basil Moreau

I WENT TO visit a student from our school who had experienced a relapse in her leukemia. I was her principal at Saint George's College in Santiago, Chile, and I wanted to be with her and her family. It was the day before Christmas. I wondered how they would celebrate the birth of Jesus Christ when their every moment was a confrontation with pain and impending death. Yet young Javiera and her family received me with great joy. Javiera wanted me to sit by her side. We ate lunch together, and I stayed the afternoon. As I celebrated Christmas Mass that night with the Saint George's community and we prayed for Javiera, I knew that she already had told all her friends her great joy that I had been to visit her that day.

We in Holy Cross are frequently brought face-to-face with the pain and crosses of our students and their families. It is precisely in these moments, when we have neither an explanation nor a word of encouragement, that Christ makes us his voice, his hands, and above all his presence to transmit his great love to them. Even though we never know who might be listening to us or what it is they are really going to understand, it is above all our presence that illuminates and transforms the lives of others. For all educators—teachers, parents, and mentors alike—it is through our very presence that we make space for Christ to enter into the minds and hearts of others.

José E. Ahumada, C.S.C.

December 28

At the last moment an angel awakens Joseph the Protector and says to him: "Arise, and take the child and his mother, and fly into Egypt; for it will come to pass that Herod will seek the child to destroy him." The order admits of no delay; the next moment, Mary and Jesus, under the protection and guidance of Joseph, are on their journey, directing their steps towards Egypt.

—Fr. Edward Sorin, C.S.C.

OUR FAITH MAKES us aware of our weakness. In the course of a lifetime, we learn that when we depend upon our own strength, we fail. Eventually, we realize that we can do nothing except by the grace of God. This is an essential spiritual insight. But the example of St. Joseph reminds us of a further spiritual truth upon which we may ordinarily reflect too little: in Christ, we have strength beyond our imagining. The lives of the saints testify that however unimpressive we may look, and whatever our circumstances may be, we can be pillars of strength for the kingdom of God.

Like St. Joseph, we should use our strength to protect others. For the weak and fearful, we should be a refuge. The innocent and idealistic should find in us shelter from cynicism and exploitation. Wherever we find holiness, we should guard and foster it. Imagine how safe you or I would feel in the physical presence of St. Joseph. In Christ, we can, in all humility, give such comfort to one another. And this is possible for any of us. Who among us has not known, for example, an elderly, seemingly frail Christian woman before whom Satan's legions would quail? When an angel spoke a word of warning to him in a dream, Joseph the Protector acted immediately and decisively to defend those entrusted to him. In that way, he preserved and sustained all that was most precious in the world. In Christ, we may do the same.

Charles B. Gordon, C.S.C.

December 29

Who cares for the poor in this world of ease and comfort? Who feels for them? This, then, is our privileged lot, to see and attend to the needs of the suffering members of our beloved Savior.

—Fr. Edward Sorin, C.S.C.

EVERY YEAR ON Christmas Day, the youth of La Luz, our Holy Cross parish in Guadalupe, Mexico, throw a party for the children from the poorest section of the parish. These are children who dwell in houses made of cardboard, tar paper, and perhaps a bit of tin for a roof. They live on dirt floors, walk dusty roads, and gather water from a common spigot. The celebration at the church is their only Christmas party. It is the only time that they receive any presents.

The parish youth do a remarkable job with this event, from planning the puppet Christmas story to going door-to-door to round up all of the children in the neighborhood on Christmas morning. Time and time again, during my years as pastor there, I was inspired by their example. They share their faith with great joy as they attend to the needs of their younger brothers and sisters in Christ.

But what touched me even more, and what I remember to this day, is one six-year-old girl. She left the party carrying many things in her arms. Just outside the church gate, however, she passed a four-year-old standing alone in the street. After walking about ten steps past him, the girl wheeled around and ran straight back to the little child. She then slowly took some of the candy that she was carrying and gave it to him, then one of her presents, a balloon, and some more candy. I couldn't believe it. She then simply turned around and literally skipped away down the street, back to her desperately poor neighborhood. That six-year-old girl models for all of us that the real gift in life, our true privilege, is to give abundantly as we have received.

Pete Logsdon, C.S.C.

December 30

Our vows bind us together as a community. We commit ourselves to share with one another who we are, what we have and what we do.

—Holy Cross *Constitutions*

THE RETIRED BROTHER—A creative inspiration to me for decades, although I met him only recently—asked to see a wood carving of mine, a figure whittled in cedar. He was intrigued that a computer teacher had a woodcarving hobby. Honored by his interest, I handed it to him. "You have a wonderful gift, brother," he said. "Keep it up!"

We were sitting among other Holy Cross brothers at Columba Hall, enjoying breakfast and sharing a savory mix of stories about handicraft projects each of us had attempted that were beyond the expected scope of our training as educators or administrators. The explanations for such "outside the box" activities differed. Some found that using their hands to create objects in wood or metal provided a meditative, peaceful focus, a release from daily tension. Several brothers told of carpentry or refurbishment projects that would not have been completed without their own response to the unexpected need. Most learned the necessary "tricks of the trade" skills on their own or from family and friends, underscoring the value of relationships that encourage and inspire. Any of us can experience similar "gift exchange" relationships, whatever vocation we follow or community we find ourselves in, if we allow others to challenge us to draw out and to share gifts and talents we might have never discovered on our own.

At last the retired brother was prompted to tell of his own response to a challenge, something he had built with his own hands. He looked up and replied, "A cathedral . . . in Uganda."

James Kane, C.S.C.

December 31

Let us enter into the Sacred Heart of Jesus forever loving and so prolific in good deeds, especially those of us honored to be priests and charged with bringing others into his heart. Let us celebrate the holy mysteries within the heart of Jesus; let us recite our office there; let us hear the confessions of our penitents there; and let us proclaim God's Word there. In a word, let us fulfill all our duties there, and he will permeate the work of our ministry with the most abundant blessings.

—Blessed Basil Moreau

"TEACHER, WHERE DO you abide?" With this question asked by the first disciples, the evangelist John begins his account of a life-changing adventure. It is the question asked by each one of us in our search for God. Characteristically, Jesus doesn't provide an immediate answer. Instead, he invites, "Come, and see." And they went and spent the day with him.

The invitation to discipleship is an invitation to discover, day by day, where Jesus abides, where God abides and, once invited to this search, to spend our days with him. Indeed, Jesus does not really reveal to his disciples where he lives until the very end of the journey, in his most intimate words to his friends, at the Last Supper: "As the Father loves me, so I also love you; abide in my love. If you keep my commandments, you will abide in my love, just as I . . . abide in his love. My Father and I will come and make our home . . . in you" (cf. Jn 15:8–10, 14:23). At long last, Jesus' remarkable answer: God now dwells within our faith-filled hearts!

Blessed Moreau's invitation echoes that of Jesus, beckoning us to make our home deep within the Sacred Heart—to enter confidently into Jesus' love and to abide there. Yet for our founder, always the zealous apostle, it is not enough simply to enter into the Sacred Heart. He simultaneously charges us with bringing others into Jesus' heart. This is not an invitation to strictly personal quiescence in Christ but rather both to abide in God's love and then to reach out in and through that love to transform the lives of others. We are to invite all to "come and see" what Christ has revealed to us—that God, in Christ, dwells with us, his Sacred Heart now abiding within our own.

Timothy Scully, C.S.C.

THEMATIC INDEX

Mercy: February 5, February 24, March 2, March 13, March 30, June 3, June 15, October 8, October 19, October 24, November 7

Mission: January 4, January 25, February 18, March 21, March 25, April 28, May 3, May 5, May 7, June 1, September 27, October 20, October 23, October 28, December 30

Mystery: April 20, June 10, September 17

Obedience: January 24, March 20, April 12, May 29, July 1, July 27, August 16, September 10, October 14, November 16

Ordination: April 2, April 10, April 29, June 24, October 26

Our Lady of Sorrows: March 28, July 18, August 5, September 4, September 15

Patrick Peyton: January 9, September 3

Perseverance: April 7, May 12, August 2, September 11, September 16, September 28, October 18, October 27, November 6, November 26

Poverty: April 22, May 31, July 3, September 26, October 4, November 22

Prayer: January 27, February 3, February 13, February 19, February 29, March 23, March 27, April 3, April 19, May 23, June 14, July 11, August 3, August 11, August 14, August 22, September 8, September 18, September 29, October 15, October 29, November 11, November 25, December 11

Reconciliation: February 24, March 30, June 15, August 4, December 7

Religious vows: January 26, February 2, March 15, March 24, April 26, August 2, September 2, October 1, December 16

Resurrection: April 20, May 8, May 19

Rules: January 21, April 4, August 18

Sacraments: January 2, January 12, October 6, December 20

Sacred Heart: January 15, April 16, June 3, June 23, July 26, September 3, October 26, December 31

Sacrifice: February 11, February 17, February 22, February 23, May 6, August 16, October 10

Scripture: August 16

Service: January 12, February 2, February 27, March 14, April 8, April 29, July 15, July 22, August 31, October 5, October 22, November 13, December 17, December 25

Solidarity: February 7, March 5, March 16, June 12, October 23, November 3, November 19

Solitude: January 17, March 6, May 16, August 29, September 24

St. André Bessette: January 7, August 9, October 17

St. Joseph: March 19, May 1, December 28

Stewardship: April 22, June 9, July 8, September 30

Study: February 13, August 27, September 23

Suffering: March 31, April 20, May 8, June 7, July 7, July 13, August 7, September 4, September 11, September 12, September 25, October 18, November 11, December 2

Surrender: July 18, October 5

Teaching: February 1, March 7, May 27, June 26, July 21, August 12, August 30, September 5, September 23, October 3, October 25, November 15, December 5

CONTRIBUTORS

Ahumada, J., September 12, December 27

Allison, J., May 15, October 26

Alonso, J., July 6

Amakyi, M., October 23, November 3

Anjus, E., February 4

Ayo, N., July 17, August 22, September 29, December 11

Banas, L., November 6

Beauchamp, W., July 29

Beaupre, R., June 22

Bednarczyk, P., May 23, July 8

Beebe, J., April 4

Belinsky, M., April 6, August 5

Berg, R., March 5

Bertone, T., December 19

Blantz, T., June 17

Blauvelt, D., February 18

Booth, A., March 26

Bracke, J., June 25

Branigan, J., May 27

Britto, J., December 22

Bullene, R., June 15

Burasa, J., July 28

Carey, J., April 8

Cecil, B., June 26

Chamberland, G., February 3, April 12, July 7

Ching, B., March 17, September 1

Cleary, H., August 29

Clementich, L., August 30

Colgan, A., March 25, August 14

Collins, A., September 13

Collins, L., July 16

Conley, J., February 9, November 26

Connelly, J., February 16, November 7

Connor, J., June 21

Connors, M., July 12

Cooper, J., January 10, November 30, December 5

Corpora, J., October 16

Couhig, M., January 2

Cregan, M., August 31

Critz, R., February 6

Dailey, W., January 18, March 15

D'Alonzo, A., June 18

DeLaney, M., June 16

DelFra, L., April 20, June 1, December 23

DeMott, M., April 15

Denning, J., January 13

DeRiso, J., February 11, May 17

Devadoss, P., September 30

Dilg, D., April 26, October 2

Dionne, G., September 18

Donato, J., May 21, August 18

Donnelly, J., August 7

Donoso, F., April 22

Dorwart, W., May 30, December 17

Dowd, R., October 13, November 19

Doyle, T., October 12

D'Rozario, B., July 21

Dziekan, T., March 1, September 27, November 12

Ebey, C., March 4

Eckert, T., June 11, July 22

Ehrman, T., January 23

Epping, B., July 23, August 3, September 11

Esparza, J., August 19

Faiella, B., February 5

Fase, M., February 27

Fenstermaker, J., November 13

Fetters, D., February 22, September 15

Fillmore, R., May 9

Foldenauer, R., February 2

Foster, J., March 31

Freel, C., December 25

Fresnais, R., June 23

Fritz, L., December 21

Gaffney, P., January 6, September 25

Gallagher, J., April 16, May 3, December 1

Rev. Andrew Gawrych, C.S.C., was ordained a priest in the Congregation of Holy Cross in 2008. He serves as the director of the Congregation's International House of Formation in Santiago, Chile. Fr. Gawrych is the editor and coeditor of several Holy Cross books, including the first edition of *The Cross, Our Only Hope; The Gift of Hope; The Gift of the Cross; You Have Redeemed the World;* and *Basil Moreau: Essential Writings.*

Rev. Kevin Grove, C.S.C., was ordained a priest in the Congregation of Holy Cross in 2010. In 2015, he was awarded a PhD in theology from the University of Cambridge. Fr. Grove is the coeditor of the first edition of *The Cross, Our Only Hope, You Have Redeemed the World,* and *Basil Moreau: Essential Writings.*

Rev. Richard V. Warner, C.S.C., is the superior general of the Congregation of Holy Cross.